MIRROR TO NATURE

Tavistock Clinic Series

Nick Temple, Margot Waddell (Series Editors)
Published and distributed by Karnac Books

Other titles in the Tavistock Clinic Series

Assessment in Child Psychotherapy
Margaret Rustin and Emanuela Quagliata (editors)

Facing It Out: Clinical Perspectives on Adolescent Disturbance
Robin Anderson and Anna Dartington (editors)

Inside Lives: Psychoanalysis and the Growth of the Personality
Margot Waddell

Internal Landscapes and Foreign Bodies:
Eating Disorders and Other Pathologies
Gianna Williams

Multiple Voices: Narrative in Systemic Family Psychotherapy
Renos K. Papadopoulos and John Byng-Hall (editors)

Psychoanalysis and Culture: A Kleinian Perspective
David Bell (editor)

Psychotic States in Children
Margaret Rustin, Maria Rhode, Alex Dubisky, Hélène Dubinsky (editors)

Reason and Passion: A Celebration of the Work of Hanna Segal
David Bell (editor)

Understanding Trauma: A Psychoanalytic Approach
Caroline Garland (editor)

Orders
Tel: +44 (0)20 8969 4454; Fax: +44 (0)20 8969 5585
Email: shop@karnacbooks.com
www.karnacbooks.com

MIRROR TO NATURE
Drama, Psychoanalysis, and Society

Margaret Rustin, Michael Rustin

KARNAC

LONDON   NEW YORK

First published in 2002 by
H. Karnac (Books) Ltd.
6 Pembroke Buildings, London NW10 6RE
A subsidiary of Other Press LLC, New York

British Library Cataloguing in Publication Data

A C.I.P. for this book is available from the British Library

ISBN 1 85575 298 0

10 9 8 7 6 5 4 3 2 1

Edited, designed, and produced by Communication Crafts

Printed in Great Britain by Biddles Short Run Books, King's Lynn

www.karnacbooks.com

CONTENTS

S ince it was founded in 1920, the Tavistock Clinic has developed a wide range of therapeutic approaches to mental health which have been strongly influenced by the ideas of psychoanalysis. It has also adopted systemic family therapy as a theoretical model and a clinical approach to family problems. The Clinic is now the largest training institution in Britain for mental health, providing postgraduate and qualifying courses in social work, psychology, psychiatry, and child, adolescent, and adult psychotherapy, as well as in nursing and primary care. It trains about 1,400 students each year in over 45 courses.

The Clinic's philosophy aims at promoting therapeutic methods in mental health. Its work is founded on the clinical expertise that is also the basis of its consultancy and research activities. The aim of this Series is to make available to the reading public the clinical, theoretical, and research work that is most influential at the Tavistock Clinic. The Series sets out new approaches in the understanding and treatment of psychological disturbance in children, adolescents, and adults, both as individuals and in families.

Mirror to Nature embodies a central and time-honoured aspect of the Clinic's work—the importance of bringing together insight

into the inner world of the individual and the family with speci-
ficities of time, place, ethnicity, and culture. As the first book in
the new Tavistock/Karnac Series, it marks a significant extension
of the scope of the Series into broader areas of the humanities,
locating clinical experience within literary, social, historical, and
political domains.

In this volume, Margaret and Michael Rustin offer an exciting
and original study. Encompassing the development of drama from
Greek tragedy to contemporary theatre, they explore the multi-
fold relationships between a psychoanalytic perspective on the
pro-tagonists' unconscious impulses and desires (especially within
marriage and between parent and child) and a broader contextual
picture of the historical and ideological determinants of the action.
The special combined expertise that the authors bring to their undertaking provides fresh illumination on a number of major works
from within the classical dramatic canon, thorough intimacy with
the psychoanalytic framework constantly informing and being
informed by an acute sociological awareness.

Nicholas Temple and Margot Waddell
Series Editors

PREFACE

This book has arisen from a class we have conducted for nearly a decade as part of the Tavistock Clinic and University of East London's Masters in Psychoanalytic Studies programme. For a term in each year, we have been exploring the meanings of a number of plays with successive groups of students who have been remarkably enthusiastic about both psychoanalysis and drama and their connections. We are also long-term theatregoers and have gained much from that experience, in settings as varied, over the years, as major London theatres such as the Almeida, the National, and the Royal Shakespeare Company, the outstanding travelling companies such as "Cheek By Jowl" that we have seen at the Theatre Royal, Bury St Edmunds, and elsewhere, our excellent local Tricycle Theatre in Kilburn, and many of the tiny theatres of the London fringe. Nor do we forget the experience of seeing our children perform in the musical theatre of Malorees Junior Primary School, of a productive academic association with the East Fifteen Acting School, then directed by its founder Margaret Walker, when its courses were first given academic recognition by the University of East London, and of seeing our friends Tony and Elizabeth Evans develop from scratch in Great

Livermere's village hall an admirable amateur company, Theatre 85, which now performs, to a high standard, at the Theatre Royal, Bury St Edmunds, twice per year. All these and many more experiences of theatre have informed and stimulated our thinking.

We bring different backgrounds to this project. One of us is a child psychotherapist, the other a sociologist. Neither of us, as may be regrettably evident to some readers, has any formal academic training in literature or drama. This is, however, our second exercise in this field in intellectual "trespassing", to borrow Albert O. Hirschman's expressive term (Hirschman, 1981). In 1987 we first published *Narratives of Love and Loss: Studies in Modern Children's Fiction*, which explored that genre of writing in a similarly interdisciplinary way. (This has just been republished in a new edition.) At around that time, in 1984–85, one of us was given a research fellowship at the Institute for Advanced Studies in Princeton to study drama, and this book is in part a belated accomplishment of what was begun by both of its authors in that year.

We are grateful to Margot Waddell and Graham Martin for reading the manuscript of the book and offering us valuable advice. We would, finally, like to thank many colleagues and friends, at the Tavistock Clinic, the University of East London, the British Psychoanalytical Society, the Association of Child Psychotherapists, the Raymond Williams Society, and the journal *Soundings*, for their interest in and support for this project.

MIRROR TO NATURE

. . . the purpose of playing, whose end, both at the first and now, was and is to hold, as 'twere, the mirror up to nature; to show virtue her feature, scorn her own image, and the very age and body of the time his form and pressure.

Hamlet, Act III, Scene 2

CHAPTER ONE

Introduction:
theatre, mind, and society

Our particular interest in the plays we discuss in this book is in the states of mind and feeling, enacted through relationships, that they represent and explore on stage. We hold that from the Greeks onwards drama has been one of the primary symbolic forms in which emotional experience has been articulated in Western culture. Audiences have been continually drawn to the drama as a space for discovery and reflection, and authorities have been drawn to control the dangerous space of the theatre through censorship.

We are also deeply interested in psychoanalysis, whose subject-matter is the understanding of states of mind and feeling, in particular as these arise in the primary relationships of generation and gender, in families and their equivalents. One purpose of this book is to draw on the perspectives and insights of psychoanalysis in reflecting upon representative and admired works of classical theatre.

We consider plays by eight dramatists, stretching in their chronology from Euripides to Pinter. Although our choice of writers and plays may seem unsurprising—even conventional—to those familiar with the mainstream tradition of the theatre, it is also unavoidably somewhat arbitrary. We are plainly not attempting to produce a historical or explanatory survey of the drama. Instead, we have chosen to explore a number of plays by significant writers, to see whether an approach and a method can be developed that bring together our understandings of contemporary psychoanalytic thinking with this dramatic tradition. If what we have to say about these plays is of interest, then it should be possible to extrapolate this way of thinking to other works. At any rate, that is our hope.

The passion for truth in drama and psychoanalysis

We believe, with many other writers on drama, that great drama has always been driven by "a passion for truth".[1] This has also been the goal of psychoanalysis, from its founding by Freud onwards. It is significant that Freud saw in Sophocles' *Oedipus the King* something similar to the psychoanalytic process. "The action of the play", he wrote, "consists in nothing other than the process of revealing, with cunning delays and ever-mounting excitement—a process that can be likened to the work of a psychoanalysis—that Oedipus himself is the murderer of Laius, but further that he is the son of the murdered man and Jocasta" (Freud, 1900a, pp. 261–262). For Freud, not only does *Oedipus the King* provide a dramatic representation of one of the foundational issues of human consciousness—the repression of primary desires—it also reveals the potential for catastrophe inherent in attempting to bring these to awareness. He sees the poet, like the psychoanalyst, "compelling us to recognise our own inner minds, in which the same impulses, though suppressed, are still to be found" (p. 263). His reference to

---

[1] "The driving force of the great naturalist drama was not the reproduction of rooms or dress or conversation on the stage. It was a passion for truth, in strictly human and contemporary terms. Whatever the later arguments, about particular conventions, it was the decisive moment, in all modern drama" (Raymond Williams, 1968, p. 385). Williams had particularly in mind here the revolution effected by Ibsen.

the fierce conflicts provoked by this insight suggests his identification with the great dramatist as the discoverer of unwelcome truths.

It was Aristotle's view (Aristotle, 1951) that poetry, including in particular the tragic plays that held such a significant position in the cultural life of Greek cities, was a crucial means of exploring reality, notably the reality of human motivation. He distinguished between the truth of particulars—the contingent facts of the everyday world, which could be represented by literal description—and universal truths, which could only be grasped by the identification of what was typical or essential. The truth established by poetry was the discovery of the universal in this sense.

Drama, according to Aristotle, depended above all on the "action" it represented. In work of substance, there are relations of necessity between the elements of an action, and this rule of necessity applies also to character. Characters do what they do because they must—that is to say, because their nature, or the interaction of their natures, makes this unavoidable. The elaboration of feelings, desires, and beliefs in characters, and the elaboration of their circumstances, are important because they clarify the "necessity" of their actions.

Psychoanalysis has also always been occupied, in its quite different way, with explaining the necessity of human actions—that is, with understanding how and why one action or state of mind follows from another, and in particular what unrecognized beliefs, desires, or compulsions make people do what they do, even sometimes seemingly against their will or against their better nature. The essential structure of a psychoanalytic case-study (and clinical case-studies have always been the building blocks of psychoanalytic knowledge, from Freud's famous case-studies onwards) is an investigation into the coherence and necessary connection of the different aspects of the self and its history, including the history of what has happened within the psychoanalytic process itself.

The written presentation and report of psychoanalytic cases is invariably highly selective. Usually, particular details—a crucial event in childhood, a revealing dream, a preoccupying symptom, a moment of recognition, understanding, or emotional change—are chosen for elaboration, and a narrative is constructed by the psychoanalytic writer suggesting how these details disclose an underlying pattern or a relation to an underlying theoretical model. Psychoanalysts differ about whether what they are seeking to find in these investigations are connections of cause and effect, or of meaning and coherence. But some notion of necessity—of what broader pattern has to be understood in order to make sense of the particulars of the patients' experience—is central to psychoanalytic writing and discovery.

Of all literary forms, drama is perhaps the most condensed and selective in its representation of human action. In three hours or so of performance we might see the struggles of a ruling dynasty, the experience of a crisis in an individual's life, or the breakdown of a family and its relationships. Sometimes, in Greek and Shakespearean drama, all these dimensions are present in the same play. To achieve this compression and yet demonstrate the necessity and connectedness of what happens on the stage, dramatists and performers need to be acutely sensitive to the significance of every possible detail, in the many dimensions of plot, character, setting, and in the forms of communication through speech, image, and gesture that sustain these.

It is because plays are such a condensed form that they give rise to so many different possibilities for interpretation—many of their implications are inevitably latent rather than manifest in the text. There are similarities between the combination of significant detail with an essential connectedness in the procedures of the dramatist and those of the psychoanalyst. In thinking about plays, and in thinking about the process of psychoanalysis, we have not felt that we were engaging in entirely divergent activities, even though we should stress that our interest in drama and its characters is not primarily from a clinical perspective. We try to demonstrate what qualities and experiences the characters in drama have in common with other human beings, not what is especially pathological about them. Indeed, psychoanalysis has always sought to establish the universality of the conflicts and difficulties found within human character and to undermine complacent distinctions between the normal and the abnormal.

In psychoanalysis and drama, understanding depends on remaining close to the language of a play or a patient, respectively, and only with reluctance and caution moving beyond this into more abstract and theoretical ways of thinking. In psychoanalysis, communication between analyst and patient can only take place when properly rooted in the language that the patient uses.[2] We have found it essential, in thinking about the plays we discuss, to remain as close as possible to their texts and to ground what we say as much as possible in the language of the text itself.[3] This does not mean that our "readings" are theoretically innocent or uninformed, since there is no doubt that our perspectives have been deeply shaped by the psychoanalytic and other conceptions with which we are familiar. But it does mean that it has often seemed unhelpful to introduce explicitly theoretical concepts into our analysis of the plays. Where we have done so, it has been simply to make the basis of our thinking more visible to our readers.

There are some other respects in which our purpose may be clarified by reference to Aristotle's theory of poetry. The first of these concerns the ways in which tragedy, in his view, is a way of exploring the contradictions of human experience, the terrible collisions that take place between conflicting aspects of human nature, or between what is desired and what is possible in human lives.[4] The central concern of psychoanalysis has also been with the question of how to live—or, more precisely, how to live without excessive mental pain or catastrophe to the self and others. The "extreme" states of mind that psychoanalysis has sought to investigate, map, and relieve or modify in its therapeutic role are analogous to the "extreme" states of mind that are the subject of many of

---

[2] This is especially the case in the psychoanalysis of children, since child patients rarely read psychoanalytic books and are unlikely to be tempted into conversational "excursions" (O'Shaughnessy, 1993) or into theoretical discussion with their therapists.

[3] Sometimes we fear that our citing of textual "evidence" for our interpretations may seem laborious, especially to readers already familiar with the works we discuss. But we are not literary specialists, and we felt that the greater danger for us was to appear to be offering interpretations that had no foundation.

[4] Aristotle puts this in terms of what will arouse pity and terror in the audience. This, he says, should arise "from the inner structure of the piece". "It should come about as the result not of vice, but of some great error or frailty" (*Poetics*, XIII). "The conflicts to be looked for from the poet are between people who are near or dear to one another—if, for example, a brother kills, or intends to kill, a brother, a son his father, a mother her son, a son his mother, or any other deed of this kind is done—these are the situations to be looked for by the poet." (*Poetics*, XIV).

the greatest plays of the Western dramatic tradition, some of which we discuss in the ensuing chapters.

Although we believe there are convergences and affinities between the "objects of inquiry" of psychoanalysis and of dramatic and other literary forms, there are also important differences between them. Drama achieves its truths to experience, and its meanings for audiences, by embodying its understandings in an imaginative construction of a world. It does not, usually, describe, theorize, or comment in "objective" terms on what it realizes in this "fictional" form, though many dramatists, including some of those we discuss here, have done this outside their dramatic work, in commentary on it.[5]

Psychoanalysis, and sociology (another of the explanatory paradigms on which we draw), do work by explicit description, categorization, and the clarification of law-like connections between phenomena, even when they seek to ground their accounts on particular truthful accounts of the actual experiences of their subjects. Drama and social scientific analysis, therefore, generate rather different forms of understanding, even if the substantive insights they provide may coincide. Drama creates imaginary worlds, from which learning among audiences and readers takes place implicitly, by the carrying over of understandings gained from a play to fields of experience beyond it. Psychoanalysis is located unusually far along the expressive and imaginative end of the continuum between the forms of knowledge usually contrasted as the sciences and the humanities.[6] But even so, the convergences and affinities between the truths of human nature and society that have been discovered by psychoanalysis and those that have been represented and realized in drama, and the influences of these

---

[5]Some dramatists—Shaw for example—have incorporated such explicit commentary within their plays. Others, like Brecht, have sought to provoke their audiences into a measure of detached intellectual awareness of the dramatic effects they were using, though without eschewing more emotionally direct kinds of engagement by audiences.

[6]Michael Rustin deals with these issues in a number of essays (see *Reason and Unreason: Psychoanalysis, Science and Politics*, 2001; *The Good Society and the Inner World*, 1991a).

traditions on each other,[7] must not obscure the important differences of method that distinguish them.[8]

We have so far been considering the connections between Aristotle's theory of poetry and psychoanalysis from the point of view of the "production" of both these forms of understanding and knowledge. There is also something to be said about their "reception" by audiences, in the case of theatre, and by those who experience psychoanalysis in its various forms as analysands or in some related way.[9] What connection might there be between these? Relevant to understanding this is Aristotle's concept of catharsis, as the most important response of audiences to tragedy.

Although Aristotle elaborated this influential idea rather little, some elements of what he meant are clear. He describes an experience for audiences of pity and terror at the events enacted on stage,

---

[7] In the earlier years of psychoanalysis, the principal direction of influence was from imaginative literature, since its traditions had anticipated many of the insights into human feeling and motivation that psychoanalysis was trying to bring within the domain of science. But subsequently, certainly so far as the novel and cinema are concerned, the influence has gone in both directions, as psychoanalytic ways of thinking have come to pervade the entire culture of the west.

[8] Meg Harris Williams and Margot Waddell have persuasively argued, in *The Chamber of Maiden Thought* (1991), that the tradition of English poetry from Shakespeare onwards and the psychoanalytic writing, especially of Bion, articulate similar conceptions of imagination and creativity as the foundations of mind. There is weight in this argument, which gains support from the actual influence of this literary tradition on modern psychoanalysis. (See also Britton, 1998.) There are, however, significant differences between the embodiment or realization of a conception of mind in literature and a discursive or theoretical account of it. Psychoanalysis works in both modes, the analytic process and its descriptions combining elements of imaginative as well as theoretical writing. But while modern psychoanalysis has been substantially nourished by literary conceptions of these kinds, its theoretical articulation provides a dimension that is otherwise lacking in imaginative representations of creativity ("the Vale of Soul-Making"), which illuminate by realized example rather than discursive argument. The earlier absence of such theory may be one reason for the gulf between scientific theories of mind and literature. The development of a psychoanalytic theory of mind may make possible some better bridge between them.

[9] Psychoanalytically based observation of infants or children, and group relations events, are now common modes of non-clinical experience of psychoanalysis.

and he considered this to be potentially transformative for them. It seems from what he had to say about the truth-bearing qualities of poetry and the element of "necessity" that held together the action of major plays, that there must be important elements of both understanding and emotion in his view of audience response. Audiences learn, and are transformed to some degree, by an experience of being induced or enabled to think in a context of strong emotional identification and engagement. Neither emotion nor abstract thought, by themselves, adequately describes this experience. Indeed, one can readily see that emotion by itself connotes superficial or sentimental theatre, and a wholly intellectual approach seems incompatible with an experience that is genuinely theatrical at all.

Catharsis, understood in these terms, is very close to the conception of "learning from experience" central to contemporary British psychoanalytic practice. Indeed, one might say that this psychoanalytic conception now offers a new resource for understanding what "catharsis" might mean in the theatre of today. This theory differentiates between "knowing", understood as reflecting on an emotional experience with which a person is in contact, and "knowing about", as a dissociated cognitive experience in which feelings are kept at a distance. The psychoanalytic process, and its therapeutic and observational derivatives, involves exposure to an emotionally significant experience, through the "transference relationship" in its various forms.[10] It is this "learning through feeling" that gives the psychoanalytic method its distinctive power and depth. This is also what makes psychoanalysis an ongoing process in which the interaction of two persons, and their conscious and unconscious responses to one another, is itself the subject-matter of their encounter and the basis for reflection and interpretation. What happens is that on the one hand analyst and analysand learn what is—what is fundamental and formative for the patient. This may itself be a relief, in so far as understanding what is really the case, rather than what is merely feared or believed to be, often provides solace of some kind. But additionally, such realization

---

[10] By the transference relationship is meant the evocation of unconscious feeling focused on the analyst and deemed to be indicative of the "internal" states of mind and feeling of the analysand.

may bring change, and a capacity to move, in feeling. This conception of self-understanding can be viewed as a kind of freeing of the self through understanding, consonant with Spinoza's view (Spinoza, 1963).

The idea that significant change in the self often has both an intellectual and an emotional and relational dimension may explain why the public symbolic space of the theatre has had importance and influence as a "mirror of the times", and as a register of new feelings and identities. It is not only a public symbolic space, but a space that powerfully brings together cognitive, emotional and relational dimensions, the last of these through relationships of transference and identification between audience and characters.

Psychoanalysis, art, and culture

Central to psychoanalysis from its beginnings has been the idea that unconscious desires and states of mind find expression in symbolic form, primarily through dreams—Freud's *The Interpretation of Dreams* (1900a) is the founding text of psychoanalysis—but also through cultural forms. Freud believed that the sublimation of drives and desires through art, science, and culture was the highest form of life, equated by him with civilization itself:

> No feature, . . . seems better to characterise civilisation than its esteem and encouragement of man's higher mental activities— his intellectual, scientific and artistic achievements—and the leading role that it assigns to ideas in human life. [Freud, 1930a, p. 94]

Later psychoanalytic writing in the Kleinian tradition has assigned an even greater importance to symbolic capacities as means by which psychic integration and development are achieved. In this tradition, "symbol formation" is associated with the capacity to acknowledge the reality and complexity of other human subjects. One of the principal functions of art, according to Hanna Segal (1952),[11] is to effect symbolic reparation to objects damaged by

---

[11] See also other essays on these issues by Segal (1986, 1997).

destructive impulses.[12] A function of art and culture, for writers in this tradition, is to establish a community of understanding between artist and audience, in which what is shared is an appreciation of the reality and value of vulnerable aspects of their world. Art and culture, in this perspective, depend for their creation both on a tenacious commitment to the "reality principle" and on the prevalence of love over hate in the self's relation to its objects. The arts and the sciences are also the most developed expressions of the "epistemophilic instinct"—that is, the human drive to comprehend our world—and they represent mental functions at their most complex. This contemporary psychoanalytic approach reinforces Freud's own commitment to art and culture as primary sources of understanding and of human values.[13]

The post-Kleinian tradition has given increasing attention to the "epistemophilic instinct" described by Klein (1930) as an innate appetite for knowledge—in its theory and practice. Klein, like Freud (1905d) before her, thought that this innate desire to know was evoked directly in the infant's experience of his parents. The early sexual curiosity that Freud scandalously (in the view of many of his contemporaries) assigned to infants was further explored by Klein and her colleagues, who gave greater emphasis than did Freud to its negative and destructive aspects. The struggle between the impulses of love and hate, and the role of a "containing environment" in determining the balance between them, is viewed in the Kleinian tradition as central to psychic development. Later, in the work of Bion (1959), the idea that the mind and its capacities might itself be a focus for internal attack became a further object of investigation, leading to greater understanding of psychotic states of mind, marked by the destruction of the reality sense and of the capacity to think. Bion argued that the containment of primitive mental states via understanding, most vitally within the mother–

---

[12] Adrian Stokes (1965, 1978), influenced by Kleinian ideas in the later period of his work, developed a theory of painting, sculpture, and architecture that drew attention to the functions of psychic attack and reparation in the construction of works of art.

[13] A variation on this theme has been notably developed by Winnicott (1971) and Milner (1987). Their understanding of the nature and importance of cultural experience has been enormously influential, the evocative power of their writing serving to heighten the power of their arguments.

infant relationship, was the essential precondition of psychic integration and the growth of mind in infants. This idea of containment through understanding has become essential to the theorization of the psychoanalytic process itself, and it has had many extensions to wider relational and institutional settings. All of these concepts are important to our own attempts to offer a psychoanalytic interpretation of the plays that we discuss in this book.

Drama is one of the art forms to which psychoanalysts have given particular attention. Freud (1916d), Klein (1963), Ernest Jones (1949), Ella Freeman Sharpe (1950), Donald Meltzer (1994), and Bennett Simon[14] (1988) are among those who have discussed major works in the classical dramatic tradition (see also Alford, 1993).[15] Their interest in drama is similar to that developed in this book—namely, that its subject matter, from Sophocles onwards, has often been focused on the inner and unconscious dramas of the family—of the relations of gender and generation—and seems therefore to provide a privileged access to understanding its essential aspects. For example, the sexual curiosity ascribed to infants by Freud (1905d, 1909b) and the epistemophilic instinct ascribed to them by Klein (1930) can be seen to find mature expression in classical drama, being represented both as the unconscious drives of characters (Oedipus, Electra, Orestes, etc.) and in the investigations of the dramatists whose imaginative creations these are. Similarly, we might see Harold Pinter as an explorer, on behalf of his audiences, of some of the more perverse and unwelcome realities of family life.

Drama and family

Of the many plays discussed in this book, all but one have as principal themes the relationships of partners within marriages—actual, anticipated, or failed—or between parents and children—

---

[14] Bennett Simon's book *Tragic Drama and the Family* (1988) puts this argument in a particularly clear way, and has been a significant influence on our own work.

[15] In *The Psychoanalytic Theory of Greek Tragedy* (1993), C. Fred Alford views Greek tragedy as offering understandings that demand a rethinking of psychoanalytic thinking, partially reversing the usual direction of the psychoanalytic interpretation of literature.

actual, remembered, destroyed, or feared. Medea kills her children; Ion ends the play of that name with two parents whom he did not know before the play began; Macbeth and Lady Macbeth are prob- ably the most notorious married couple in the history of the drama. *A Midsummer Night's Dream* ends with the joyful and simultaneous marriage of three couples. Ibsen's Hedda Gabler kills herself rather than have a child by a husband she does not love. John Gabriel Borkman kills himself when he understands that he has betrayed his love for one twin sister and married the other, for the sake of his ambition. Chekhov's *Three Sisters* live in mourning for their dead parents: one is unhappily married, one is abandoned by her lover, and one renounces marriage to look after the others. In *Uncle Vanya*, Sonya mourns her dead mother and Vanya his sister, and both are denied marriages of their own. Ranyevskaia in *The Cherry Orchard* is a mother who cannot provide for her children, and in this situation the marriage that her daughter Varya desires does not take place. Wilde, in *Lady Windermere's Fan*, shows an "ideal marriage" nearly destroyed by the impact of the truth, but surviv- ing to allow some emotional development to take place. In *The Importance of Being Earnest* grown-up children struggle with the consequences of having had parents who are entirely uninterested in them, but nevertheless luckily succeed in finding the marriage partners they believe they want. In Arthur Miller's *All My Sons* and *Death of a Salesman*, and in *A View from the Bridge*, all three central male figures—two of them fathers, one taking on the role of father to his niece—die, having failed in their all-important relationship to their children.

Perhaps less obviously, at the other end of the chronology of the plays we discuss, Beckett's *Happy Days* has a married couple on stage throughout, and in *Endgame* Hamm's aged parents inhabit dustbins and die during the action. In Pinter's *The Caretaker*, one character's mother has authorized the electro-convulsive therapy that has nearly destroyed his mind, and another character claims to have left his wife after two weeks of marriage. In *The Homecoming* a family of men frequently make reference to the wife and mother who has died years before; the play ends with the invitation to a sister-in-law to join this "home" in her place, abandoning her hus- band and children to do so. The only one of the plays we discuss in which these primary relationships of family are absent, *Waiting for*

Godot, takes place in a world in which families have disappeared, perhaps as a result of a devastation of some kind, and the only kinds of relationship that are left are between survivors who remain friends in spite of everything, and between a master and his slave.

The plays we have chosen focus on themes that are central ones for the Western dramatic tradition. In the Oedipus plays, in the plays about the successive catastrophes surrounding the House of Atreus, and in most of Shakespeare's work (even the history plays have this as one of their key dimensions[16]) we see how "familial" in its subject matter drama has always been. The Jacobeans also explored family relationships, though in more perverse and extreme forms than did Shakespeare. Racine constructed tragedy from the contradictions between sexual passions and social rules. Restoration dramatists made comedies from the contradictions between affections and interests. Later, Strindberg, Lorca, Synge, O'Casey, and Friel, and the Americans O'Neill, Tennessee Williams, Albee, and Mamet, explored tensions in the relations of generations, and between the sexes, which expose the structure of entire societies in different states of crisis. In sum, there seems little doubt that relations of gender and generation provide much of the primary subject matter for plays that make up the entire classical tradition of Western drama.

The relationships between the sexes, and between parents and children, are also, of course, a primary subject-matter of psychoanalysis. While the understanding of what happens in the conscious and unconscious interactions of members of the intimate family network has been developed substantially in the century since Freud's early writings, the importance accorded to unconscious phantasy and the belief that such phantasy defines the nature of what is now often called the "internal world" have remained fundamental.

In contemporary clinical approaches, the aim is not primarily to recover actual memories of early events or experiences. Rather, the idea is that the unconscious templates—or, in Joyce McDougall's

---

[16] Prince Hal has to choose not only between indulgence and responsibility, but between a father to whom he is tied by duty and Falstaff, to whom he is joined by love.

(1986) term, unconscious "scripts"—that organize modes of feeling, thought, and action will be revealed in the intensity of the transference relationship with an analyst, and can be understood, and to some degree modified, as a consequence of the shared understanding achieved between analyst and analysand of what is happening within their relationship. [Other related contemporary formulations for these "unconscious templates" are "memories in feeling" (Klein, 1975), "internal working models" (Bowlby, 1981), and "internal representations" (Fonagy, 2001, pp. 118–119).[17]] The emphasis on the understanding of the transactions between analyst and patient in the "here-and-now" of the consulting-room is especially relevant to a psychoanalytically informed understanding of drama. Drama only succeeds if it is able to create interactions between characters in the "here-and-now" of the action on stage, as a number of dramatists, from Ibsen to Pinter, have memorably said in describing their own methods of writing.

We need to reflect on how it is that the themes of so much classical drama, and those of psychoanalytic investigation, overlap to such an extent. Although some might contend that this is a matter of perspective—the psychoanalytically minded seeing their own preoccupations reflected everywhere—the thematic evidence of this "convergence" does seem overwhelming. But before we answer this question, we should clarify some other aspects of our approach to these plays.

Structures of feeling

A second point of departure for our work has been our interest in Raymond Williams's concept of "structures of feeling" as he developed this in the study of drama (Williams, 1961, 1966, 1968; Matthews, 2001). One of his concerns was to explore the evolution of dramatic form and its relationship to changing social relations and institutional practices. Although he wrote powerfully and insightfully about individual dramatists and particular plays, his broader subject was the investigation of genres and conventions in

---

[17] The coexistence of these concepts, and their similar referents, signifies some convergence between psychoanalytic thinking and attachment theory.

drama and the kinds of expression of social experience and aspiration that they made possible or obstructed. The crucial concept of "culture" in Williams's work signifies a practice of learning taking place within a whole society, and drama is an exemplary instance for him, not least because of its public nature, of how this learning is enabled to proceed by innovations in representative form and content.

The concept of "structure of feeling" deliberately yokes together apparently incompatible ideas: the rigidity and mechanistic quality of structures on the one hand, and the fluidity and evanescent quality of emotions on the other.[18] Williams found this concept an essential analytic resource because he believed social and individual development to be the outcome of continuing tension and conflict between received ways of thinking, representation, and action and emergent aspirations and experiences which as yet lacked self-understanding or recognition. The concept of "structure of feeling" connotes the compromise established at any one time within the work of an individual writer—such as Ibsen, whose life-work Williams (1968) saw as embodying the potential of a new epoch of realist drama—or within a genre of playwriting, such as naturalism.

Williams was generally unsympathetic to what he saw as the doctrinal system of psychoanalysis, which he criticized as based on an unduly rigid and negative view of human possibility.[19] But in reality, the commitment to "learning from experience" and to the facilitating "containment" of new thought in modern psychoanalytic practice is not far distant from Williams's broader conception of the learning process embodied in culture. One reason for this is that both conceptions draw significant inspiration from literature, and from aspects of romanticism in particular. Our interest in

---

[18] Williams deployed other attractively oxymoronic concepts, such as that of the "long revolution", in his work. In fashioning these terms, Williams was attempting to transcend long-established contradictions and exclusions in received thinking and to create new openings in thought and social practice. His overriding commitment, embodied both in the idea of "structure of feeling" and "long revolution", was to the development of a fully democratic culture.

[19] Whereas Williams viewed psychoanalysis as upholding ideas close to those of original sin, we view it as a developmental humanism, grounded in realism.

drama as a public symbolic space that enables audiences and societies to learn, comparable to psychoanalysis as a private space that enables individuals—and by extension and the dissemination of ideas, societies—to learn, was influenced by Williams's work.

It is, however, clear that there is a considerable gulf between Williams's concept of "structures of feeling" as a description of states of social consciousness as these are reflected in drama (and in other cultural forms), and the idea of feeling as this might be used by psychoanalysts. Emotions in their broadest sense are certainly included in Williams's reflections on states of social consciousness, both in literature and in life, and he could be insightful and penetrating on the consequences for intimate relationships of prevailing social relations. But "intimate" emotions were simply not Williams's main interest. He was more concerned with the broader social relations of class and power, and it is these to which he mainly refers to explain the emergence or decline of dramatic conventions. One might explain Williams's particular focus of interest, and what it tended to leave out, by reference to his formation in a society still dominated by an ethos of production and collective kind of struggle, in contrast to the more individualized and feminized culture of recent decades.

This all means that while we have remained attentive to the broader social relations explored in these plays, and sometimes to the conflicts between emergent and dominant cultures that they reflect, we have needed to move beyond Williams's own frame of reference. Particularly central to the "social" dimension of our analyses has been the sphere of gender-relations and the representation of the usually subordinate experience of women. We argue that the social function of Western drama has been as much to give articulation and "voice" to female subjectivity and agency as to the suppressed agencies of class. Even *Macbeth* offers some compassionate insight into the plight of women in a male-dominated and violence-ridden society, though of course it has harsher insights to offer as well. We have also found it necessary to substantially elaborate and extend the descriptive and explanatory language implicit in the "feeling" component of "structures of feeling". Indeed, the thinness of Williams's theoretical vocabulary of feeling, not least in its unconscious aspects (whatever may be said about his interpretations of particular plays), is one of the weaknesses of his approach. Since those concerned with the production and performance of plays must take an interest in the detailed dimensions of affect, relationship, and motivation in order to think out what they wish to represent, this relative lacuna in Williams's work may also have limited its influence on dramatic production. One reason why we have chosen to present our thinking in the form of detailed analyses of particular plays is because we think that the questions that occupy theatre directors and actors—what is going on in this scene, what is a character feeling, why does she do or say this or that?—are of such interest.[20]

Families and societies

If we were one-dimensional and reductive in our approach to psychoanalysis and drama, we might be tempted to answer our own question about the remarkable convergence of thematic focus between drama and psychoanalysis without reference to any larger societal dimensions. There are fundamental facts of human nature, such an argument might go, and psychoanalysis and the classical drama have been primary forms of investigation of these. This would, however, just be to replace one dominant preoccupation— for example, with the relations of social class, or with changing dramatic conventions, or forms of rhetoric—with another exclusive focus, this time on "human nature". This is not our intention—our object is to bring together different perspectives, not to pull them further apart.

What links a "sociological" interest in drama as an expression of social conflicts with a psychoanalytic interest in it as an exploration of primary relationships of sex and generation is the way in which such relationships are repeatedly represented in drama as crucial indicators of societal well-being or malaise. This connection is made in the earliest days of Western drama in the most forceful

---

[20] Incidentally, this is also the method we have adopted in the seminars we teach on Psychoanalysis and Drama, with postgraduate students of psychoanalytic studies. We have sought to work by reflecting on the meanings of a particular play, for ourselves and our students, and to proceed to make theoretical links only from this basis.

way by Sophocles, in *Oedipus the King*. Thebes has been brought to
the edge of disaster by the unwitting violation by Oedipus of the
"natural laws" prohibiting parricide and incest, and only if this can
be recognized and admitted can the city be saved.

These connections continued to be a central theme—perhaps
even *the* central theme—of drama thereafter. The most intense and
powerful means of exploring a social crisis that were available to a
dramatist remained the representation of its implications for the
most primary relationships. This is not, of course, to argue that
family relations are the source of all good and evil in society. It is,
rather, that they are among the most sensitive barometers of societies' capacities to care for their members. It is bloody war that sets
the Macbeths off on their cruel course, and it is a decaying economic and social order that leaves Chekhov's families so stranded.

What explanations can be offered for the extraordinary strength
of this connection? One must be a sociological one. Societies do,
after all, only reproduce and sustain themselves through the production and formation of new generations, and the process of succession between one generation and other, and their inevitable
difficulties and conflicts, are plainly a constant sphere of risk and
crisis. New generations are formed by couplings of men and
women, and much seems to hang on the qualities—of dominant
love, trust, and cooperation or, alternatively, of hate, mistrust, and
conflict—of such couplings. It is a striking fact that even where
drama (as for most of its history) represents women as subordinate
to men, often with little effective voice or agency, nevertheless the
quality of relationships to them, external and internal, are represented in drama as crucial to well-being. The fact that women may
have had to take second place in most areas of life does not alter the
fact that it is disturbed or poisoned relationships with loved
women that contribute to the destruction of Hamlet, Othello, Lear,
and Macbeth, with catastrophic consequences for the societies in
which these men are powerful figures. It is as if the great dramatists
have continued to remind the world that women are as significant
as men to the survival and well-being of society, however much a
dominant patriarchal order has preferred to pretend otherwise.

There are unconscious dimensions to these links between
the world of intimate relationships, and the wider public sphere.

Freud (1930a) explored the basis of political and social order as dependent on a kind of unconscious transference to authority figures, or in the sphere of religion to gods, whom he conceived as projected parent figures (Freud, 1927c, 1939a). Later psychoanalytic work by Klein, Bion, and others has characterized other kind of unconscious social ties, such as the "basic assumptions" by which Bion explained differences in group phenomena (Bion, 1961). The ideas of paranoid-schizoid and depressive anxiety and their consequences are now probably the most fertile in psychoanalytic thought. When paranoid-schizoid fears and anxieties are most in evidence, relations of care and respect in the private sphere are apt to suffer. This forms part of our argument in relation to several plays. Unconscious anxieties also undermine the capacity to think. In paranoid-schizoid states of mind, this can be severely eroded or, put to perverse use, as we see with Macbeth's recourse to the witches or in the intermittent collapse into verbal or physical violence of some of Pinter's characters.

Connections between the intimate and the public spheres are also made in the imaginations of audiences. For most citizens of most societies, primary relationships within families, or their surrogates, provide the most fundamental ties that link them to a wider society. For human beings, childhood is an extended period (persons are not like birds who fledge in three weeks and may become wholly independent in ten, or like tadpoles who grow to maturity without acquaintance with any adult frogs), and it is this "natural fact" of extended nurturance—physical, psychological, and cultural—which explains why familial relationships are socially so central.[21] From the point of view of audiences, the imagined relationships of family members provide a natural point of identification and a powerful metaphor for reflecting on whatever anxieties there might be about their social conditions.

---

[21] Evolutionary biology and psychology also have something to offer to the understanding of these issues, in suggesting that priorities accorded to reproduction and to kin in human and other species are to a degree innate. These ideas need not minimize the significance of cultural dimensions in human life, but do bring awareness of a biological substratum to these. One might see this perspective as a biological materialism. (For stimulating overviews see Dennett, 1995; Hrdy, 1999; Jones, 1999; Pinker, 1997; Ridley, 1994, 1997.)

The conventions of classical and modern drama

Different dramatic conventions explore the links between family relationships and wider social relations in different terms. We are not primarily interested in this book to analyse dramatic conventions, still less changing conventions of performance that have been a major theme of writing about modern theatre, but we do take note of major developments that have occurred towards more "democratic" forms of drama.[22]

Within the conventions of Greek, Elizabethan and Jacobean, and French classical theatre, principal characters were invariably represented as leading figures in the hierarchical societies in which plays were set—heroes and heroines for the Greeks (these were also usually rulers or their rivals) and kings, queens, and aristocrats in sixteenth- and seventeenth-century drama in England. (The French classical theatre recreated in its own idiom much of the setting and action of Greek tragedy.) The effect was to ensure that the fate of the main figures of these plays would be inseparably tied to the fate of the societies over which they ruled. Oedipus begins his quest to understand his own origins because of the plague that has befallen Thebes, and the popular demand on him as its king to do something about it. One of the soldiers in *Hamlet* famously says that "something is rotten in the state of Denmark", signifying that whatever may secretly be going on between Ham-

---

[22] In particular, we have not explored the specific convention of tragedy as an organizing concept of our work, even though it looms large in much analysis of drama. The reason for this is that we have found the links between primary relations (and their interior aspects) and a wider social well-being to be key themes in plays in several genres, and not only in tragedies. In comedies such as *A Midsummer Night's Dream* and *Ion*, disaster lies waiting as a possibility, giving gravity to actions despite their ultimately benign outcomes. Although Ibsen and especially Miller create some equivalents to earlier tragic forms in their work, the "heroic" form of tragedy does generally diminish as a consequence of more "democratic" dramatic conventions. While Chekhov deliberately rejected the term "tragedy" for his plays, we regard those discussed here nevertheless as social tragedies—even though they are tragedies of failed possibilities rather than of disaster or death. Bion and Pinter create worlds that are beyond or "post" tragedy, which, if it any longer exists, has taken place long prior to the action of the plays. The scope of our argument, in other words, is not confined to the forms traditionally characterized as tragedy.

let, his dead father, his uncle, and his mother has alarming implications for the whole state.

This dramatic convention reflects the ideology of monarchical and patriarchal rule, which holds that states and societies live in a state of obedience and dependence on their rulers, and that without their power they would be prey to invasion in war, or vulnerable to internal collapse. The other side of this state of affairs is that rulers have an obligation to ensure the well-being of their dependent citizens, and they deserve blame if they fail in this.[23] Several of Euripides' plays criticize the ruling generals and kings of the Homeric age for pursuing their own ambitions and passions at the expense of their people's sufferings—his descriptions of the brutal consequences of the destruction of the mythical Troy remain a powerful indictment of war to this day and were, no doubt, intended to call into question the fever aroused by the Peloponnesian War. Shakespeare leaves his audiences in no doubt what abuses of kingly power, or civil war, can mean for ordinary citizens, whether in *Julius Caesar*, *Richard III*, or *Macbeth*. The Jacobean dramatists made clear on a more domestic scale what a greedy and brutal court can do to the society from which it draws its wealth. Here, for example, is Vindice, hired at court to be agent of the seduction by Lussurioso of his sister in the country:

VINDICE: I have been witness
To the surrenders of a thousand virgins,
And not so little;
I have seen patrimonies washed apieces,
And in a world of acres,
Not so much due to the heir 'twas left to
As would gravel a petition.

[Tourneur, *The Revenger's Tragedy*, Act I, Scene 3, lines 48–54]

---

[23] Raymond Williams comments in "The Social History of Dramatic Forms" in *The Long Revolution* (1961) that the Elizabethan theatre was sustained by the support of court and aristocracy against the hostility of the (puritan) commercial bourgeoisie, who closed all the theatres in the 1640s. This social context may help to explain why Shakespearean drama offers such a sustained meditation on the potential of monarchy, for both good and ill. Free in thought as it was, this theatre was nevertheless held within the magnetic field of a traditional constella-

The idea that virtuous or vicious rulers could shape the fate of whole societies, fundamental to this pre-modern dramatic convention, was always in large part an assumption, even an ideology, of these traditional societies, rather than their full reality. The real scope of power of monarchical authority in pre-modern societies was limited, even if it claimed to be absolute.[24] But the effect of this assumption was to enable audiences to experience dramas that featured representations of ruling elites—usually displaced into other times and places, but still recognizable as analogous to their own aristocracies—as directly relevant to their own lives. We could say that the transferences involved in monarchical and patriarchal rule were available to be reproduced and mobilized in the theatre, with the possibility of, in their turn, influencing feelings and attitudes towards dominant powers in the "real world" outside it. It is in this way that we can see Shakespeare's cycle of history plays, in particular *Henry IV, Parts 1* and *2*, and *Henry V*, as an epic of English nation-building, and, indeed, Greek tragedy as exemplifications of, and implicit arguments for, rational and dialogic ways of negotiating conflicts in society by means other than lawless violence.

Drama therefore brought the public realm of government, politics, and war and the private realm of family, marriage, and parenthood into very close proximity. This proximity is enforced in pre-modern drama by the fact that in monarchical and aristocratic societies dynastic succession and inheritance was the primary means by which power and wealth were transmitted between generations. What happens within the relations of kinship, marriage,

---

tion of power and looked away from the religious and political dissidence that would soon divide the country. The Jacobeans' picture of a wholly venal and brutal court has a different inflection—nothing good can come from it. Here is a distillation of bitterness and cynicism towards those who hold power.

[24] Michael Mann (1986) and Anthony Giddens (1981), in their macro-historical accounts of the origins of modern societies, demonstrate that the scope of power of the rulers of traditional agrarian societies was extremely limited, despite their claims to absolute authority. Communications of all kinds were poor, and the mobility of armed forces slow. By contrast, in modern industrial societies, while political authority is formally constrained and divided, military and economic power can be exercised on a global and almost instantaneous basis, while ideologies (such as those supporting markets, or democratic citizenship) are also diffused on a global scale.

and generational succession among ruling families really did affect political realities. Individual passions had somehow, in these societies, to be harnessed to the demands of dynastic power if the dominant order was to be maintained and reproduced. Sons who rebelled against their fathers, brothers who opposed brothers, daughters or sons who demanded to marry those whom their passions chose for them, children who were jealous or envious of their parents, or parents of their children, all constituted threats not only to familial but also to political order.

The discovery of psychoanalysis, made through the analysis of individuals from bourgeois societies, has been that the reproduction of families from generation to generation rarely takes place without tension and crisis. Taking up the roles of son or daughter, brother or sister, father or mother, through the different moments and phases of the life cycle, invariably involves inner conflicts and the presence of passions and desires that are sometimes difficult to accommodate within the framework of what is expected. The common trials of adolescence, which provide one contemporary frame of interpretation for Hamlet's states of mind, are easily recognized examples of such conflicts, but all points of growth and change involve some conflict and pain.[25]

The conventions of pre-modern drama—we might call it "dynastic drama" for this reason—make it possible to see the direct effects of such intra-familial conflicts on "public life". Audiences are invited to respond to the action "as if" they were themselves affected by the crises in the lives of their rulers, through the rhetoric of leading figures, or by the presence on stage of more ordinary citizens like themselves, or by reported events befalling ordinary people offstage. We might say that they experience in the theatre the transference to parental ruling figures that Freud argued, in *Civilisation and its Discontents* (Freud, 1930a), was the essential emotional basis of political authority.

---

[25] For example, in the context of the adoption and fostering of children, of the "mid-life crisis" theorized by Elliott Jaques (1965), in serial marriages and reconstituted marriages, and in the context of the ageing process, whose risks and pain was most eloquently captured by Shakespeare, in *King Lear*, and, with a more benign outcome in *The Tempest*. Another agenda for psychoanalytic inquiry into the life cycle is suggested by the ubiquity of migration and the reconstitutions of identity that this implies in a globalized world.

In "modern" dramas, for example those written by Ibsen and Chekhov, the leading figures are no longer rulers but are, instead, drawn from the "middle classes" of their contemporary societies— small landowners, members of professions like doctors, clergymen, architects, journalists, or professors. It was the essence of this new realist drama that its dramatized subjects were representative in their lifestyle, wealth, and occupation of at least a substantial segment of their audiences. Audiences were invited to identify with characters on the stage who were like themselves, rather than with figures who are manifestly their social superiors. There is probably still some element of an upward social gaze in the bourgeois theatre, since its major figures are persons of significant substance, whereas many readers and audience members will have been much lowlier than this. But still, it remains true that the bourgeois drama invited a more equal social identification, and less awe and deference, than was the case for the drama of the preceding epoch. This was also an important factor in its capacity to shock and disturb.

Later "moderns", such as Arthur Miller and his American contemporaries, and the Irish dramatists of the turn of the century, become still more socially inclusive, with heroes who include a salesman, dismissed because he has become too old to compete, and a dockworker, in Miller's case, and cottagers and a publican in J. M. Synge's work.[26] Beckett and Pinter extend this social range even further, creating leading characters out of criminals, outcasts, persons of no fixed abode, and individuals who have been stripped by unnamed catastrophes of any definite social identity.[27] In their plays audiences have to encounter characters who are without status or position. Identification with them requires more universal and inclusive human sympathies, both with victims of violence, terror, and abuse and with its perpetrators, if audiences are to make use of drama to explore such unrecognized and unwanted aspects of themselves.

---

[26] For useful overviews of modern drama and its changing conventions, see Gilman (1987) and Styan (1981).

[27] Brecht sought to represent subjects who would be explicitly representative of a collective experience—another kind of extension of dramatic range.

Yet still in these plays, which, we suggest, are representative of their eras, the assumption seems to have remained constant that what happens at the primary level of "gender and generation" has a powerful social significance in the public sphere. Characters in the plays of realists such as Ibsen and Chekhov are now perceived to be representative of a wider society not because they have great power over it, but because they can be seen as exemplars of a shared social experience, within and beyond their social stratum. As social hegemony in these nineteenth-century societies gradually shifts from aristocratic to bourgeois classes and their respective ways of life, so the understanding of who can serve as appropriate figures in the drama of these societies also changes. It remains the case that it is the failures of these major characters—often, especially in Chekhov, deliberately denied the status of "heroes" or "heroines"—in the spheres of marriage and parenthood that often identify a larger crisis for their class, and for the society in which this class exists.

Oscar Wilde exploited an older comic tradition in choosing the aristocracy as the principal social locale of his plays, reflecting perhaps the continuing influence of class in English life, even during the period in which democracy was emerging. *Lady Windermere's Fan* explores the oppressive and potentially disastrous effects of conventional attitudes to marriage, locating the possibility of change for the better in the experience and courage of women. The farce-like structure of *The Importance of Being Earnest*, almost surrealist in its representations of upper-class social attitudes, disguises the extreme social tensions that are implicitly present within it. This makes it difficult to see all that is at stake in its action. The sublime Lady Bracknell's indifference to the feelings of those close to her is at one with her contemptuous attitudes to the lower orders. In a different and more "serious" theatrical convention, this ruthlessness might have been shown to have direct affinities with a violent counter-revolutionary response to the social crisis which is faintly discernible in the play, but this is, after all, the England of compromise.[28]

---

[28] We could say that Wilde was the individual victim of such a response in his trial and imprisonment. Unlike many of its continental neighbours, the English *ancien régime* escaped revolution (Mayer, 1982).

This close link between the integrity of intimate life within the family and the state of society is also a central theme in Arthur Miller's work, where the crisis of a society that is extreme in its individualism, and thus places more pressure than is bearable on the family unit of parents and children, is dramatized in the collapse of the men of these families. Miller reinvents a kind of explicit heroism, returning to the model of Greek tragedy to do so, to emphasize his sense that these crises are exemplary ones in the society in which he is writing.

Beckett and Pinter create characters whose level of disorganization and suffering has taken them beyond the capacity to maintain conventional family relationships of any sort. This incapacity is, however, also one of the most powerful indices of the trouble with which their societies are faced. Pinter explores the connections between the public and the private in a more explicitly political way in some of his later work, when he shows the relationships between partners and between parents and children under deliberate attack by torturers.

Our contention is that the private and the public spheres are essentially connected, and that the theatre has been one of the principal cultural resources of Western society for exploring these linkages. It is through sexual partnerships and the nurturing of children that future generations are made. This is how societies survive, reproduce themselves, and develop within their distinct clusters of value and meaning, and how they confront the threat of death and annihilation, by ensuring that beyond one generation there is another that will continue.[29]

What happens in the main tradition of Western drama is that this "crisis of reproduction"[30] is explored in the lives of representa-

---

[29] A moving Australian play, *Stolen*, by Jane Harrison, is about the forcible abduction of aboriginal children and their fostering and adoption by white families. This practice continued in Australia for over a century, until the 1970s. The play was written during the 1990s as the outcome of discussions with people who had themselves been victims of this practice, as parents or as children. Performed in 2001 at the Tricycle Theatre, in London, this play explores the vital significance for a people of the links between generations and the extreme pain caused by their rupture.

[30] Most influential in developing a sustained theory of social reproduction, which includes the sphere of artistic production, has been the sociologist Pierre Bourdieu (see, e.g., Bourdieu, 1993).

tive individuals, depicted in a variety of social milieux and according to a variety of dramatic conventions. Because for "real" individuals, the issues of sexual partnership, relations to parents, and relations to children *are* usually fundamental to identities and the fulfilment of life-goals, dramas can speak to their audiences in ways that are felt to be meaningful within their experience. Societies are made up of myriads of individual lives, bound together by structures and cultures that bring about remarkable commonalities between them. This is why the crises of individuals on stage can reflect crises of a much wider kind. It is the central importance of what Money-Kyrle (1978) called the "facts of life" of gender, generation, and mortality in each individual's life, which explains why this apparently "private" and "intimate" realm provides the most resonant and universal indicator of a wider social well-being and one of the most powerful means of exploring it imaginatively.

Space of the theatre: space of the mind

Both psychoanalysis and drama achieve understanding of the realities of human experience, through their different kinds of investigation. Indeed, one can view the theatre, and psychoanalysis, as each contriving to create a ritual[31] space within which intense emotional experiences can be "produced" and reflected on, for the pleasure and illumination of audiences in the former case and of the participants in the "psychoanalytic drama" in the latter. Both practices depend on the existence of a common desire to understand the life of the emotions. Both set out to clarify a dimension of reality by means of the elaboration of "fictions"—the "pretend" world created by plays in the theatre, and the phantasies mani-

---

[31] "Ritual" refers to the processes by which the intensity of experience is heightened by the establishment of symbolic boundaries of place and time and by recognized norms and conventions that "frame" an occasion or practice in which states of feeling are to be shared. Religious services, pilgrimages, ceremonies of all kinds are typical instances. We suggest that the theatre and the psychoanalytic consulting-room share these "ritual" attributes. The idea that ritual could be seen as a social device for the production of emotion was suggested to us by Perri 6. (On the social attributes of ritual see, for example, Douglas, 1970, 1982, 1992; Durkheim, 1915; Thompson, Ellis, & Wildavsky, 1990; Turner, 1969, 1974.)

fested in dreams and investigated in the transference relationship within psychoanalysis.[32] Our contention is that there are striking overlaps and convergences between these two kinds of "psychic drama".[33]

We believe that both the sciences, which aim to achieve generalized kinds of knowledge supported by empirical evidence, and the arts, whose methods are imaginative and, we might say, conjectural, are able justifiably to make truth-claims for the descriptions and representations of experience they set forth. Both are valued because they convey understanding and truth about human experience.

The relation between human understanding and its subject-matter is essentially dialectical and interactive, whether in drama or in psychoanalysis. The understanding by human beings of their experience becomes an aspect of the experience itself, then acquires the attributes of a cause, with effects on mind and action. Thus the process of "interpretation" in psychoanalysis has as its intention to facilitate psychic change, as patients come to see their experience, and indeed their own ways of thinking, differently. The understanding achieved within drama also has its effects, and this is one reason why its works are valued and sometimes bitterly opposed, rather like the analyst's interpretations. Ibsen's *The Doll's House* caused a scandal because the representation of a conventional wife and mother as a person without freedom or fulfilment in her life was recognizable to audiences and, with the effect almost of an interpretation, may indeed have enabled some of them to transform their view of themselves. To those able to respond to this possibility of emancipation, Ibsen became a hero. For those threatened by this new perception of conventional bourgeois marriage, he was viewed as subversive. Euripides seems to have been a

---

[32] We are "realists" in regard to each of these fields of inquiry, holding that each seeks to establish truths about human nature and motivation. We are also "realist" in regard to the investigation of social relations, holding that these can clarify the social forces that constrain human existence.

[33] In "Give me a consulting-room . . . the generation of psychoanalytic knowledge", Michael Rustin (2001) has argued that the consulting-room can be seen as a "laboratory" designed for the investigation of unconscious states of mind.

controversial and sometimes unpopular figure in ancient Athens, since his continued reminders to his audiences of the dangerous violence that underlay Athenian society, which could be mobilized and exploited in times of war, was unwelcome to many. The admiration for and love of Miller's work among some of his audiences in the United States must be due to the fact that he gave a voice and a meaning to the sufferings of individuals trapped in a system that subjected them to too much pressure, so that even the ordinary bonds of family became difficult to sustain. The blame by parents of their children, and by children of their parents, must have been a particularly resonant and recognizable aspect of common experience that Miller brought to recognition in his work.

Drama is a highly particular public space, among the arts. Audiences gather, enjoy and suffer an experience together, and contribute to the experience through their response. The power of the theatre to function as an interpretive medium for a society depends on the ways in which what is shown on stage is felt to encompass the experience of those who form the audience. This sense of the representative can take different forms, depending sometimes on a transference towards patriarchal figures whose roles are a fusion of parental with political authority, sometimes on more democratic identifications, sometimes via identification based on a strong sense of the "otherness" of those on stage, to whom audiences relate in an explosive mixture of horror and compassion.

It is notable how many of the greatest dramatists—both the Greek tragedians and Shakespeare, for example—were at pains to represent on their stages almost the full range of those who watched their plays. Choruses of ordinary citizens and slaves are part of the action of Greek drama, and Shakespeare populates his plays with an inclusive galaxy of citizens ranging from kings and queens to gravediggers, hangmen, and robbers. (Many have argued that this social inclusiveness partially explains the unrivalled range and depth of Shakespearean drama.) It is because there are so many points of potential identification for audiences in these plays, and also because differences within audiences mirror those represented on the stage, that they are such powerful evocations of the central tension and dilemmas of their societies—and, since hierarchies and social differences persist in recognizable ways, in contemporary societies too.

Access to the consciousness and "mentalities" of societies other than our own is not easy to obtain. Meaningful access to the consciousness and mentalities of citizens outside our own social and working worlds is also not so easy to obtain.[34] Literature, however, does furnish audiences and readers with an imaginative understanding of how others live, in situations not directly accessible from personal experience. The understanding we obtain from what are ostensibly "fictions" (whether these be films, soap operas, novels, or plays) are in many ways more vivid, more believable, and more influential than the descriptions we obtain from more "objective" documentary or scientific reports. What is created in drama and fiction, but is difficult to reproduce in literal descriptions, whether penned by journalists or social scientists, is the sense of agency, coherence, and "being there". Knowing a person or persons "from outside" is not the same as knowing a mind "from inside". Drama enables audiences, through a process of identification, to imagine what it would be like to be someone else, or to be in a close relationship to them, and sometimes both of these, in rapid alternation.

Because drama offers this privileged and unusual access to "mentalities", we think it might be a means by which the broader applicability of modern psychoanalytic thinking could be tested against this densely textured and evocative evidence. One question concerns the universality, or otherwise, of psychoanalytic ideas. Does psychoanalysis falsely generalize from Freud's high bourgeois patients to other social milieux to which it has no application, or have Freud and his successors been right in their conjecture that they were discovering universal attributes of human nature itself? Might we at any rate identify, through the study of drama, those respects in which psychoanalytic ideas may require modification to take account of social and historical contexts?

We hope that our analyses of particular texts show that the discriminations between feelings and the understanding of the unconscious dimensions of motivation made available by contem-

---

[34] Consider the superficiality of the understanding of social experience obtained from market research and its equivalents, which underpins much of our political life.

porary psychoanalysis can illuminate dramatic action in enriching ways. Dramas depend on the creation of an illusion that the characters on the stage are in some ways credible as people, to whom audiences (and other characters, of course) impute feelings, intentions, and indeed histories. To act in, or direct, plays requires making assumptions about what such feelings, states of mind, and individual histories might be. We hope that our conjectures might be illuminating to those who work in and go to the theatre.

We were struck as we proceeded by just how relevant the conceptions of contemporary psychoanalysis are.[35] It does not seem that one needs to posit a human nature "different" from the one known from our own experience, and from psychoanalytic practice, to understand Medea and Jason, Creusa, Xuthus and Ion, Macbeth and Lady Macbeth, Titania and Oberon, or the characters of the more modern dramas we discuss. The test of this must be the adequacy of our interpretations to the plays themselves, and this readers must assess for themselves. The conclusion we come to, as believers in the possibility of understanding the realities of nature, is that there is indeed evidence that human nature has many universal attributes, and that these universalities are particularly located in the primary experiences of the relationships of gender, generation, and our shared mortality and, no less significantly, in an inherent human desire for self-understanding and for the freedom to change that this makes possible.

We hold that the classical tradition of drama, and contemporary psychoanalysis are convergent in their understandings, and that each can and should illuminate the insights of the other.

---

[35] The same point has been made by James Fisher in his book, *The Uninvited Guest: Emerging from Narcissism towards Marriage* (1999), and by Beta Copley in her *The World of Adolescence: Literature, Society and Psychoanalytic Psychotherapy* (1993).

CHAPTER TWO

Medea:
love and violence split asunder

The story of *Medea*, which must be one of the most disturbing plays ever written, is well known. Medea, whose grandfather was the Sun-god, has, in a heroic exploit that long precedes the action of the play, assisted Jason in the capture of the Golden Fleece. It was Medea's courage and ruthlessness that brought this adventure on Jason's ship to a successful conclusion: to achieve this outcome she has killed her brother, and induced the daughters of Pelias to put their father to a horrible death. The couple have returned to Jason's city, Corinth, where they have had two sons. However, Jason has now married for a second time: his wife, Glauce, is the daughter of Creon, the king. It seems that Jason's prior marriage to Medea can be disregarded, since she is not a Greek but a "barbarian". Jason presents his new marriage to Medea as a straightforward matter of interests—not only his own, as the husband of King Creon's daughter, but also of the sons of Jason and Medea, who can now look forward to a life of wealth and honour. Why doesn't Medea simply accept this, he asks her—if she did, she could remain in Corinth, living in comfort at least, with her sons close at hand.

Medea, however, is distraught with rage and grief. Creon is afraid of what damage she might do to the royal house in this state of mind, and he banishes her. She pleads to remain in Corinth for a single day longer, just to arrange her affairs, as she deceivingly puts it to Creon, but in reality in order to enact her revenge. Medea has a bitter row with Jason. At this point, Aegeus, an Athenian and a friend who is seeking advice on his childless state from the oracle at Delphi, appears. She explains her mistreatment to him and offers him help, in return for sanctuary for herself in Athens. Aegeus agrees and swears an oath to this. Medea asks to see Jason again, talks with him and now deceives him too, saying that she repents of her earlier bitterness and that it is best that her sons remain in Corinth with Jason and his new wife. Medea offers presents to her to be delivered by the children as part of their plea to remain. The royal princess, Jason's new wife, is reported charmed by the children and the gifts, and she agrees to their remaining. But the wedding presents—a golden dress and golden coronet—are poisoned, and when Glauce puts them on, she dies in agony. Creon, trying to save her, is consumed by the poison and also dies. Medea then kills her two sons. Jason enters to learn what she has done, while she is raised up high on a chariot, with their bodies. He curses her; she justifies her actions. They quarrel over who is to undertake the children's burial and mourning rites. She takes them away in her chariot, leaving Jason to a wretched death foretold.

Euripides' interest in female experience

One of the principal themes of *Medea*, and one reason for its lasting appeal and its frequent productions in recent years, is the experience of women in relation to men, on which the play offers a deep meditation. The play explores both what is distinctive about the life-experience of women, in Euripides' perception, and what is universal to both men's and women's experience, both in actuality and possibility. Euripides represents Medea as irrevocably committed to Jason, as he is not to her—as if sexual passion for a woman is of a different order from sexual passion for a man. A less admirable face of femininity is represented in Creon's daughter's vanity—she is seduced by the golden dress and coronet offered to her as gifts and by the reflection of herself, wearing them, in a mirror:

MESSENGER: So, when she saw those lovely things, she was won
        over,
    And agreed to all that Jason asked. At once, before
    He and your sons were well out of the house, she took
    The embroidered gown and put it round her. Then she placed
    Over her curls the golden coronet, and began
    To arrange her hair in a bright mirror, smiling at
    Her lifeless form reflected there. Then she stood up,
    And to and fro stepped daintily about the room
    On white bare feet, and many times she would twist back
    To see how the dress fell in clear folds to the heel.

[lines 1156–1165][1]

The intensity of Medea's love of her children is also represented as being of a different order from Jason's. Jason cares for them and has some feeling for their interests, but he was willing to send them away with her, having married a new wife, and he is expecting to have further children, who will be more important to his inheritance. But for Medea, the children born to her are part of both her and Jason, her lover, and the love she feels for them as children they have had together turns to hatred when she is rejected; she then resolves to drive these former loved objects out of herself. Such intensities of passion are foreign to Jason.

The play is in large part an exploration of Medea's state of mind, having suffered the outrage to her feelings and dignity of Jason's abandonment of her.[2] Medea's love for Jason has turned into bitter hatred before the play begins, but even its negative image in Medea's despair and hatred makes plain the intensity of

---

[1] Extracts from *Medea* are taken from *Euripedes: Medea and Other Plays*, translated by Philip Vellacott (Harmondsworth: Penguin, 1963).

[2] *Medea* can be compared with another of Euripides' plays, *Alcestis*: where *Medea* is about an abandoned wife who refuses to go quietly, *Alcestis* is about a wife who volunteers to spare her husband, when Death arrives to claim him, by agreeing to die in his place, abandoning her two children to do so. *Alcestis* being a comedy, she escapes this fate, but the play is in its own different way as deep an indictment of male claims to superiority as *Medea*.

passionate love she felt, and the pain and rage it has also un-
leashed. Delineating this process of disillusioned love in a woman
is eloquently accomplished by Euripides. Medea is described by
the Chorus as having been "wild with love" when she set sail from
her father's house. Jason adds humiliating insult to the injury he
has already inflicted on Medea by his marriage when he refers to
her passion with condescension:

> JASON: I admit, you have intelligence, but to recount
> How helpless passion drove you then to save my life
> Would be invidious; and I will not stress the point.
> Your services, so far as they went, were well enough.
> But in return for saving me you got far more
> Than you gave.
>
> [lines 529–534]

and he then generalizes his contempt for women, as he justifies his
calculated actions:

> JASON: Was such a plan, then, wicked? Even you would approve
> If you could govern your sex-jealousy. But you women
> Have reached a state where, if all's well with your sex-life,
> You've everything you wish for; but when *that* goes wrong,
> At once all that is best and noblest turns to gall.
> If only children could be got some other way,
> Without the female sex! If women didn't exist,
> Human life would be rid of all its miseries.
>
> [lines 568–575]

Euripides is the brilliant ancestor of August Strindberg and
Edward Albee in his understanding of the dynamics of matrimo-
nial quarrels.

Medea is not in the least understood by her husband, and the
potential for understanding provided by the chorus and other
members of her household also fails to encompass adequately her
explosive passions. As is customary in Greek tragedies, the chorus
can observe and reflect on the action but not influence its outcome.

The voices of nurse, tutor, and chorus, who witness all that
takes place in Medea's house, provide an important contrast to
Medea's own extreme state. They look for a "middle way", recom-
mending a spirit of compromise in human life that is unacceptable
to Medea. But the limitation of their power lies not only in the

conventional disregard of the ordinary people by the royal figures at the centre of the drama, but also in their own evasion of the full reality with which they are faced. The play in fact opens with the nurse's evocation of the problem of tolerating reality—if only something had never happened, is her cry:

> NURSE: If only they had never gone! If the Argo's hull
> Never had winged out through the grey-blue jaws of rock
> And on towards Colchis!
>
> [lines 1–3]

This is a wish-fulfilment thrown back in time, and it reminds us that the apparent good sense of the ordinary folk who urge caution and acceptance is mixed up with their feeling overwhelmed by the emotional storm they are witnessing. Their apprehensive acknowledgement of Medea as "a frightening woman" marks the limit of what they can imagine.

Primitive breakdown

Without any containment of her agony of sexual jealousy, Medea is in the grip of a murderous obsession. Her gift of a golden dress and coronet tempts Glauce through her desire to be attractive to Jason, metaphorically injects poison into their marriage bed, and turns Glauce's body into tortured and horrible fragments. The horrific description of her body melting and imploding gives meaning to Medea's choice of poison as her method of killing: her rival is forced to endure in physical reality the kind of torture that Medea has been experiencing psychologically—the melt-down of her identity brought about by Jason's betrayal of her. It is as if she says to Jason: now love this woman if you will! Her decision to employ her children to poison Jason's new wife follows Aegeus's visit and their discussion of his childlessness. She seems to be put in mind of the possibility that new children will be conceived in Jason's and Glauce's bed, and she sends Jason's children to Glauce to make sure this will not happen, almost as if they are being invited to act unconsciously on jealousies of their own, imagined for them in present or future by their mother in identification with them.

It is also significant that Medea arranges that Creon and his daughter will die together, when Creon is trying to save his daughter. Medea has betrayed her father, and in her murders she attacks a loving relationship that contrasts with the relationship with her own father that she has destroyed but now desperately needs. Here is the Messenger's report of Creon when he finds his daughter lying dead:

MESSENGER: But suddenly her father came into the room.
He did not understand, poor man, what kind of death
Had struck his child. He threw himself down at her side,
And sobbed aloud, and kissed her, and took her in his arms,
And cried, "Poor darling child, what god destroyed your life
So cruelly? Who robs me of my only child,
Old as I am, and near my grave? Oh, let me die
With you, my daughter."

[lines 1202–1209]

Medea has been socially dishonoured and shamed by Jason's abandonment of her, as a woman who was once at least Jason's equal in their adventures together. Indignation and rage at her shame and dishonour provide some relief and escape from the pain of her abandonment, which otherwise threatens her with total breakdown.

She at first cannot eat or sleep, only weep, and she is poised unstably between murderous and suicidal impulses:

MEDEA: Oh, oh! What misery, what wretchedness!
What shall I do? If only I were dead!

[lines 95–96]

Do I not suffer? Am I not wronged? Should I not weep?
Children, your mother is hated, and you are cursed:
Death take you, with your father, and perish his whole house!

[lines 112–114]

Come, flame of the sky,
Pierce through my head!
What do I gain from living any longer?
Oh, how I hate living! I wait
To end my life, leave it behind and die.

[lines 143–147]

Oh, may I see Jason and his bride
Ground to pieces in their shattered palace
For the wrong they have dared to do to me, unprovoked!

[lines 164–166]

It is easier for her to think and speak in the register of injustice than that of suffering. She goes on to make a rather formal speech to the Chorus in her own justification:

MEDEA: Women of Corinth, I would not have you censure me
So I have come . . .

[lines 214–215]

She finds in resort to a more generalized kind of feminist advocacy a relief from her agony, even when she is describing her despair, and this long and apparently rational speech seems to enable her to regain control of herself and plan her revenge:

MEDEA: Life has no pleasure left, dear friends. I want to die.
Jason was my whole life; he knows that well. Now he
Has proved himself the most contemptible of men.
      . . .
Surely of all creatures that have life and will, we women
Are the most wretched. When, for an extravagant sum,
We have bought a husband, we must then accept him as
Possessor of our body. This is to aggravate
Wrong with worse wrong. Then the great question: will the
      man
We get be bad or good? For women, divorce is not
Respectable; to repel the man, not possible.

[lines 225–234]

It is noteworthy, however, that neither Jason's nor Medea's descriptions of marriages as instrumental contracts bear much truthful relation to the reality of their own passionate history, so far from psychic reality has their quarrel taken them. Euripides understands not only the moral and logical force of feminist arguments, but also the psychic functions rationalizations can have in managing mental pain.

Medea has, however, been made exceptionally vulnerable by Jason's abandonment of her. She is not merely far from home and a non-Greek foreigner in Corinth ("No woman, but a tiger; a

Tuscan Scylla, but more savage", Jason calls her in his final rage).
She has deceived her father to elope with Jason; she has killed her
own brother; her ruin of the house of King Pelias, in which she
made the King's daughters his murderers, has further turned her
into a moral outcast. Her abandonment by Jason, as a barbarian,
now leaves her to bear all the guilt for their shared violent adventure, and the pain that engulfs her is that of feeling herself now the
victim of what she knows she inflicted on others. Hence, her despair.

As Jason says, cursing her after she has killed their children:

> JASON: I am sane now; but I was mad before, when I
>   Brought you from your palace in a land of savages
>   Into a Greek home—you, a living curse, already
>   A traitor both to your father and your native land.
>   The vengeance due for your sins the gods have cast on me.
>
> [lines 1328–1332]

Mother love turned to violence

Although Medea hates Jason from the beginning of the action of
the play, it is important to recognize that she continues to love her
children, even as she resolves to kill them. Even at the last, her
tenderness towards them nearly moves her to abandon her plan:

> MEDEA: Parted from you,
>   My life will be all pain and anguish. You will not
>   Look at your mother any more with those dear eyes.
>   You will have moved into a different sphere of life.
>
> [lines 1035–1038]

The passion and intensity of a mother's love for her children is
memorably represented in this play—something that is not ne-
gated in any simple way by Medea's murder of them. Medea describes their impending death as "my sacrifice"; this is a significant
description which starts from the confusion between Medea's own
sense of aliveness and the lives of her children. They are not fully
conceived of as separate beings but felt to be a part of herself, hence
their death is felt to be "her" sacrifice. This is "mother love" of a

very primitive kind.[3] The murder of the children is in fact an act
with several levels of meaning. Most openly, it is Medea's means of
revenge on Jason, killing the one thing she possesses—the children—that he still values. But she has also already polluted the
boys, as she had earlier polluted the daughters of King Pelias, by
making them instruments of death, so they can now have no hon-
ourable life. (Jason comes to save them from death at the hands of
Creon's family, only to find that she has already killed them.) In
killing her children, Medea is also killing an aspect of herself and
ensuring her own lifelong grief and misery. Whatever damage she
has been able to do to Creon, his daughter, and Jason, she cannot
escape her share of the huge burden of shame and guilt, the consequence of all that has happened previously. Her sacrifice has the
significance and weight it does, as an act of expiation as well as of
revenge, not because the children have ceased to be of account to
her, but because they are what has been dearest to her. It is hinted
that it is this experience of extreme suffering and sacrifice that will
later enable Medea, like Oedipus at Colonus, to live out her days in
a kind of honoured sanctuary in Athens, as a representative of guilt
and suffering for an entire society.

The catastrophic potential of arrogance

However, the three central figures of the play—Medea, Jason, and
Creon—while they each speak with compelling eloquence in defence of their positions, are all enmeshed in a mode of thought that
allows them only a partial recognition of what they are doing. The
tragic outcome depends on their shared incapacity to escape their
limitations. Creon and Jason believe they can rewrite emotional
reality without cost. Medea feels shame and guilt to be such intolerable emotions that she must give up on mere mortal existence,
with all its painful aspects, and resort to her links with the gods to
escape it. Her arrogance[4] as the granddaughter of the Sun-god is
her protection from her tormenting situation, her manic defence:

---

[3] On mother love from a psychoanalytic point of view see Rosita Parker
(1995), "Torn in Two": The Experience of Maternal Ambivalence.
[4] See Bion, "On Arrogance" (1967).

MEDEA: Come! Lay your plan, Medea; scheme with all your skill.
On to the deadly moment that shall test your nerve!
You see where you now stand. Your father was a king,
His father was the Sun-god; you must not invite
Laughter from Jason and his new allies, the tribe
Of Sisyphus. You know what you must do. Besides
        [*turning to Chorus*]
We were born women—useless for honest purposes
But in all kinds of evil skilled practitioners.

[lines 400–408]

As the Chorus responds:

Streams of the sacred rivers flow uphill,
Tradition, order, all things are reversed.

[lines 409–410]

Medea is turning the world upside down. Women are to pride themselves on their capacity to deceive and kill and to forswear their traditional womanliness as "skilled practitioners" of evil.

John Steiner has pointed out (Steiner, 1985, 1990, 1993) that the Oedipus of *Oedipus at Colonus* has become a different and less admirable individual from the figure of *Oedipus the King*. Where in the earlier play he was a man of extraordinary courage in the pursuit of truth, at whatever cost to himself, at Colonus he has become self-righteous and complacent, able to make use of the exceptional burden of guilt and pain he is carrying to assert his own will. "I have already endured so much, more than anyone could imagine, so who can now ask more of me?" he seems to say. The ruthlessness displayed by Medea in defence of her honour and in pursuit of justice and revenge against Jason may point to a similar future of arrogant pride. By destroying her own loved children, she already feels that she is ripping out her own heart. What further reparation could possibly be asked of her? This is how she may be imagining her own later years when she strikes up her deal with Aegeus. She is to bring fertility to him, a somewhat goddess-like role, distancing her from her despair about her own lost children through whom the meaning of her life might have lived on.

The place of shame and guilt as two primary emotions in the play is not easy to disentangle, and perhaps the struggle of the reader in this respect is linked to Medea's problem in understanding these different but related feelings. Shame, loss of honour, is the ultimate disaster in the moral universe of the Homeric heroes, and this is a powerful dynamic in both Medea's and Jason's actions. Medea states clearly that it is shame that she will avoid if she murders her children:

> MEDEA: What makes me cry with pain
> Is the next thing I have to do. I will kill my sons.
> No one shall take my children from me. When I have made
> Jason's whole house a shambles, I will leave Corinth
> A murderess, flying from my darling children's blood.
> Yes, I can endure guilt, however horrible;
> The laughter of my enemies I will not endure.
>
> [lines 790–796]

As Medea carries off the children's lifeless bodies at the end, Jason calls on the gods to witness the outrage of Medea's cruel contempt for him:

> JASON: I long to fold them in my arms;
> To kiss their lips would comfort me.
> MEDEA: *Now* you have loving words, now kiss for them:
> *Then* you disowned them, sent them into exile.
> JASON: For God's sake, let me touch their gentle flesh.
> MEDEA: You shall not. It is a waste of breath to ask.
> JASON: Zeus, do you hear how I am mocked,
> Rejected by this savage beast
> Polluted with her children's blood?
>
> [lines 1398–1406]

Earlier, Medea hardened herself to do the deed precisely by invoking the unbearable humiliation of being laughed at. She thus deals a fatal blow to her tender feelings towards both herself and the children:

> MEDEA: Dear sons, why are you staring at me so? You smile
> At me, your last smile—why? Oh what am I to do?
> Women, my courage is all gone. Their young, bright faces.
> I can't do it. I'll think no more of it. I'll take them
> Away from Corinth. Why should I hurt *them*, to make
> Their father suffer, when I shall suffer twice as much
> Myself? I won't do it. I won't think of it again.

What is the matter with me? Are my enemies
To laugh at me? Am I to let them off scot free?
I must steel myself to it. What a coward I am,
Even tempting my own resolution with soft talk.

[lines 1040–1050]

There is no picture available to her of grief shared but only a dread
that it will be a source of mockery; suffering is shown as failing in
Medea's mind to evoke sympathy either internally or externally,
inciting, instead, further cruelty. Though she speaks of preferring
guilt to shame, her magical escape at the close gives the lie to the
notion that guilt can be faced. This, we suggest, echoes the ultimate
failure of character in the Oedipus portrayed by Sophocles.

Parents and children

There is a further dimension in the collapse of Medea's love for her
children and the extreme state of mind that leads her to their
murder. Envy undermines her identification with their future: she
cannot bear the picture of children who could retain a sense of
having a home, a country, a future, and a mother and a father who
love them, at least to a degree. This benign constellation is not
available in her inner imaginative reality because of the abandonment of home and family she herself chose in her pursuit of Jason.
The idea that her children could have so much while she has to
tolerate so little maddens her. Even her happiness with Jason had
been flawed, since it was obtained at the cost of so much guilt.
Once the external trappings of honour and respect are taken away,
she has no internal resources left to sustain her.

It is the children's looking at her with bewilderment—a smiling
and trusting hopefulness that their mother's distress might abate,
we could perhaps speculate—that first softens her and then twists
her into a hardening resolution. In fact, neither Jason nor Medea
can stand the reality that they shared a part in the birth of their
children; the envy between the couple is most cruelly evoked when
Jason holds forth with his plausible and insulting plan to set them
all up in Corinth in luxury by means of his marriage into the royal

family. After reproaching Medea smugly with her sexual jealousy, he concludes:

> JASON: If only children could be got some other way,
>   Without the female sex! If women didn't exist,
>   Human life would be rid of all its miseries.
>
> [lines 573–575]

Neither parent can protect the children, given the violence at the heart of their relationship, which has now rebounded and is imploding the family from within.

The violence underlying "civilization"

Another way of reading this tragedy is as the working-out of the continuing and unavoidable consequences of the violence on which Euripides thought "modern" and "civilized" cities like Corinth and Athens had been built. Jason's "heroic" adventures had been in reality murderous ones, involving offences against nature. He seeks to distance himself from Medea, his heroic partner in these deeds, who had at that time transcended the conventionally subordinate and gentle role of women to enable *him* to succeed and win honour and renown. King Creon is happy to have Jason as his son-in-law, so long as his barbarian first wife can be got rid of. But it turns out that these "heroic" qualities are not so easily disowned. If their moral burden is not shared and acknowledged, they will return in all their original savagery and destroy everyone. This is what happens in *Medea*, when Jason, abetted by the equally shallow King Creon, seeks to discard the obligations and meanings of his own past, placing them all on Medea with the choice he gives her of either living in Corinth in shame or being cast out on her own into a friendless world.

The issue of how the meaning of violence is to be defined and acknowledged remains, of course, a pressing one. Most modern states have been founded on acts of violence, revolution, conquest, or usurpation, yet to their subjects all preach peace and conformity to their law. Movements that are "terrorist" from the point of view of legal authorities may be characterized as struggles for national liberation by their supporters and members. What are defined as atrocities and crimes against humanity from one perspective may be represented as merely regrettable misfortunes of war from another. Rational discussion and negotiated conflict-resolution is made impossible when such definitions do not match. By forgetting or denying the violence that has been routinely perpetrated during its own establishment of political legitimacy, a state or regime can lose the capacity to acknowledge the possibility that others may view their actions in a comparable way and may in their own eyes have reasonable justification for doing so.[5] This is not the main theme of *Medea*, but the contemptuous dismissal of its heroine by Jason and Creon, disregarding her vital contribution to Jason's renown, does have something to say about its dynamics. Euripides was no supporter of the warlike political faction in Athens, but he plainly thought it better to recognize than to deny the realities of political violence.

The personal and the political intersect in another of Euripides' themes: his exploration of the differences between men's and women's expectations of life and the meanings they attribute to experience. As we have shown, the play has much to say of value on this topic. Euripides asks his audience to experience an extraordinary reversal of its conventional assumptions, by imagining what it would be like if a Homeric kind of Greek hero were represented by the figure of a woman, instead of, as was usually the case, a man. It is Medea, with Jason as only a secondary participant, who has performed the heroics that have led to the capture of the Golden Fleece, and it is Medea, not Jason, who has behaved as the ruthless warrior and Odysseus-like trickster:

---

[5] One could give many examples of such conflicting definitions and their consequences. In Northern Ireland, some measure of recognition by the British Government, and by the Protestants, of the frame of reference of the Republican movement's armed struggle was a prerequisite of negotiation. In Israel and Palestine, recognition of the legitimacy of the claims of both sides is the vital precondition of progress. The "war against terrorism" unleashed by the attacks of September 11th has produced similar manifestations of blindness, in which only the violence and hatred of adversaries can be acknowledged by each side.

MEDEA: I will begin at the beginning. When you were sent
    To master the fire-breathing bulls, yoke them and sow
    The deadly furrow, then I saved your life; and that
    Every Greek who sailed with you in the Argo knows.
    The serpent that kept watch over the Gold Fleece,
    Coiled round it fold on fold unsleeping—it was I
    Who killed it, and so lit the torch of your success.
    I willingly deceived my father; left my home;
    With you I came to Iolcus by Mount Pelion,
    Showing much love and little wisdom. There I put
    King Pelias to the most horrible of deaths
    By his own daughters' hands, and ruined his whole house.
    And in return for this you have the wickedness
    To turn me out, to get yourself another wife,
    Even after I had borne you sons!

[lines 473–489]

It is Medea, not Jason, who experiences the compelling claims of
honour and the need to avoid shame characteristic of the heroic
culture. It is she who is bound by the demands to exact revenge
typical of this kind of warrior-band, clan society. Its most familiar
equivalent in modern times are Mafia or gangster cultures of respect and vendetta, though it is clear that states behave in comparable ways. It is Medea who behaves in Homeric fashion by
deceiving her enemies—first Creon, then Jason—turning apparent
impotence into great destructive power.[6] Euripides thus required
his audience to experience the story of a Homeric kind of hero from
a completely unexpected perspective, with the hero as a valiant
woman who has to overcome and overturn in this role all the
normal "civilized" expectations of how women, wives, and mothers are supposed to conduct themselves. The tragic qualities of the
play lie in large part in the fact that these dilemmas and contradictions have to be experienced internally by Medea herself, who
has to destroy one large part of her nature in order to keep faith
with another. By ascribing these "heroic" qualities to a woman,
Euripides enables his audiences to reflect on their limitations and
consequences as a universal value-system, one that was probably
linked to contemporary militarism in his eyes.

---

[6] If one thinks of Medea's children as aspects of herself, she can be seen to
acquire some of the power of the suicide bomber by murdering them.

A number of major classical scholars[7] have explored how in Greek tragedies two different moral universes—one a world of heroic violence, honour, and revenge, the other a world of civilized obligation, law-abiding behaviour, and moral reflection—are juxtaposed to one another, and their conflicts explored. The drama provided a symbolic space in which the implications of these different moral orders for Greek citizens could be explored. (The political life of the *polis* provided another such space.[8]) This was not, for the Greeks, merely a matter of coming to terms with history and tradition in their then "modern" world, since war with its reassertion of traditional martial values, remained for them, as for us, a continuing reality. The Peloponnesian War with Sparta in the event led to the defeat and ruin of Athens. Disillusion with the prosecution of the war and its effects on Athenian society seems to have led to Euripides' self-exile from Athens. In a parallel way, Shakespeare's plays explore the continuing significance of an earlier era of uncontained violence and civil war for his contemporary more pacified society, as we try to show in our discussion of *Macbeth* (chapter 4).

Euripides introduces a further paradox. In the civil context of the play it is Medea who is the outsider and the barbarian, outranked not only by Creon and his daughter, but also patronized by Jason, who is at least a Greek. Her rage is that of someone who is treated as an inferior and an outsider by the socially more established, who have used her superior energy and courage and then cast her aside. Euripides' audience has to encounter Medea's "extremism" in relation both to her "outsider" status and to her violation of the normal expectations of women's subordination and docility. But, in contraposition to this, in the larger universe it is

---

[7] Among influential works are E. R. Dodds (1951), *The Greeks and the Irrational;* Bruno Snell (1953), *The Discovery of the Mind: The Greek Origins of European Thought;* Jean-Pierre Vernant & Pierre Vidal-Naquet (1990), *Myth and Tragedy in Ancient Greece.* Moses Finley's *The World of Odysseus* (1954) describes the earlier Homeric world-view. Valuable sources on the plays and their context are Simon Goldhill, *Reading Greek Tragedy* (1986); H. D. Kitto, *Greek Tragedy* (1961); and P. E. Easterling (Ed.), *The Cambridge Companion to Greek Tragedy* (1997). Valuable psychoanalytic approaches to Greek tragedy are by Bennett Simon (1988) and C. Fred Alford (1993).

[8] On the political life of ancient Greece, see Finley (1983).

Medea who outranks Jason and Creon, not they her, since she is the granddaughter of the Sun-god and it is from this godly inheritance that her powers derive. Although Aegeus's agreement to give her sanctuary in return for advice on his childlessness ("I know certain drugs whose power will put an end to your sterility. I promise you will beget children") is presented as a prudential and unheroic act on his part (he refuses to help her leave Corinth, merely saying that he will protect her if she can find her own way to Athens), nevertheless its effect is to give her the protection of the highest-ranking Greek city—and, of course, the city in which Euripides' plays were performed. There is further significance in the fact that Medea is ultimately taken to Athens in the chariot of the Sun-god. Her terrible actions are thus endorsed in the play by the protection she is given both by Athens and by a god.

Euripides insists that his audience recognize the states of mind and sense of value that drive both sides in this catastrophic struggle. The play suggests that we cannot live as a society without acknowledging the justice of both.

CHAPTER THREE

Ion:
an Athenian "family romance"

*I*on is a remarkably modern play, nearly 2,500 years old. The 1994 translation of this seldom-read play, by David Lan (1994), and its productions in 1993 and 1994 directed by Nicholas Wright,[1] arose from a recognition of its many contemporary resonances. It is an extraordinary feature of Euripides' play, as with other works of classical Greek tragedy (Alford, 1993; Simon, 1988), that it explores states of mind similar to those that were later to become the principal subject-matter of psychoanalysis. As in the case of *Medea*, the central concerns are with relationships. In *Ion*, the initial focus is on the impact of earlier loss and separation on the mother–child relationship. There is also exploration of the meaning for a child of substitute care (a sort of fostering) and of the impact of infertility within a marriage. These intimate family issues also have a wider social significance, as we shall attempt to show.

---

[1] Nicholas Wright was the author and director of *Mrs Klein* (1988), an impressive though controversial play about the life and work of Melanie Klein, and he is no stranger to psychoanalytic ways of thinking.

The play

We shall begin by telling the story of the play, as it is not as familiar as the better-known Greek dramas. Ion was abandoned by his mother soon after his birth and was brought up in the temple of Apollo at Delphi by the priestess known as the Pythia. When the play opens, he is described by Hermes, messenger of the gods, as having grown up at the temple, where he has become, in his youth, its chief caretaker. He seems innocent and without a care as he goes about his duties in the temple precincts. We see him sweeping the floor, scaring off birds, showing visitors around and taking an interest in them.

Two such visitors are Creusa, daughter of the king of Athens, and her husband, Xuthus—a "foreigner", as she tells Ion, who "won her" through his services to Athens in a war with Athens's enemies. Why have they come? asks Ion.

> CREUSA: He has only one question. He'll put it to Treophonius, and then to Apollo.
> ION: What is it? I'll guess. Will your harvest be fruitful? Will your children be healthy? In my experience, it's one or the other.
> CREUSA: We have no children.
> ION: None at all?
> CREUSA: Ask Apollo if I speak the truth.
> ION: I see why you're distressed. I'm sorry. Poor woman.[2]

Creusa changes the subject:

> CREUSA: Let's talk about you, shall we? Who are you?
> I'm sure you're the envy of your mother's friends.

Ion's replies reveal that he knows only his life in the temple and nothing at all of his origins. This exchange is a poignant evocation of the pain of infertility and the longing to bear children.

But Hermes has already told the play's audience much of the story. Apollo has made love to Creusa, and she has had his child. On Apollo's instructions, the birth was kept secret and the baby exposed. Hermes' task, as the gods' messenger, was to bring the

---

[2] Extracts from *Ion* are taken from *Euripedes: Ion,* translated by David Lan (London: Methuen, 1994).

baby to Delphi, where he has been brought up. And there we see him.

Creusa and Xuthus, we learn, are at this point an unhappy couple. They want a child and heir, both for themselves as a couple and for Athens. The temple at Delphi, where they have come for help, turns out to contain powerful memories for both of them, recalling their younger passionate days before their marriage. Delphi is the temple of Apollo, so Creusa is visiting the place of the god who seduced her, abandoned her, and, for all she knows, left her child to die. Xuthus is visiting a place where, as a kind of tourist on an earlier visit, he had a fling with a "handmaid of the temple"—probably a local girl available for the entertainment of male visitors to the temple district.

Xuthus goes into the temple to see the god. When he comes out, he greets Ion effusively as his child. Ion does not understand. Xuthus explains what Apollo has told him—that the first man he sees when he comes out of the temple will be his son. "If you're my father, you know who's my mother," says Ion, and Xuthus has to explain that Ion's mother is not Creusa, Xuthus's wife, but perhaps an unknown "handmaid".

Xuthus decides that Ion will come home with them to Athens. He proposes a cover story, and the fact that Ion is his son will for the time being be a secret between them.

But Creusa learns what has happened and feels that she is being betrayed. Supported by her ancient servant, who is loyal to her father and her line of descent and who stirs up her sense of outrage, she decides to kill Ion in the midst of the celebration which Xuthus is holding. Apollo intervenes to save him, and Creusa flees from the death sentence passed on her, taking refuge in the sacred precincts of the temple.

Here the mystery is revealed to both Ion and Creusa. The Pythia, Apollo's priestess and Ion's foster-mother, produces the basket in which Ion was brought to Delphi. Creusa recognizes it and learns that Ion is her own lost son, not Xuthus's, and Ion learns that Creusa is his lost mother. Their earlier hatred of each other gives way to love. Athene explains that once the news was out about Xuthus and his son, Apollo had no choice but to send Athene, his goddess sister, to sort things out. She outlines the glorious future of Ion, his descendants, and Athens.

Athene offers a further consolation. She tells Creusa that she and Xuthus will also have sons of their own. Apollo's final instruction is that Xuthus is not to know that Ion is not, in fact, his son. In the end it is to be Xuthus, not Creusa, who is to be kept in the dark.

"The family romance"

This story of separation of mother and child at birth and the later reforging of parent–child bonds is the prototype for many later works of literature. It is a theme well known to us, particularly through Shakespeare's final plays. Loss, melancholic preoccupation, confusion, and guilt precede any possible resolution.

In circumstances where parent and child have remained unknown to each other, a large space, both conscious and unconscious, is created for speculation about what each may in fact be like. Freud pointed out, in his paper on "Family Romances" (1909c), that the habit of mind of imagining parents different from the actual ones does not arise only when literal separations have taken place. He describes the way in which many children imagine that they really come from families that are more grand or distinguished than their own, and he suggests the function of this phantasy as part of the normal process by which children need to detach themselves from idealization of and dependence on their parents. It also serves as a kind of wish-fulfilment in which denigration of the parents' unwelcome sexuality displaces oedipal desires. Additionally, the idea that siblings may not have shared the same parentage may legitimize incestuous desires between siblings.

There may be an inverse phantasy in the minds of parents: that a child who is disappointing their expectations is not their "real" child, or that a child who might have been born to other partners would have been a better bearer of their hopes.

Thus the "extreme" circumstances of actual separation and children brought up in an unknown adoption elsewhere give a more definite and concrete form to phantasies that widely occur in more ordinary conditions of family life. Just as Freud saw in Sophocles' *Oedipus* a literal enactment of a "normal phantasy", so we can see in Euripides' *Ion* a parallel enactment and exploration of universal states of mind.

Seeing and not-seeing

John Steiner (1985) has argued that the most striking fact about King Oedipus is not his incestuous and parricidal desires and their enactment, but his inability to notice evidence that was clearly before his eyes of the dangers to which these desires were exposing everyone. The tragedy of Oedipus, Steiner pointed out, was his heroic search for what should already have been obvious to him. In considering the clinical parallels to this tragedy of unacknowledged aspects of the self, Steiner found that it was the "turning a blind eye", the refusal of the truth, that was the most intractable and significant issue. Steiner's attention to what is known and yet cannot be acknowledged grows out of Bion's extension of psychoanalytic theory to encompass our minds' relationship to knowledge, including knowledge of ourselves, and the crucial importance of the distinction between truth and lies for mental development.

Creusa and Ion are unable, until tragedy has almost struck them both, to recognize the truth that is before their eyes. Creusa tells Ion that she knows a woman who has suffered as his mother has, and that it is on her behalf that she has come to Delphi. This woman has slept with Apollo; she has given birth to his child; the child was got rid of. Ion refuses to believe her, and we see the anxiety stirred by hearing his mother's story—a mixture of the refusal of oedipal knowledge of parental sexuality and the pain of the multiple abandonments being described:

> CREUSA: Then listen ... my friend ... Apollo ... he slept with her
> ION: With a woman? A mortal? That's impossible.
> CREUSA: It's true!
>   And there's more! She gave birth to his child.
> ION: I won't listen!

Creusa, on her side, is equally blind to the meaning of the facts that she and Ion are putting together.

> ION: How long ago did all this happen?
> CREUSA: If the child were alive, he would be more or less your age.
> ION: And since then she's had no more children? Her story's as sad as my own.
> CREUSA: What you say is true. Somewhere a mother is yearning for you.

The question is, what brings Ion and Creusa so close to, and yet so far from, recognition of the truth? Why does Ion's acknowledged desire to find his lost mother, and Creusa's longing to know what has happened to her abandoned baby son, not lead them to recognize in each other their deepest objects of love, given these promising clues?

Love and hate

Different levels of explanation for this situation are elaborated in the play. Before Creusa and Ion are reunited as mother and son, Creusa has tried to have him killed, and he seeks to deliver her to a death by stoning to which she has been condemned when her plot was discovered. It is only when these murderous desires have been mutually recognized that there is space for what becomes a reconciliation between them. Creusa believes it is Xuthus's son by another woman, not her own son, whom she is trying to kill. Ion thinks that Creusa has no good reason to wish him dead. Beneath these surface misapprehensions of identity, Euripides draws our attention to deeper truths.

As Creusa is planning Ion's death with her old servant, they discuss the human inheritance.

OLD SERVANT: The earth's first sons were giants.
CREUSA: Yes!
OLD SERVANT: But slaves to the children of Zeus. So,
    To help them conquer the gods, Earth bore
    A monster, the Gorgon, a hideous girl.
    From each breast a snake spat poison.

Athene helped Perseus kill the Gorgon, but Creusa explains that she gave to Creusa's father, Erechtheus, the founder of Athens,

CREUSA: Two tiny drops of Gorgon's blood.
    One's a cure for any illness.
    The other kills. No remedy.
OLD SERVANT: She gave them to a baby? How?
CREUSA: Locked inside a golden bracelet.
    When Erechtheus died it came to me.
    And here it is.
    This drop flowed from the wound that killed her.

No one who drinks it will ever die.
The drop is venom from the gorge of the serpents.
No one who touches it can live.

Human nature, for such is the implication of this story of descent from Earth, is thus essentially composed of capacities both for love and hate. Melanie Klein's idea (1935) of the "good and bad breast" have frequently been derided as absurd, but here in the myth of the Gorgon's breasts is perhaps its first representation. When a baby does not confirm a mother's sense of her own goodness, through the acceptance of her maternal care and through the reassurance offered by her baby's growth that mother's milk is indeed a life-giving substance, the mother's psychic equilibrium is put at risk. Without such confirmation of her goodness, she is vulnerable to extreme anxiety, even to madness. We can see this process in Creusa's violent turning against the wished-for son who does not recognize her in the action of the play.

The terrible sense of painful rejection and loss is rendered dangerous by being linked to jealousy. Creusa tries to kill Ion because she cannot tolerate the thought that her husband now has a son while she is still deprived of hers. If Ion is not to be her son, he is certainly not to be anyone else's. Her love turns to hatred, the desire for life to the desire for death. In *Medea*, if the children are father's and not Medea's, they must be destroyed as part of the father. In a similar way Ion is now the fruit of two lovers, first Apollo, and now her husband Xuthus. This explains Creusa's passion to kill him.

Euripides shows himself as sympathetic to the situation of women in a patriarchal world in *Ion* as he does in *Medea*:

CREUSA: Life is harder for women than for men:
They judge us, good and bad together, and hate us.
That is the fate we are born to.

Ion's feelings are symmetrical to Creusa's. He is full of rage and indignation when he discovers what has been plotted against him. But this is also doubly determined. Creusa has just tried to have him killed, which is bad enough. But there is also the question of his mother and why she abandoned him as a baby. He has heard Creusa's story about a woman who left her child on the rocks to die.

CREUSA: I know a woman who's suffered as your mother has.
It's for her I've come here ahead of my husband.

Creusa's speaking for a woman who has lost her baby establishes her in an as-if relationship to Ion as his lost mother. She invites Ion to link her with the image of a mother searching for her son, and he responds accordingly, just as in a therapeutic relationship a patient may feel quite concretely that the analyst is, rather than represents, the lost object. Thus the mother he wants so much to find has tried to murder him—and by poisoning what he was about to drink from a cup! Here is an echo of elemental infantile terror of mother's food. And this is a second attack, for he was abandoned as a baby and was never nursed at the breast. So his love, like Creusa's, is transmuted into hate.

Under the impact of such intense fear and hatred, the capacity for reflection is lost. Creusa is afraid to think the thought that Ion might be her lost son; Ion too afraid to think that Creusa might be his mother. So they act out the thought instead, but in its negative form. This "no-mother" and "no-son" must be destroyed. Bion's description (Bion, 1962b) of the way in which our powers of thought can be suffused either with love or hate illuminates these psychic events. Creusa's and Ion's minds are now dominated by fury and hatred, and their thinking is consequently distorted. This creates a peculiar kind of mad logic in which their actions appear reasonable to themselves. Creusa's violent rush of feeling is "rationalized" for her by the disclosure to her that Ion is not the son she would like to have had ("I'm sure your mother's the envy of her friends") but, instead, Xuthus's son by another woman. Her husband's disregard for her feelings intensifies her rage. But its roots also lie in a more normal process of splitting, the other side of a normal idealization of the baby as a part of the self, when it becomes apparent, as it must, that this is never the entire reality. The extreme ambivalence shown in this play by mother towards son and son towards mother thus acts out universal potentialities.

Creusa's old servant, who is loyal to her royal line of descent, and the Chorus, also identified at this point with Creusa and Athens, become paranoid in their hatred of these outsiders, Xuthus and Ion, who, they fear, are going to contaminate their ethnic purity. The old servant constructs what has happened at the temple as

Xuthus's plot against Creusa and imagines that it is intended to end in her death. Here is another version of the absolute intolerance of difference, of the knowledge that two distinct elements (male and female) must combine to create life. The narcissism of the parent wishing to destroy the child who is alien to her is rationalized reference to a larger political reality: the narcissism of a society's commitment to ethnic purity becomes both a cover for an individual's hatred, and, of course, the two in interaction amplify the violent self-justification required to commit murder. Both Creusa and Ion are plunged, by the action of the play, into an exceptional exposure to these powerful infantile feelings. Creusa is having to come to terms with the fact that her marriage to Xuthus is childless. It was a marriage of political expediency, and she thinks back longingly to the passionate moment of Ion's conception. By coming with Xuthus to Delphi she is revisiting, if not the geographical, then at least the emotional setting of this earlier event. Perhaps they both have the idea that if they come here, a place full of memories of an earlier sexual aliveness for them, something creative may happen and give them the child that they want.

The conjunction at Delphi of licensed excess (drinking, the "handmaids of the gods") and spiritual nourishment suggests that this is the recognized function of visits to the temple of Apollo. Analogies with modern tourism come to mind, as the visitors to Delphi marvel at the sculpture and its half-remembered cultural references and haggle about how much they want to pay. When the feast is prepared, it is clear that the temple can put on quite a show.[3]

Adolescence

Ion is approaching adolescence—a moment at which his own identity and his differentiation from his parents become important. Is he just an institutional child, born to live contentedly around the

---

[3] Religious celebrations take many forms, and the Dionysian side of Greek mythology has its modern equivalents. From an anthropological perspective, rock festivals may be as much ritual events as church services. Visits to Delphi seem to have combined spiritual guidance with sensual pleasure.

temple? His enthusiasm in setting up the tent in which the feast to celebrate the discovery of his origins is to take place shows that he relishes new outlets for his capacities. His continuing annoyance with the birds around the temple is not merely because they make a mess of the buildings:

> ION: Oh no! Birds
> Streaming down from Mount Parnassos!
> Don't land here! Get away!
> Keep away from my capitals, my cornices!
> Doves! Swallows! Why do you do this
> every morning? Can't you see
> that I've just swept there?

They have also come to breed:

> ION: Where've you flown from? Do you think
> I'd ever let you build a nest
> of sticks and straw right in the eaves
> of a golden temple? Think again.
> I'll cut your throat.

This boy does not want to be reminded at this point of where babies come from. But when Xuthus tells him that he is his father, his curiosity is immediately aroused. The deprivation of being able to digest the facts of sexuality and generativity a little at a time as a child in ordinary family circumstances can therefore lead to a desperate urgency for knowledge. But Ion has no one to help him with the meaning of his discoveries, and he is overwhelmed by his intense reactions. There is no containment available for this shattering process, external or internal.

He urgently questions Xuthus about the circumstances of his conception. Learning, as he believes, who his father is only stirs in him a desire to know his mother, which is much stronger than his somewhat reluctant acknowledgement of Xuthus.

> ION: Shall I touch the flesh that is my flesh?
> XUTHUS: Touch it? Embrace it! Enfold it!
> ION: My father.
> XUTHUS: My son!
> ION: Mother. Where are you? My longing
> to find you, to see you, is greater

than ever, more painful. Whoever
you are. Wherever you've got to.
My arms ache to hold you.

But what he learns about his origins from Xuthus is not reassuring.
He establishes that Xuthus had been to Delphi before, around the
time when Ion would have been conceived. Ion knows quite well
what happens when visitors come to Delphi.

ION: And you stayed . . .?
XUTHUS: At a tavern.
ION: And there were some . . .?
XUTHUS: Possibly, one or two—what do you call them?
ION: Handmaids of the godhead.
XUTHUS: Exactly.
ION: And you drank?
XUTHUS: Well, there *was* wine . . .
ION: Then that's it! That's where I come from!

This story of his supposed origins in casual sex also explains why
Ion is unconsciously so angry with mothers and is so ready to
believe the worst of Creusa.

The temple at Delphi

The temple at Delphi is represented in the play as having a
well-established role in its society. Ion himself is familiar with the
problems normally brought by visitors, usually concerning bad
harvests and the health of children. There are routines of sacrifice,
payments, questions asked of the oracle, and answers that are
notoriously ambiguous—"riddles". We can think about this pro-
phetic function both at an individual, or familial, level and at a
social and political one, since in answering the questions and responding to the needs of Xuthus and Creusa, both dimensions are
involved. Creusa is the daughter of the king of Athens, and Xuthus
is her husband. Thus the future of the city seems to be at stake in
their situation. In Greek and much later classical drama, kings and
queens who must face the terrors, conflicts, and passions of human
life in stark forms represent the human situation on behalf of the
whole society. The patriarchal social order carried with it the pos-

sibility for everyman to identify with a royal family's engagements with the fundamental issues of life.

Beneath the literal story of whose child Ion is, or is said to be, we can see an imaginary or phantasied story inseparable from the experiences surrounding the adoption of children. Suppose we think of Xuthus and Creusa as above all needing a child and being given one, at Delphi, as a modern childless couple might be given a child by an adoption agency. What kinds of feelings and phantasies might this experience involve for them? What feelings might be evoked in a son who was adopted in these circumstances, like Ion, whose temple upbringing we could think of as that of rather exceptional long-term foster-care? How far do the states of mind enacted in this play help us to understand these modern, everyday states of mind?

This correspondence is not as fanciful as one might suppose if one approaches Creusa's, Xuthus's, and Ion's thoughts about what actually happened in the past as a metaphorical exploration of this issue. How easily does a child adopted by parents who have been unable to produce biological children come to feel to each of them to be the child of *their* marriage, rather than a child of only one of them, or indeed of neither of them? Does it happen that parents are at risk of becoming divided by this experience, one identifying with the child as if it were "naturally" theirs while the other feels excluded? Do earlier good memories of loving relationships and of relationships with parents in a family of origin influence in phantasy the conception of a child as a possible child born out of love? Do earlier dominant bad memories of this kind risk having a toxic effect on identifications with the new child?[4]

Creusa recalls that her father slaughtered her sisters, for interests of state, but that her mother saved her life. She has been forced to abandon a child by the combined pressure of fear of her father and the instructions of her god–lover. This traumatic fact of her life seems to make her vulnerable to complete despair at the thought of her own capacities to be a mother, and to fear that she will be punished for her failure to be one. It takes the generosity of the

---

[4] All of these constellations will be familiar to therapists engaged in clinical work with children and parents in substitute families.

Pythia, Ion's foster-mother, and Ion's own predominantly undamaged capacity for love (which must owe much to the Pythia's devotion to him) to enable Creusa to recover her confidence in the idea that she could become a mother.

Xuthus has a memory of good times at Delphi, consorting with the euphemistically titled "handmaids of the godhead". But he too has a grievance and a source of self-doubt. His wife describes him as having "won her", as if she had been a prize in a competition, and the Chorus and the old servant convey considerable hostility and suspicion towards him as a scheming outsider. Xuthus's omnipotent wish to set up Ion as his heir, and his complete indifference to the role of a mother in Ion's life (whether this be Creusa in the future, or whatever mother Ion was born to), can also be seen as a defence brought about by his isolation as a man who is seen to have brought military muscle to Athens but not much else.[5]

Ion is the least damaged of the three protagonists. He wants a mother and a father. When he learns who his father is, he wants to know about his mother. When he learns who is mother is, he wants to know about his father. He is troubled that he is not the child of both Xuthus and Creusa, and angry with both of them for the casualness with which he fears they have brought him into the world and taken no care of him from that moment. He does not like the idea that he was conceived unintentionally. He is suspicious of his mother's story that she had lain with a god, seeing that as merely a way of avoiding shame.

All this has the potential to end in catastrophe, and it almost does so. Xuthus nearly drives his wife mad by his eager espousal of the idea that his son by another woman is going to be his sole pride and possession. Creusa fears that she is going to be usurped and fears for her family inheritance. Her servant puts the idea into her head that she is the victim of a plot:

OLD SERVANT: Did he
Share your sorrow like your fortune? Did he!
No, he beds some slave girl. A brat's born,

---

[5] This is reminiscent of some adoptive couples where the father seems to deal with the anxieties aroused by infertility by becoming very active in producing a baby through adoption in such a way that the baby seems to be the father's clone.

Farmed out to a friend here in Delphi. It grows.
So does his guile. He says all you need's
To consult great Apollo. . . .

When Ion feels subject to his mother's hatred, his inner memories of being abandoned drive him towards revenge. He denounces her as a harpy and a witch. The form of his revenge is to inflict on her what his baby self had felt exposed to at the time of his abandonment. He was left on a rock, she is to be stoned to death.

The temple resolves the problem of these conflicting desires, but only through several different moves. It is if the temple were trying to practise a sort of psychotherapy with each member of this family separately and is finding great difficulty in bringing together all the narratives constructed in this process. Xuthus is all right so long as he believes that Ion is his alone. Creusa can accept Ion as her son if she believes that he is the outcome of her seduction by Apollo. Ion needs to believe that Xuthus and Creusa are both his parents, or are both going to become his parents. The problem, of course, is that not all of these things can be true. What is certain is that Ion is not the son of Xuthus *and* Creusa. Therefore, if he is Xuthus's son, he is not Creusa's, and if he is Creusa's, he is not Xuthus's. All the ingenuity of the temple is needed to resolve these contradictions.

Reconstituting the family

But a resolution is what Apollo and Athene (the male and the female halves of this therapeutic couple) eventually bring about. How do they do this? One way of describing this process is as a set of deceptions. Xuthus is to be allowed to believe one thing, Creusa and Ion another. The adoptions of earlier decades in our times, which were based on concealment, come vividly to mind. But can this be all that there is to it? Is the lesson of Euripides' temple of Delphi that inconsistent narratives are needed to allow family life to proceed? Lies and denials are a dangerous place to start from, as Euripides so clearly expounded in *Medea*, and here too, if we turn to the level of unconscious identifications, an interesting idea emerges. We can perhaps suggest that the psychological truth re-

vealed in the play is that Xuthus and Creusa need to be able to feel
a separate sense of identification with their adopted son, before his
parenting can be fully shared by them. Ion may also need to believe
that the mother who abandoned him nevertheless loved him, if he
is to accept an adoptive mother. The deeper "truths" from which
the oracle's wisdom is derived may concern what inner beliefs
(what kind of internal objects) these family members may need to
gain access, if their difficult external transitions are to be successfully made. The prophecy that Ion will eventually have four sons,
and that Xuthus and Creusa will have two of their own, suggests
that change and development are not yet finished with, and that
from this rocky start a new family can be constituted. The parents—and the child—who discover belief in themselves may indeed recover creativity and fertility. But the reversal of years of
deprivation at multiple levels usually takes years to work through,
and this time-span is hinted at in the text.

The temple at Delphi has a hard time with its two visitors,
whose questions have implications not merely for their own well-
being but also for the city-state of Athens. Apollo has to improvise
to meet the needs of the situation. First, Xuthus is given the son he
wants. No one except Xuthus and Ion are supposed to know this.
But when the Chorus, loyal to Creusa, report what they have
heard, Apollo has to intervene again, this time via a convenient
spillage and a dove, to prevent Ion drinking from a poisoned cup.
When Creusa flees to the temple steps, pursued by Ion, it becomes
necessary to tell her, and also Ion, another version of the truth.

When Pythia the priestess appears, addressing Ion, her foster-
child, as "my son!", Ion, who is in a fury with Creusa, calms down
a bit, as he feels held by his beloved foster-mother. She produces
the basket in which Ion is supposed to have been brought to Delphi
as a baby, and in which Creusa recognizes the work of her own
hands—a woven image of the Gorgon's face. Creusa is then able to
feel more reconciled to her abandoning seducer, Apollo (by the
evidence of being held in mind at Apollo's temple, we might say),
and she joyfully accepts Ion as her own child.

But Ion's state of mind is still profoundly confused, as it must
be. Making sense of having more than one set of parents is inherently confusing. When Ion thought that Xuthus was his father, his
mother was a "handmaid". Now, when he learns that Creusa is his

mother, it at first seems wonderful. He begins to believe her solemn story that Apollo had lain with her. But his abandonment comes back into his mind, and he becomes suspicious again.

> ION: What if a young girl fell in love
> and then fell in
> with whatever her lover wanted and then
> to save herself and him from shame
> she accused Apollo of seducing her?
> That's what happened, isn't it?

Creusa denies this, and Ion is puzzled about what Apollo is said to have done.

> ION: But then what I can't make sense of is . . .
> He gave me to someone else. He did.
> He told me Xuthus was my father.
> CREUSA: It sometimes happens if a man has sons
> he might give one to a friend who's childless
> so he has an heir. That's what the god did.
> ION: But he lied! How can a god lie?

Ion says that if the gods lie, we can never know the truth, and he is about to confront Apollo himself. In the background is Ion's dread that his whole "family romance" will collapse and he will turn out to be the outcome of a casual act of sex. At this new moment of crisis, Athene appears.

> ION: Who's this rising over the temple?
> Skin streaming light, eyes like suns
> facing the East. Run, mother!
> No mortal may look into a god's face . . .
> Unless my time to do so has come.
> ATHENE: Don't be afraid. Am I against you?
> No, I wish you nothing but good
> Here in Delphi and in Athens my city.
> For I am Athene. Apollo sent me.
> He thought it best not to come himself
> in case it sparked an angry scene
> relating to events that occurred long ago.

It is only now that a fully acceptable story is produced, with the authority of Athene's presence.

ION: Athene, daughter of world-winging Zeus,
      I hear and believe each word you say.
      This is my mother, my father's Apollo.

Creusa can now also become fully reconciled to her situation.

CREUSA: Athene, I want to confess something.
      When I came to this city, Apollo I loathed.
      The walls of his temple crushed me. Now
      Every stone smiles. I praise him.

This secret Creusa and Ion must, however, now keep from Xuthus, who is left to believe that Ion is his son. However, Xuthus and Creusa, made happier by the arrival of Ion, can now go on to have children of their own, the prophecy informs us. Yet we can be sure that the collusion of Creusa and Ion against Xuthus leaves a problem yet to be solved.

The story has a political as well as a familial outcome, upholding a founding myth of Athens. The assertion, in the sacred precincts of the temple, that Ion is the child of Creusa and Apollo establishes the divine origin of the Athenian royal family and of the Greek tribes. It consecrates the mythical origins of the Greeks as products of a marriage of Earth and the gods. Xuthus and Creusa will have descendants, who will found new tribes. Athens has thus been given a way of incorporating into its dynastic succession what might be called (in later terminology) the "ethnically impure" blood of foreigners, which had already been needed in practice to renew the vitality of their line. The difficulty in acknowledging the full humanity of barbarians—that is, non-Greeks (also a prominent theme of Euripides' *Medea*)—has been resolved through the intervention of the gods. This is a comment on the inherent difficulty for human beings of the acceptance of otherness—the gods who have a wider perspective have to help us, just as we can say that inner parental objects who have a concern for all the children in a family are needed to support more generous impulses between siblings. At a wider level, this argument holds within society as a whole, and in principle (however difficult to uphold) also within international relations.

This play therefore functions on many levels. On the one hand, we can analyse the psychic conflicts that form the relations between parents and children, of which Freud's "family romance" is one instance. These conflicts are intensified and sometimes brought to extreme crisis by actual separations and losses and by attempts to reconstruct families after these have taken place, but they occur in some form in all families.

There is also the wider political dimension, as the play invites its audience to enjoy the enactment of the myth of origins of Athens's royal family (which we suggest is a civic version of a "family romance"). Yet—as the authors of its modern English versions, Philip Vellacott and David Lan both point out[6]—the play also invites its audience's scepticism, and leaves questions yet to be resolved. Doubts that the gods are all that they are traditionally cracked up to be are placed in the mouths of characters in the drama. There are parallel doubts about the veracity of the human figures. Xuthus is said by Creusa's servant to have invented the story of Apollo's prophecy, so he could take back to Athens an illegitimate son whom he had farmed out years before. Ion accuses Creusa of inventing her seduction by Apollo to avoid the shame of a love affair. Ion is described as Apollo's, Creusa's, and Xuthus's child, but he cannot be the child of all of them (except perhaps metaphorically, after his adoption.) The priestess's production of the newborn baby's basket, in its pristine condition, might not be all that it seems. Even Athene's flaming presence can be interpreted as stagecraft, using the glare of the setting sun over the temple to simulate a supernatural effect.

Ion denounces the gods for their wanton behaviour, drawing attention to the contrast between how we might expect them to be, as moral examples, and how they were represented in the standard mythology. His recognition that the gods are not above reproach is connected with his growing up as a result of experience, and the way in which the god-like importance of parents for young children is subjected to a sceptical reworking in adolescence. Sex is not divine but human.

---

[6] Philip Vellacott (1954) and David Lan (1994) both draw attention to these issues in the introductions to their English translation (Vellacott) or modern version (Lan) of the play. Vellacott describes a larger context in which Euripides' disenchantment with Athenian "nationalism" and the domination of its war party eventually led him into voluntary exile.

ION: The truth is this: if that day came
       when you, your brother Poseidon and Zeus
       paid fines for all the women you'd seduced
       your temples would be bankrupt. You give in to every urge.

But more unsettling to traditional belief than this picture of the
gods taking their pleasure with humans is Euripides' representation of their difficulties in solving the human problems brought to
them. They are shown as dramaturges not unlike himself, rewrit-
ing their script as they go along, manipulating the action on the
human stage from within their temple.[7] Athene, in her final appearance to Ion and Creusa, explains that the gods have ordained
everything not only for their good, but for that of the Greeks too.
But while the story she tells is flattering to their Athenian identity,
it surely has the idealized quality of a fairy-tale that grown-ups—
and his audiences—might be expected not to believe fully. Intel-
lectually, this suggests that Euripides is calling into question the
basis of the Athenian civic religion, but in a playful spirit. How,
after all, could such a benign outcome cast any shadows? Nonetheless, through the character of Ion, the play elaborates an adolescent scepticism about the values of the grown-up world, and
the failures of the parental generation to live according to these
values.

What sustains the meaning and emotional force of this play
across so many generations, despite such enormous changes in
social and cultural context? Perhaps there is a universal human
truth in this portrayal of the psychological need of parents to have
children, and of a child to have parents. The temple of Delphi
seems to find itself dealing with the anxieties of both, as it takes in
and brings up children who are otherwise parentless, and as it
receives unhappy parents wanting children. What Euripides' ancient and modern audiences take away from the theatre is an understanding of how human deprivation and pain can be overcome,

---

[7] A contrast can be drawn between the role Euripides' assigns to the gods in
Medea, one of his first plays, and in *Ion*, which was written many years later.
Whereas in *Medea* the gods seem to sanctify the heroine by carrying her off, in *Ion*
the audience seems to be invited almost to question their existence, and instead
to see human beings as wholly responsible for their own fate.

when people learn to accept that even if all circumstances are not what they would like them to be, new beginnings can take place just the same. The precondition of this seems to be "a presence" that can contain hate and anxiety and offer an element of understanding and love. In *Ion*, this benign presence is assigned to Apollo's temple. The temple is a sheltering, parental space,[8] contrasting with the bare rocks on which Creusa says she was assaulted and the stone on which she exposed her baby. Theatre, *pari passu*, provides its audiences with a protected space within which to share experiences of emotional deprivation, with the help of playwrights and performers, and to feel the hope offered by understanding.

---

[8] To the sheltering space of the temple is added the basket produced by the Pythia. Rank, as Freud (1909c) pointed out, drew attention to the frequent occurrence of baskets in the many mythical family romances—e.g. the basket in which Moses was found.

Shakespeare's *Macbeth*: a marital tragedy

What is the nature of the contradiction between the "universal facts of life" (see Money-Kyrle, 1968) and the unconscious phantasies, desires, or anxieties of the dramatic characters in *Macbeth*? This is the question we will try to explore in this chapter.

It seems to us that *Macbeth* represents the crisis of an emergent kind of intimate family. It shares this quality with *Romeo and Juliet* and also, though it is a less central issue in the latter play, with *Julius Caesar*.[1] It is paradoxical that a play that is often regarded primarily as the representation of a monstrous couple does, in our opinion, depend for its tragic force on the implicit understanding that they also represent an emblematic kind of "modern" marriage, though of course one that fails in disastrous ways.

Macbeth and Lady Macbeth do not live out a sexually fertile and creative life together or accept their due place in a natural

---

[1] For reflections on this relation to other plays, see "Thinking in *Romeo and Juliet*" (Rustin, 1991b) and "Coups d'Etats and Catastrophic Change: Shakespeare's *Julius Caesar*" (Rustin & Rustin, 1994).

order of generations, which prescribes respect for parents and the rearing of children, who will eventually replace them. On the contrary, they murder the king and symbolic father, Duncan, and make violent war on all the other families who exist in the play. Macbeth has no children of his own; instead, he seeks to destroy all the children of his rivals, who might both remind him of his childlessness and threaten his kingdom and its barren succession. Perverse symbolic children are made by the three witches, at Macbeth's request, with the intention of providing him with magical powers through which he can retain his usurped kingdom.

The normal social order represented in the play is subjected to brutal tyranny by the warrior Macbeth. Macbeth and Lady Macbeth are shown to be gripped by overpowering phantasies, made up of both violent greedy desire, compensating for what they do not otherwise possess, and persecutory anxiety resulting from the crimes they have committed. The catalyst for this upsurge of uncontainable desire is a state of war—indeed, civil war—in which the basis of life, political obedience, and civil well-being is placed at risk.

We wish to suggest that the "historical moment" of Macbeth involves the conjunction of a modern ideal or vision of family with an extra-familial political order that is violent, patriarchal, and unstable. There is therefore no sufficient social containment for intimate relationships between spouses or between parents and children, of the kind that Lawrence Stone (1977) termed "companionate" marriage—a concept that includes the affectionate care of children.[2] The emotional intensity released by the possibility of this intimacy is, we may say, perverted into savage violence and envy of the good, which is so absent from the lives of the Macbeths.

We argue that classical tragedy articulates moments when such conflicts between primordial desires and their social embodi-

---

[2] Lawrence Stone (1977), *The Family, Sex and Marriage in England 1500–1800*. Stone describes what is essentially a new bourgeois form of marriage. But while Macbeth is represented as a member of a warrior clan society and in no way a bourgeois, we can note that Lady Macbeth and he plot their "career" together as a project that depends on their mutual efforts, rather than on birth or royal favour. Audiences may then and now have identified with their "achievement orientation" and individualism, filtering out these historical trappings.

ment or realization cannot be contained and when this leads to catastrophic breakdown. Out of these imagined breakdowns, contemplated in the experience of the drama, arise insight and self-understanding for playwright, players, and audiences. The cultural function of tragedy, in articulating and reflecting on these moments, is to find ways of reintegrating into contemporary understanding these unfamiliar desires and fears.[3]

It is a paradox that Macbeth resonates with us because of its representation of the possibility of a form of marital relationship that it scarcely articulates in positive terms at all. The "facts of life" of gender, generation, and succession that shape the roles of the characters are universals of human existence. But of course their embodiment in this particular form of intimate sexual relationship within marriage is far from a universal fact of existence. To this extent, Macbeth is historically specific.

Just as Raymond Williams's idea of a "structure of feeling" may seem to be a contradiction in terms, so equally may seem our concept of a tragic contradiction between primordial universals of human experience and historically specific worlds. The "primordial" dimensions of gender, generation, and succession are themselves inevitably mediated and defined within a social context. But the potential for contradiction between the desires and anxieties nurtured within such a "structure of feeling" and the social order within which they seek fulfilment nevertheless remains.

This contradiction is the basis of tragedy.

The private and the public spheres

The public and private spheres impact upon one another powerfully in Macbeth. The play begins and ends on the battlefield, but in between its action takes place indoors, in Macbeth's castle, and in Macbeth and Lady Macbeth's private rooms within the castle. There are moments of intense intimacy in conversations between

---

[3] For additional discussion of this theme of "catastrophic change", see chapter 5, footnote 7.

Lady Macbeth and Macbeth and later in Macbeth's devastated reflections on his wife's death. In the contrasted family of Macduff, in Lady Macduff's and Macduff's thoughts about each other after Macduff has abandoned her, and in Macduff's grief-stricken reaction to her and their children's deaths, there is similar evidence of private passion. Both Macbeth and Macduff endure the death of their wives, and both are also much preoccupied with the fate of children dead or unborn.

There are also, in this tragedy, battles, assassinations, political meetings, and a formal banquet. The play seems centrally to be about the impact of a terrible, cruel, and unpredictable public world, on sensibilities and values that belong to the private sphere of family.

It is the essence of our view of classical tragedy that this should be the case. Values consonant with the primordial imperatives of generation and gender are, in tragedy, contradicted by social forces or contexts indifferent or antagonistic to them. Tragedies represent the consequences of these contradictions, in which their audiences can be presumed to recognize their own situation to some degree.

The extraordinary aspect of *Macbeth* is its contrasting of a recognizably contemporary conception of intimate marriage and affectionate parenthood with the harsh order of a militarized and violence-ridden society. The play perhaps gains its continuing resonance from the correspondences we can see between the extremes of civil war, regicide, and brutal tyranny and the more mundane forms of power-seeking, ambition, and patriarchy familiar to most audiences of the play.

Macbeth explores perverse as well as merely violent and brutal states of mind. Beyond invoking the states of anxious anticipation of events usual in dramatic narrative, it makes problematic the orderly temporal framework in which life is conventionally lived. It represents its characters as so torn apart by desire and anxiety that they become unable to think or are led to adopt strategies of psychic defence (obsessional guilt, death-defying courage), which preserve a coherence of identity only at the price of a state of virtual isolation. Shakespeare's poetry is, of course, the primary means for the representation of these many dimensions of the imagined action.

The unconscious in a state of war

The action of *Macbeth* begins on a battlefield, represented at its
outset as a location of the perverse:

> WITCHES: Fair is foul and foul is fair.
>   Hover through the fog and filthy air.
>
> [Act I, Scene 1, lines 10–11][4]

It is the confusion of categories of good and evil at the outset of the
play that renders the air poisonous. Banquo, Macbeth's companion, recognizes the danger of madness that confronts him and
Macbeth in their encounter with the witches, while Macbeth is
immediately seduced by them:

> MACBETH: Would they had stayed!
> BANQUO: Were such things here as we do speak about?
>   Or have we eaten on the insane root
>   That takes the reason prisoner?
>
> [Act I, Scene 3, lines 82–85]

Banquo later tells Macbeth:

> BANQUO: I dreamt last night of the three weird sisters:
>   To you they have showed some truth.
>
> [Act II, Scene 1, lines 20–21]

Banquo can distinguish dream from reality, and he struggles to
hold on to his powers of thinking. "I think not of them," says
Macbeth, and in the soliloquy that follows "Is this a dagger that I
see before me", he reports his state of confusion. He is not able to
resist the enchantment of the "wicked dreams" that "abuse the
curtained sleep":

> MACBETH: Art thou not, fatal vision, sensible
>   To feeling as to sight, or art thou but
>   A dagger of the mind, a false creation,
>   Proceeding from the heat-oppressed brain?
>
> [Act II, Scene 1, lines 36–39]

---

[4] Extracts from *Macbeth* are taken from *The Arden Shakespeare*, edited by
Kenneth Muir (London: Methuen, 1951; reprinted London: Routledge, 1988).

Lady Macbeth persistently attacks Macbeth's capacity for thinking, believing that this will undermine their project. "Consider it not so deeply," she says (Act II, Scene 2, line 29), and:

LADY MACBETH: These deeds must not be thought
    After these ways; so, it will make us mad.

[Act II, Scene 2, lines 33–34]

and

LADY MACBETH: Be not lost
    So poorly in your thoughts.
MACBETH: To know my deed, 'twere best not to know myself.

[Act II, Scene 2, lines 70–72]

She persuades Macbeth that his best self is his worst, and his worst his best. Meanwhile the witches offer him the promise of a magical, wish-fulfilling form of delusion, which is a perverse substitute for reason.

The catalyst for the disruptive surge of uncontrolled phantasy or unconscious desire that dominates the action of *Macbeth* is a state of war,[5] which soon becomes, with the reported treachery of the Thane of Cawdor, civil war. In such a war, anything can happen—the outcome of such battles, in early modern Europe, might be determined in ten minutes, by whether or not soldiers run away, or by whether a leader is killed.[6] What happens is that Duncan, who is nearly defeated, is saved by Macbeth and Banquo.

Rational judgement, in these situations of extreme fear and uncertainty, often disappears—Duncan has been wrong about the Thane of Cawdor, though, it turns out, not as wrong as he thinks, as the Thane dies with grace and dignity.

MALCOLM: Nothing in his life
    Became him like the leaving it.

[Act I, Scene 4, lines 7–8]

---

[5] The state of war in Macbeth has some of the properties of the state of war in Hobbes' near-contemporary writings. The consequences of the removal of limits and boundaries to ambition and aspiration are what Durkheim later described as a "state of anomie". The play can be understood sociologically as a meditation on what Talcott Parsons later, drawing on the problems posed by Hobbes and Durkheim, called the "problem of order" (Parsons, 1937).

[6] This observation was made to us by Roger Owen, in discussion.

He is then wrong again about Macbeth, the new Thane of Cawdor. In these life-or-death situations, judgement goes out of the window, even for men generally thought of as good rulers, like Duncan. Reflection on experience is replaced by a variety of omnipotent states of mind, which are felt to provide protection from the threat of death. Macbeth's omnipotence grows out of his real valour. It is a quality of willed fearlessness, though in someone we know to be capable of extreme anxiety and virtual collapse at other moments.

The psychic world is turned upside down by the brutal experience of battle, in which life hangs on a thread and survival is only at the expense of meting out extreme violence upon enemies. The witches represent this upside-down world, articulating, as in a malign dream, phantasies that would not in other circumstances be entertained, but which turn out in the conditions of battle to have some plausibility.

A number of dimensions to Macbeth's ambition are sequentially revealed as the play proceeds. The revelation of the fallibility and weakness of the king–father is one trigger of his limitless desire. A benign and saintly disposition, such as that attributed to Duncan later in the play, is not the character most called for in a state of war. However, Duncan also shows scant loyalty to his friends. He turns promiscuously from one favourite—the first Thane of Cawdor—to Macbeth and Banquo, but he then provokes intense rivalry between these quasi-brothers by suddenly pronouncing Malcolm his legitimate successor. Malcolm is his son, but he has not earned his good fortune by feats of valour like Macbeth's. Macbeth is thus provoked, both by the king's actions and the witches' prophecies, to attack not only the kingly father, but also the principle of filial succession itself. Macbeth's envy of the filial tie leads him to the attempted murder of Fleance and the murder of Macduff's children. The importance of the relationship with a father is further emphasized by Lady Macbeth's admission of her feelings about Duncan:

LADY MACBETH: Had he not resembled
My father as he slept, I would have done't.

[Act II, Scene 2, lines 12–13]

The absence of a child to succeed Macbeth contrasts with the images of paternal fertility that surround him.

The boundless and destructive nature of the phantasies un-leashed in aspirants to kingship is elaborated in a later speech in which Malcolm pretends to set out what he would become if he were king. This description must evoke for his listener, Macduff, and for the play's audience, the nature of Macbeth's own tyrannical rule, and in this description are also laid out the temptations before any absolute ruler. By putting these temptations into words and re-nouncing them, Malcolm, the future king, inspires trust in Macduff. Malcolm is able here to share his thoughts with Macduff, whereas Macbeth has had his attempts at self-understanding rebuffed by Lady Macbeth as unmanly weakness, and thereafter he can only think alone, in soliloquy, or in monologues with subordinates.

Phantasies of omnipotent power are unspoken, but all the more compulsively acted out by Macbeth:

MACDUFF: Not in the legions
    Of horrid hell can come a devil more damned
    In evils to top Macbeth.
MALCOLM: I grant him bloody,
    Luxurious, avaricious, false, deceitful,
    Sudden, malicious, smacking of every sin
    That has a name: but there's no bottom, none
    In my voluptuousness: your wives, your daughters
    Your matrons and your maids, could not fill up
    The cistern of my lust, and my desire
    All continent impediments would o'erbear,
    That did oppose my will. Better Macbeth
    Than such a one to reign.
MACDUFF: Boundless intemperance
    In Nature is a tyranny; it hath been
    Th'untimely emptying of the happy throne
    And fall of many kings.

                                    [Act IV, Scene 3, lines 55–69]

The fact that the desires driving Macbeth onwards are not articu-lated makes them all the more powerful and disruptive. He is driven by what he does not understand to commit more and more terrible crimes.

The compulsive power of tyranny is explored with respect to its effects on its victims. They lose their capacities for both thought and faithfulness. Terror leads them to collude with the power of the tyrant and then suffer terrible guilt in their turn for what they have done. This is the tragic meaning of Macduff's desertion of his family and is the context for Malcolm's testing him out by his false declaration of his own prospective wickedness. The possibility is set out that nothing good will survive. The bereft Lady Macduff and her son try to make sense of what has happened to them, the boy reproaching his mother for the same disloyalty for which she reproaches Macduff. But both are quick to defend him when the murderers arrive, for they have not lost all belief in his goodness:

SON: My father is not dead, for all your saying.
LADY MACDUFF: Yes, he is dead. How wilt thou do for a father?
SON: Nay, how will you do for a husband?
LADY MACDUFF: Why, I can buy me twenty at any market.
SON: Then you'll buy 'em to sell again.

[Act IV, Scene 2, lines 37–41]

Even the witches are accused of treachery to their sex—that is to Hecate, the goddess of sorcery—in becoming too excited by their dealings with Macbeth. They have to be warned that he offers nothing to them:

HECATE: And, which is worse, all you have done
       Hath been but for a wayward son,
       Spiteful and wrathful: who, as others do,
       Loves for his own ends, and not for you.

[Act III, Scene 5, lines 10–13]

Macbeth encounters the phantasy that literally anything is possible in company with Banquo. Banquo is also the subject of the tempting prophecies of the three witches:

FIRST WITCH: Lesser than Macbeth, and greater.
SECOND WITCH: Not so happy, yet much happier.
THIRD WITCH: Thou shalt get kings, though thou be none.
   So all hail, Macbeth and Banquo!
FIRST WITCH: Banquo and Macbeth, all hail!

[Act I, Scene 3, lines 66–69]

The "three witches" sequences, and the unspoken "wishes" they offer to gratify have the enchanted quality of repetition of a fairy tale. The witches seduce Macbeth, and nearly Banquo, into the loss of their reason:

BANQUO: Were such things here as we do speak about
Or have we eaten on the insane root
That takes the reason prisoner?

[Act I, Scene 3, lines 83–85]

The fact that Banquo is tempted, as well as Macbeth, establishes that these are temptations that could disturb anyone. This is the psychic threat lurking in the battlefield situation of a disrupted and fragile social order in which no one's place is secure.

Once the first crime has been committed, desire and ambition are replaced by persecutory anxiety as Macbeth's compelling obsession. One murder leads to another, as the burden of anxiety from each mounts up. The extreme guilt arising from his initial act of parricide is manifested in Macbeth's repeated attempts to shift the blame onto the bereaved sons—first Malcolm and Donalbain, later Fleance—for their fathers' murders—an attribution whose implausibility is pointed out by one observer of these events:

LENNOX: Who cannot want the thought, how monstrous
It was for Malcolm and for Donalbain
To kill their gracious father? Damned fact!
How it did grieve Macbeth! Did he not straight,
In pious rage, the two delinquents tear,
That were the slaves of drink and thralls of sleep?
Was that not nobly done?

[Act III, Scene 6, lines 8–14]

The monstrousness of Macbeth's crimes leads him to become fearful of revenge by these falsely accused sons, who must thus be exterminated like serpents before they can grow up, and the surviving father (Macduff). It is the idea of a united family that seems most to frighten Macbeth. The news of Macduff's resistance sends Macbeth off to the witches for a further reinforcement of his ruthless cruelty. The prophecy made to him made by the witches' second apparition, a bloody child, evokes a strange vision:

SECOND APPARITION: Be bloody, bold, and resolute!
Laugh to scorn
The power of man, for none of woman born
Shall harm Macbeth.

[Act IV, Scene 1, lines 79–81]

This provokes Macbeth to murder Macduff's wife and children as a means of destroying the power of fecundity in his rivals. Macbeth's state of mind enables us to see with horrible clarity why children are included in acts of genocide. Children have to be killed because they are imagined, consciously or unconsciously, as future agents of retribution and revenge. Macbeth is then magically reassured by the prophecy. Since he has shown he is strong enough to kill normally born children of every rival family, there can be none left powerful enough to threaten him.

The modern marriage of Macbeth and Lady Macbeth

It is a striking feature of the play that despite Macbeth and Lady Macbeth's wickedness, we become deeply identified with them and can mourn their fates.

In this violent world, they are a curiously modern couple. Macbeth is full of terms of endearment for his wife ("my dearest partner of greatness", "my dearest love", "dearest chuck"). He writes to her to tell her his extraordinary news. They talk to each other and form a plan of action together. Their dialogues touch on many different moods. Lady Macbeth is acutely sensitive to Macbeth's state of mind and tries to help him, as she thinks, to get over his attacks of panic and weakness. They each attempt to understand and control their individual states of mind, and they also have a subtle and rapidly evolving division of emotional labour. Lady Macbeth becomes identified with the witches, as ministers of the devil, after she has read Macbeth's letter about them, and she takes on responsibility for destroying both the tender aspects of her own and Macbeth's nature.

LADY MACBETH: Come, thick night
And pall thee in the dunnest smoke of hell,
That my keen knife sees not the wound it makes,
Nor heaven peep through the blanket of the dark,
To cry "hold, hold!"

[Act I, Scene 5, lines 51–55]

It is because Lady Macbeth has taken this responsibility that she is later overwhelmed with guilt. Where Macbeth always has the option of externalizing his pain in violent action, Lady Macbeth can act only through the agency of her husband. She is later abandoned by Macbeth as he becomes addicted to evil. He tells her he is going to the witches for more of the poison that they feed him:

MACBETH: I will tomorrow
And betimes I will, to the weird sisters;
More they shall speak, for now I am bent to know
By the worst means the worst. For mine own good
All causes shall give way. I am in blood
Stepped so far that, should I wade no more
Returning were as tedious as go o'er.

[Act III, Scene 4, lines 134–141]

Lady Macbeth is thus soon left to suffer the emotional burdens of guilt and remorse on her own. The woman, in this modern marriage, is already the specialist in the management of feelings. Macbeth presciently sounds out the Doctor as a prospective psychiatrist ("Cannot thou minister to a mind diseased"), pointing out the space that modern patterns of emotional life would several centuries later require to be filled by new professional specialisms.

Their conversations often carry the expectations of instant mutual understanding of an intimate marriage, though they are painful to hear because the couple often find themselves out of touch with each other. In the following passage, the rapid monosyllabic exchange conveys how much is usually taken for granted between them:[7]

LADY MACBETH: My husband!
MACBETH: I have done the deed. Did'st thou not hear a noise?
LADY MACBETH: I heard the owl scream, and the crickets cry.
   Did you not speak?
MACBETH: When?
LADY MACBETH: Now.
MACBETH: As I descended?
LADY MACBETH: Ay.
MACBETH: Hark!
   Who lies i' th'second chamber?

[Act II, Scene 2, lines 13–19]

---

[7] A well-known article in the field of phenomenological sociology by Peter Berger and Hans Kellner described modern marriage as above all an evolving conversation (Berger & Kellner, 1964).

The child they do not have figures as a negative in Lady Macbeth's reproaches to Macbeth, urging him to the violent action that has taken the place of bearing children together:

LADY MACBETH: I have given suck and know
How tender 'tis to love the babe that milks me:
I would, while it was smiling in my face,
Have plucked the nipple from his boneless gums
And dashed his brains out, had I so sworn as you
Have done to this.

[Act I, Scene 7, lines 54–58]

The play also has a second representation of an intimate marriage, in Macduff and Lady Macduff, the contrasting yet similar couple. This household makes clear how strongly the conception of family is present as an alternative source of positive identities and identifications. This marriage, like that of Macbeth and Lady Macbeth, also fails disastrously, but also in its failure demonstrates the potential fulfilment that has been lost. Macduff has abandoned his wife and left her and their children to be slaughtered by assassins:

LADY MACDUFF: What had he done, to make him fly the land?
ROSS: You must have patience, madam.
LADY MACDUFF: He had none:
His flight was madness. When our actions do not
Our fears do make us traitors.
ROSS: You know not
Whether it was his wisdom or his fear.
LADY MACDUFF: Wisdom! To leave his wife, to leave his babes
His mansion and his titles, in a place
From whence he himself does fly? He loves us not.
He wants the natural touch; for the poor wren,
The most diminutive of birds will fight,
Her young ones in her nest, against the owl.
All is the fear, and nothing is the love;
As little is the wisdom, where the flight
Runs against all reason.

[Act IV, Scene 2, lines 1–14]

Feminists might note here that the heroic wren Lady Macduff is describing defending the nest is a mother.

Lady Macduff's speech, and later Macduff's guilty and repent-
ant response to his family's slaughter, represent a conception of
family life that has been violated but nevertheless stands in the
play for the most natural of all social bonds.

Most obviously, women and familial virtues are placed at risk
or sacrificed in the conditions of war. (This is also Portia's rebuke to
Brutus in Julius Caesar.) Lady Macduff suffers abandonment; Lady
Macbeth adopts the opposite but equally terrible strategy of becoming her husband's partner and comrade in violence and political conspiracy. None of the other characters—Malcolm, Duncan,
Banquo—have female partners. The witches represent another version of femininity, perhaps the degraded sexuality of war with its
two poles of prostitution and rape, and hate-filled revenge of
women for the degradation inflicted on them in conditions of disorder and violence.

But there is a more disturbed vision of sexuality and perverse
procreation in the play. At the root of Macbeth's envious hatred
and cruelty seems to be the fact that he and Lady Macbeth have no
child to succeed them. It is the inability to constitute a procreative
couple that leads Macbeth and Lady Macbeth into their alliance,
which denies the normal differences of gender and banishes tenderness; they compete with each other to be the more ruthless.
There is a suggestion that violence is a substitute for sexual potency
for Macbeth, for example in the Porter's jokes about doubtful
sexual potency in Macbeth's castle, and in the comparison Macbeth
makes between himself as Duncan's murderer, who

> MACBETH: With Tarquin's ravishing strides, towards his design
> Moves like a ghost.
>
> [Act II, Scene 1, lines 55–56]

Lady Macbeth violently denies the more tender part of herself
when she claims she would have plucked her baby from her breast
and dashed its brains out rather than break an oath such as
Macbeth has made to her. This is also the imaginary baby they do
not have, and for which their quest for usurped power is a substitute. Lady Macduff's children, abandoned by their father and murdered by Macbeth, are victims of a hatred of fertility. Even the two
sleeping grooms seem like frightened children, and this arouses
pity and guilt in Macbeth:

MACBETH: But they did say their prayers, and address'd them
    Again to sleep.
LADY MACBETH: There are two lodged together.
MACBETH: One cried "God bless us!" and "Amen" the other,

[Act II, Scene 2, lines 24–26]

In the place of creative sexual reproduction, there is the witches'
cauldron of bad "part-objects", a magical production of monster
babies:

FIRST WITCH: Round about the cauldron go;
    In the poisoned entrails throw.
    Toad, that under cold stone
    Days and nights has thirty-one
    Swelter'd venom sleeping got,
    Boil thou first in the charmed pot.
ALL: Double, double, toil and trouble;
    Fire burn, and cauldron bubble.

[Act IV, Scene 1, lines 4–11]

One might see the sweltered venom got in 31 days and nights
as a reference to the product of a perverted menstrual cycle. The
playful but perverse attraction of children to the idea of the
witch's cauldron of slimy things reminds one how universal is this
unconscious phantasy that babies may be made perversely and
omnipotently, without the need of the hated and envied parental
intercourse. Two of the three apparitions that come out of the
cauldron are children.

When the witches are seen for the second time, the first witch is
engaged in an attack on a couple, the sailor being made to "dwindle, peak and pine" in punishment for the sailor's wife's refusal to
give the witch a "chestnut" (perhaps a testicle?) from her lap.

The king offers an image of omnipotent asexual[8] reproduction
when he rewards Macbeth:

---

[8] One can see a contrast in the play between a homosexual world of soldier
comrades, enemies, and bitter rivalries in which, as in *Coriolanus*, hand-to-hand
combat is imbued with sexuality, and a suffering heterosexual world of families
whose women must either be abandoned to murder or must attempt to become
as fierce as their men, destroying all their own and their men's tenderness in
order to do so. While it is not very popular to represent matters in this way, it
does seem that this is an important ordering principle of this play, as it is of *Julius
Caesar*.

KING: Welcome hither.
I have begun to plant thee, and will labour
To make thee full of growing.

[Act I, Scene 4, lines 28–30]

Having rewarded Macbeth, however, the king immediately provokes both jealousy and envy by an act that he attributes to his
limitless potency:

BANQUO: There, if I grow
The harvest is your own.
KING: My plenteous joys,
Wanton in fullness, seek to hide themselves
In drops of sorrow. Sons, kinsmen, thanes,
And you whose places are the nearest, know
We will establish our estate upon
Our eldest Malcolm, whom we name hereafter
The Prince of Cumberland.

[Act I, Scene 4, lines 33–40]

Although marriage is a tragic failure in Macbeth, it is in fact the
main positive point of reference in the universe of the play. We
could see the play as a meditation on this emerging new form of
modern life and intimacy, and the great pressures upon it in a
world dominated by considerations of male violence and unre-
strained conflict. The prophecy that Banquo's heirs will eventually
provide a line of kings, and his loved son's Fleance's escape from
the murderers, holds out some hope that a social order based on
families will eventually prevail.

Macbeth's and Lady Macbeth's virtues

Macbeth is a heroic figure. It is his bravery and his capacity to
"seize the time" and rescue his kingdom that also gives him the
opportunity and temptation to become a tyrant. The opening report of Macbeth's valour goes thus:

CAPTAIN: For brave Macbeth—well he deserves that name—
Disdaining Fortune, with his brandished steel,
Which smoked with bloody execution,
Like valour's minion carved out his passage

Till he faced the slave;
Which nev'r shook hands, nor bade farewell to him,
Till he unseamed him from the nave to the chops,
And fixed his head upon our battlements.

[Act I, Scene 2, lines 16–23]

The play tells us that the qualities of a Greek hero of battle that might be needed in some circumstances often come with other qualities that might be wanted rather less—a dilemma that has not lessened over subsequent centuries of war.

A still more interesting paradox is that it is Macbeth's capacity for guilt and remorse, not his hardness, that drives him on to such terrible deeds, murdering first Banquo and then Macduff's wife and children. Macbeth, and Lady Macbeth, suffer a terrible internal struggle with persecutory anxiety. Not everyone who seizes power in Shakespearean drama has a moral sensibility. Henry Bolinbroke (*Henry IV*), Prince Hal once he becomes Henry V, and Octavius Caesar are examples of rulers who are hard enough to grasp absolute power and who are not unduly troubled by the damage they may effect when they do so. This is why they appear as relatively one-dimensional, instrumental figures, far short of tragic. Macbeth, however, does have to struggle with this more sensitive part of himself. In killing his enemies, he is also killing aspects of himself that have been projected into them. Lady Macbeth at once realizes that Macbeth's feelings of guilt and remorse threaten their whole enterprise and rebukes him:

LADY MACBETH: Who was it that thus cried? Why, worthy Thane
    You do unbend your noble strength, to think
    So brainsickly of things. Go get some water,
    And wash this filthy witness from your hand.
    Why did you bring the daggers from the place?
    They must lie there: go carry them, and smear
    The sleepy grooms with blood.
MACBETH: I'll go no more.
    I am afraid to think what I have done;
    Look on't again I dare not.
LADY MACBETH: Infirm of purpose!
    Give me the daggers. The sleeping and the dead
    Are but as pictures. 'Tis the eye of childhood
    That fears a painted devil. If he do bleed

I'll gild the faces of the grooms withal,
For it must seem their guilt.

[Act II, Scene 2, lines 43–56]

The function of smearing blood over the grooms is not only a stratagem diverting the blame for Duncan's murder but already a projection of the guilt that Lady Macbeth feels, despite her denials. Later she suffers even more deeply than Macbeth from her guilt, and of course she goes out of her mind and takes her own life.

Banquo has the relation of a double to Macbeth. He is subject to, and attracted by, the temptations put before Macbeth. When Macbeth has Banquo murdered, he is killing his better self, and Banquo's appearance in his chair in the banqueting tells us again that Macbeth is encountering his double—a split-off better part of himself.

Macbeth decides as the play goes on to suppress his thoughts and instead to rely on actions:

MACBETH: Strange things I have in head that will to hand,
Which must be acted 'ere they may be scanned.

[Act III, Scene 4, lines 140–141]

He becomes more peremptory, abusive, and threatening to those around him. He withdraws from Lady Macbeth, ceasing to talk with her. He adopts a psychic strategy of self-sufficiency, shaping an armoured self to cope with both internal and external threats. But even as this is taking place, Macbeth retains his capacity for self-understanding, noting the impotence of the doctor to cure the ills of the mind in both individuals and peoples and recognizing, after Lady Macbeth's death, that he has nothing that is worth remaining alive for:

MACBETH: My way of life
Is fall'n into the sear, the yellow leaf,
And that which should accompany old age,
As honour, love, obedience, troops of friends,
I must not look to have;

[Act V, Scene 3, lines 22–26]

We can note here the implied loss, the conception of a rich fulfilled life against which his violent tragedy and end must be measured.

Macbeth's resort to arms at the end of the play is determined psychologically, as well as by military necessity.

MACBETH: I'll fight, till from my bones my flesh be hacked.
    Give me my armour.
SEYTON: 'Tis not needed yet.
MACBETH: I'll put it on.

[Act V, Scene 3, lines 32–34]

Time in Macbeth

The catastrophic role of the sphere of the unconscious in this play, in its various dimensions of desire and anxiety, is represented in the ways in which the passage of time is repeatedly brought to the audience's attention. Time in the play is lived in many different modalities—of perverse delusion in which phantasy is the only reality (the witches); of manic excitement (in battle); of anxious suspense (the time of Macbeth's murders); and of depression, in which future time stretches out as a dead space. The alternate hurrying-up, slowing-down, and anxious suspense of the action, and the self-conscious reflections on the passage of time for this or that person, are particularly marked features of Macbeth.

The literary critic Peter Brooks has argued (Brooks, 1984) that the structures and forms of literary narrative can be illuminated by psychoanalysis. His argument is particularly pertinent to the characters' relation to time in this play. Narratives, he suggests, represent deferrals of satisfaction—that is to say the interplay of external realities with the pressures of desires and intentions. This perspective seems particularly fruitful in considering Macbeth. Audiences cannot avoid becoming keenly aware of the pain suffered by its various characters in living through different kinds of moments of impatient longing, fear, guilt, and despair.

Preoccupation with time is indicated in the very first word of the play:

FIRST WITCH: When shall we three meet again?
    In thunder, lightning, or in rain
SECOND WITCH: When the hurly-burly's done,
    When the battle's lost and won.

THIRD WITCH: That will be ere the set of sun.

[Act I, Scene 1, Lines 1–5]

The outcome of a battle is being decided in a space of time defined
by the witches—in enchanted time, so to speak.

The witches are then perceived by Banquo to have the gift of
seeing into the future:

BANQUO: If you can look into the seeds of time,
And say which grain will grow and which will not,
Speak then to me, who neither fear
Your favours nor your hate.

[Act I, Scene 3, lines 58–61]

They appear to Macbeth and Banquo to have the capacity to disrupt in a magical way the natural temporal sequence of events.
When Macbeth is greeted from the king as "Thane of Cawdor", he
protests:

MACBETH: The Thane of Cawdor lives: Why do you dress me
In borrowed robes?
ANGUS: Who was the thane lives yet
But under heavy judgement bears that life
Which he deserved to lose.

[Act I, Scene 3, lines 108–111]

Of course, the smaller of the witches' prophecies having once been
fulfilled, belief in the larger ones proves irresistible.

The meaning of these exchanges, early in the play, is that they
establish the priority of the mental space of desire and phantasy
over that of external reality, of which temporal order is a key
marker. The action of the play is marked by the pressures of unconscious impulse and motivation upon the "reality principle". The
attention that is so frequently drawn in the play to time, as disordered, unbearable, tormenting, or in some other way problematic,
marks the precarious boundary of the reality principle and the
unavailing struggle of the play's two tragic figures to hold themselves in some reflective relation to it.

Once Macbeth has heard the witches' prophecies and been told
by the king's messengers that he is Thane of Cawdor, he and Lady
Macbeth become driven by a compulsion to act instantly, under the
pressure of their compulsive desires. However, this impulse con-

flicts with Macbeth's awareness that reality cannot simply be anni-
hilated by an act of will and that actions have consequences:

> MACBETH: If it were done when 'tis done, then 'twere well
> It were done quickly. If th'assassination
> Could trammel up the consequence, and catch
> With his surcease, success, that but this blow
> Might be the be-all and end-all—here,
> But here, upon this bank and shoal of time,
> We'd jump the life to come.
>
> [Act I, Scene 7, lines 1–7]

Lady Macbeth enters, to bring her husband's troubled meditation
to an abrupt end:

> MACBETH: How now! what news?
> LADY MACBETH: He has almost supped. Why have you left the
> chamber?
> MACBETH: Hath he asked for me?
> LADY MACBETH: Know you not he has?
>
> [Act I, Scene 7, lines 28–30]

Soon it is Macbeth who is taking his turn to insist on instant action,
to the two murderers of Banquo:

> MACBETH: Your spirit shines through you. Within this hour at most
> I will advise you where to plant yourselves,
> Acquaint you with the perfect spy 'o the time
> The moment on't; for 't must be done tonight,
>
> [Act III, Scene 1, lines 128–131]

The repeated knocking at the door, after the murder of the king,
reminds Macbeth and Lady Macbeth, and the play's audience, that
the time of reality does exist after all.

> MACBETH: Whence is that knocking?
> How is't with me, when every noise appals me?
>
> . . .
>
> LADY MACBETH [*Knock*]:   I hear a knocking
> At the south entry. Retire we to our chamber.
> A little water clears us of this deed:
> How easy is it then! Your constancy
> Hath left you unattended. Hark! more knocking.
> Get on your nightgown, lest occasion call us

And show us to be watchers. Be not lost
So poorly in your thoughts.
MACBETH: To know my deed, 'twere best not know myself.
[*Knock.*]
Wake Duncan with thy knocking! I would thou could'st!

[Act II, Scene 2, lines 57–73]

The Porter's speech then elaborates a metaphor that reminds his listeners that this time of reality signifies men's mortality and their fate in the afterlife:

PORTER: Here's a knocking indeed! If a man were porter of hell gate, he should have old turning the key.
[*Knock.*]
Knock, knock, knock! Who's there, i'th' name Beelzebub?

[Act II, Scene 1, lines 1–4]

Time is the explicit topic of many less important exchanges. For example, the witch torments the sailor by disrupting his sense of time:

FIRST WITCH: Weary sev'nights nine times nine
Shall he dwindle, peak and pine.

[Act I, Scene 3, lines 22–23]

The King expects to find Macbeth at his castle before him but seems in some doubt whether he has in fact arrived. Banquo and Fleance set out to establish what time it is, establishing a time-marker for the audience at the outset of Act II, just as the witches' speeches did at the beginning of Act I.

BANQUO: How goes the night, boy?
FLEANCE: The moon is down; I have not heard the clock.
BANQUO: And she goes down at twelve.
FLEANCE: I take it sir, 'tis later.

[Act II, Scene 1, lines 1–3]

Lady Macbeth notes the owl's sinister cry, marking the termination of a life, as Macbeth is assassinating Duncan:

LADY MACBETH: Hark! Peace!
It was the owl that shrieked, the fatal bellman,
Which giv'st the stern'st good-night. He is about it.

[Act II, Scene 2, lines 2–4]

The old man's remarks to Ross establish a larger temporal context in which the murder of Duncan can be located:

OLD MAN: Threescore and ten I can remember well:
Within the volume of which time I have seen
Hours dreadful and things strange, but this sore night
Hath trifled former knowings.

[Act II, Scene 4, lines 1–4]

The entry of the Messenger to warn Lady Macduff of the danger she is in has no other dramatic purpose than to create anxiety about the events to come. The disruption of time in the play is frequently linked with blurring of the boundary between night and day. Not only is night the location of wickedness, but lack of sleep threatens reason. Lady Macbeth's sleep-walking is a sign of her mental disorder. She has earlier sought to explain her husband's troubled state of mind:

LADY MACBETH: You lack the season of all natures, sleep.
MACBETH: Come, we'll to sleep. My strange and self-abuse
Is the initiate fear that wants hard use.
We are yet but young in deed.

[Act III, Scene 4, lines 142–145]

Macbeth's reply, appearing to agree but in fact announcing his final commitment to violence, are the last words he speaks to Lady Macbeth in the play. Macbeth returns to the witches and arranges the death of Macduff's family. Lady Macbeth goes mad and kills herself from guilt.

At the end of the play, when Macbeth hears of Lady Macbeth's death, present and future time is immediately emptied of meaning for him. The frenzy of excitement, persecution, and guilt that has sustained them through the action vanishes, and the underlying state of nothingness is revealed.

MACBETH: Wherefore was that cry?
SEYTON: The Queen, my lord, is dead.
MACBETH: She should have died hereafter;
There would have been a time for such a word.
Tomorrow, and tomorrow, and tomorrow
Creeps in this petty pace from day to day,
To the last syllable of recorded time;

And all our yesterdays have lighted fools
The way to dusty death. Out, out, brief candle!
Life's but a walking shadow, a poor player
That struts and frets his hour upon the stage
And then is heard no more. It is a tale
Told by an idiot, full of sound and fury
Signifying nothing.

[Act V, Scene 5, lines 15–28]

After these moments of reflection, in which the undamaged part of Macbeth's mind contemplates the present meaning of his life, he reverts again to an anxious engagement in the moment, as he prepares to die in battle:

Enter a messenger
MACBETH: Thou com'st to use thy tongue; thy story quickly!

[Act V, Scene 5, line 29]

The way in which the disruption of time serves as a metaphor of the disruption of the capacity for thought, or reason, is similar to the pell-mell rush to action in *Romeo and Juliet*,[9] where the disturbance of time is also a measure of the disturbance of the reality principle.[10] Shakespeare's understanding of this prefigures the ex-

---

[9] For this argument, see Rustin (1991b).

[10] Time in the sixteenth and seventeenth centuries: it is in this period in which Macbeth was written that time was in fact beginning to be recategorized by scientists as a homogeneous, abstract, and measurable category of explanation. It was soon to be removed from its earlier associations with a classical, multi-dimensional cosmology in which explanatory, moral, and aesthetic dimensions of meaning were inseparably linked together. Calvinist doctrines of predestination can be understood in this context as a final, dogmatic attempt to reimpose the idea that men's lives could be wholly understood within the framework of a divine temporal order.

In *Macbeth*, as in many others of Shakespeare's plays, the role and meaning of time is rendered problematic in remarkably explicit ways. One can see this mainly as one consequence of Shakespeare's psychological insight into the fragile boundaries of the mind. The experience of time is thus represented as magical, delusional, or terrible, as reason comes under pressure.

But it is also possible that the explanation for this problematization of time is a deeper one. It may be that the anxious awareness in *Macbeth*, and other plays, of the fragility of a frame that might so easily have been taken for granted signifies that the frame itself was beginning to feel unreliable. These most intense

plorations of emptied-out time in Chekhov, and of timeless disloca-
tion in Beckett.

The death of Lady Macbeth

That Macbeth is a tragedy of modern marriage is made most clear
at its end, when Lady Macbeth's death is reported to Macbeth. He
has previously worried over her, with the doctor. He is brought
back, by "The cry of women, my good Lord", to a memory of a
more vulnerable aspect of himself that he has armoured himself
against, and which is associated in the play with Lady Macbeth,
who shared his knowledge of this part of himself:

> MACBETH: I have almost forgot the taste of fears:
> The time has been, my senses would have cooled
> To hear a night-shriek, and my fell of hair
> Would at a dismal treatise rouse and stir
> As life were in't. I have supped full with horrors.
> Direness, familiar to my slaughterous thoughts,
> Cannot once start me.
>
> [Act V, Scene 5, lines 9–15]

Macbeth's speech on learning of the queen's death announces that
his life has instantly lost all its remaining meaning, and even in
retrospect now appears quite empty. Their lives were built on their
relationship with each other. Lady Macbeth is driven into madness
when she is left to bear the burden of their joint guilt alone.
Macbeth can function alone, as "bearlike, I must fight the course",
but now in full knowledge that this can lead only to his death. Now

---

meanings were perhaps being sought and elaborated in men and women's
relationships to the markers of time just as these life-ordering frames of meaning
were being destabilized by the development of scientific rationality. A teleologi-
cal and animistic conception of the universe, as Shapin (1996) puts it, was being
replaced by a mechanical and depersonalized one. Here, time is abstractly conceived and measured, and the clock becomes an important symbol of this new
mechanistic world view. The meanings of human lives have to be made, and can
no longer be inferred from signs given by nature.

Psychoanalysis, like classical drama, is most interested in concepts of time in
relation to their emotional meanings for individuals and within relationships.

that Lady Macbeth is dead, he takes on a burden of remorse, or depressive guilt, telling Macduff:

> MACBETH: Of all men else I have avoided thee.
>   But get thee back! My soul is too much charged
>   With blood of thine already.
>
> [Act V, Scene 8, lines 4–6]

Macbeth's speech tells us that he and Lady Macbeth have held together in his mind, despite his external abandonment of her. They are the only couple to do so. Macduff has abandoned Lady Macduff to her death, thus signifying her secondary unimportance to him, and the other nobles have no partners. Male group ties seem otherwise to be central in this warrior society.

It is the passion for each other, displaced into ambition and then lost in mutual guilt, that is the Macbeths' doom.

CHAPTER FIVE

Shakespeare's
A Midsummer Night's Dream:
further meditations on marriage

A *Midsummer Night's Dream* was probably written during
the same two years as *Romeo and Juliet*[1] and offers another
exploration of the themes of love and marriage, a comedy
to match the tragedy. Scholars suggest that the two plays were
often performed close on each others' heels. But, as with all Shakespeare's comedies, there are serious themes at the heart of the play.
It is important that the violent and dangerous states of mind that
are explored in these comedies are not wholly buried beneath their
playful surfaces, so that audiences realize what is really at stake.
The comedies explore "what might have been", much as the tragedies do, but in a different and happier register. So in this play, we
need to feel the panic of Hermia, the jealous fury of Helena, the
confusion of Demetrius and Lysander, and the latent violence of
the powerful Theseus and Oberon, even though the framing makes
it clear for audiences from early on that nothing terrible is in the
end going to happen to them. We shall be arguing that a deep

---

[1] Harold F. Brooks's introduction to the Arden edition (1979) suggests that
this was in 1595 or 1596.

understanding of feelings and relationships is achieved in *A Mid-summer Night's Dream* as much as it is in *Macbeth*, though it might seem that one play is to be taken seriously in a way that the other is not. Whereas we suggest that in *Macbeth* a modern, companion-ate conception of marriage is tested to destruction in conditions of war and violent political competition, we see *A Midsummer Night's Dream* as a meditation on the attributes of mind, and the containing social relations,[2] that might be required to make possible a "mod-ern" marriage lastingly based on both passion and affection.

In *A Midsummer Night's Dream* there are six couples whose fortunes we follow: Theseus and Hippolyta, the king and queen whose impending marriage frames the play; Demetrius and Helena and Lysander and Hermia, the Athenian lovers who lose themselves in confusion in the night woods; Oberon and Titania, the Fairy King and Queen, Titania and Bottom, who become a couple during the enchantment brought about by Puck on Oberon's orders, and Pyramus and Thisbe in the rustics' play. The thoughts and feelings of these lovers allow Shakespeare to explore the excitement and anxieties of sexual love in gloriously moving drama. Some of the characters report their experience of dreaming, and sleep and waking, darkness and light, are significant polarities, but it is the play as a whole, with its intertwining themes, that we will argue is a meditation on the vagaries of love to which both conscious and unconscious mind contribute. Dream is the record of our experience of unconscious thought, as Shakespeare well knew, anticipating Freud and psychoanalysis, and it is the integration of the dream-thoughts that allows for the happy ending to the play.

Our contention is that it is the dream-like quality of the play that allows its exploration of the meanings and implications of love and passion. Most of its action takes place at night in a wood in which Lysander and Hermia fall asleep; love-potions are adminis-tered, which induce strange states of mind and rapid changes in the objects of passion; a fairy King and Queen enact a bitter quar-rel; the fairy queen falls in love with a rustic weaver wearing an ass's head. Hermia, awaking alone in the wood, actually recounts a dream, which we shall show to be a meditation on her imminent

---

[2] *Romeo and Juliet* explores what happens when these are absent (Rustin, 1991b).

sexual initiation as the marriages of the young people are imagined and prepared for. There are no clear boundaries set between these different worlds: indeed, the whole point of the setting and action of the play is to bring many different worlds—aristocratic and rustic, young and old, everyday and magical—together. The fact that for Shakespeare and his contemporaries the boundaries between these different spheres of existence were less clearly demarcated than they are in a modern world shaped by scientific rationality was a positive resource for him in exploring human experience. This is as much the case in tragedies such as *Macbeth* or *Hamlet*, where witches and ghosts could give texture and substance to what we might think of as fantasy, as in *A Midsummer Night's Dream*, where Oberon and Titania are such unexpectedly central figures. Poetry provided the expressive form that enabled Shakespeare and his audiences to move so freely between these different domains of experience and reference, making it possible for him to refer to and reflect on scientific as well as magical or mythical spheres.

Subsequent to the scientific revolution, psychoanalysis has tried to reclaim these "irrational" spaces for rational understanding, seeing in the representations of dreams, and within play in the psychoanalysis of children, traces of an inner world of experience that was in early modern times less sharply demarcated from the "real world".[3] By comparison with poetry, its methods often seem clumsy and over-literal. Because psychoanalysis seeks to be systematic, if not scientific, it is obliged always to connect its reported fragments of imaginative life to generalizing concepts, moving between the inner world of phantasy and the outer world of ideas in a way quite unlike the flow of a play or poem. But we think that nonetheless it comes closer than any other explicit discourse to

---

[3] An important aspect of this modern "disenchantment of the world" (to use Max Weber's description—1930, 1965) has been the decline in the saliency of religious belief, which has surrendered most of its explanatory claims to the sciences. Freud interpreted religious belief psychoanalytically as a projection of unconscious anxieties, thus putting forward psychoanalysis as an intellectual rival to religion. Imaginative literature transcends these problems of legitimacy, by avoiding in its representations of experience competition with "scientific" truth-claims. This is one reason that this and the other arts have seemed so deep a source of wisdom and insight for psychoanalysts from Freud onwards.

capturing the essence of inner experience, and that is why we consider the juxtaposition of psychoanalytic insights whose ultimate source is the consulting-room with the texts of plays like *A Midsummer Night's Dream* an illuminating one, in both directions.

At the start of the play, Theseus the warrior king addresses Hippolyta, his captured bride, with the promise that though he "woo'd thee with my sword", the wedding will be "in another key". The time set aside to wait for the marriage day—four days—represents the more civilized spirit Theseus is now embracing: rape, capture, and war are to be replaced by mutuality. There must be time for anticipation, and a tolerance of delay. Within these days, truncated in the action of the play into a night and a day, the meaning of an impending marriage is to be explored.[4]

The first theme is the adolescent discovery of being able to see with one's own eyes and to separate oneself from one's parents. This is the precursor of the capacity to fall in love and emerges in Hermia's defiance of her father's patriarchal rights in relation to her marriage.

THESEUS: What say you, Hermia? Be advis'd, fair maid.
　　　To you your father should be as a god:
　　　One that compos'd your beauties, yea, and one
　　　To whom you are but as a form in wax
　　　By him imprinted, and within his power
　　　To leave the figure, or disfigure it.
　　　Demetrius is a worthy gentleman.
HERMIA: So is Lysander.
THESEUS:　　　　　In himself he is;
　　　But in this kind, wanting your father's voice,
　　　The other must be held the worthier.
HERMIA: I would my father look'd but with my eyes.

[Act I, Scene 1, lines 46–56][5]

---

[4] The action of *Romeo and Juliet*, by contrast, takes place under extreme pressure of time, depriving its participants of space in which to reflect on the implications of their actions. (This view is developed in "Thinking in *Romeo and Juliet*", Rustin, 1991b.)

[5] Extracts from *A Midsummer Night's Dream* are taken from the *Arden Shakespeare*, edited by Harold F. Brooks (London: Methuen, 1979; reprinted London: Routledge, 1988).

Alongside this assertion of individuality is the painful discovery that it involves not only conflict with the parental generation but also a disruption of the earlier comfortable patterns of same-sex friendship. Hermia and Helena, old school friends, are split by the betrayal to which Helena is drawn by her desperate jealousy of Hermia's good fortune. Sexual love is more potent than intimate friendship, and the painful experience of envy and jealousy over-whelms her.[6]

> HELENA: For, ere Demetrius look'd on Hermia's eyne,
> He hail'd down oaths that he was only mine;
> And when this hail some heat from Hermia felt,
> So he dissolv'd and show'rs of oaths did melt.
> I will go tell him of fair Hermia's flight:
> Then to the wood will he, tomorrow night,
> Pursue her; and for this intelligence
> If I have thanks, it is a dear expense.
> But herein mean I to enrich my pain,
> To have his sight thither and back again.
>
> [Act I, Scene 1, lines 242–251]

Helena's wry recognition that she may not get much out of this betrayal of her friend's tenderly given confidences is a hint of the idea promulgated by the wise Bottom, in our first encounter with the "mechanicals" as they discuss the proposed production of "Pyramus and Thisbe" in honour of the Duke's wedding. Bottom enquires: "What is Pyramus, a lover or a tyrant?" The tyranny of love is certainly what the distressed perplexities of the young Athe-nians reveal for us: they are at the mercy of their extreme feelings, their belief that life itself depends on the possession of the beloved. Other aspects of themselves are cast aside under the "doting" power of love. Helena abandons her friend, Demetrius his former

---

[6] René Girard's *A Theatre of Envy: William Shakespeare* (1991) has brilliant analyses of the significance of what he calls "mimetic desire" (desire for what another desires) in this and other Shakespeare plays. Girard's original and ex-tremely perceptive accounts are contraposed to "orthodox" psychoanalytic theo-ries, but he seems remote from contemporary British psychoanalytic writing, and to relate his concepts of those of our tradition would be a difficult though worthwhile task.

beloved (as does Romeo his Rosalind in *Romeo and Juliet*) under the impact of romantic passion.

In the woods at night to which all the lovers wend their way, the power of magic holds sway, for the night is the territory of the Fairy King and Queen. Oberon and Titania are quarrelling, and their quarrels have led to a deep estrangement. Oberon's unfaithfulness (more betrayals here) are being countered by Titania's refusal to hand over the boy-child of her votress, and the night-world is full of danger while this quarrel persists:

> PUCK: The King doth keep his revels here tonight;
> Take heed the Queen come not within his sight;
> For Oberon is passing fell and wrath,
> Because that she as her attendant hath
> A lovely boy, stol'n from an Indian king—
> She never had so sweet a changeling;
> And jealous Oberon would have the child
> Knight of his train, to trace the forests wild:
> But she perforce withholds the loved boy,
> Crowns him with flowers, and makes him all her joy.
>
> [Act II, Scene 1, lines 18–27]

The child, we might argue, has been stolen from its true inheritance, as child of a father and a mother, and instead is being claimed as a son by Titania and kept within the feminine world of the Queen and her votress. This challenge to the paternal principle provokes Oberon's rage, especially as it is added to by oedipal jealousy—Titania and the charming boy become the happy couple, with father–Oberon the furious bystander.

The battle between Oberon and Titania has much more hanging on it than the everyday family events it chronicles, for the falling-out of the Fairy King and Queen affects the lives of all the mortals in the enchanted wood. The royal pair are fully aware of their power and the destruction of creative love that their quarrel brings about. Titania reproaches Oberon for his jealous "forgeries", his spoiling of her fairy dances, and describes the deadly outcome:

> TITANIA: Therefore the winds, piping to us in vain,
> As in revenge have suck'd up from the sea
> Contagious fogs; which, falling in the land,
> Hath every pelting river made so proud

That they have overborne their continents.
The ox hath therefore stretch'd his yoke in vain,
The ploughman lost his sweat, and the green corn
Hath rotted ere his youth attained a beard;
The fold stands empty in the drowned field,
And crows are fatted with the murrion flock;
The nine-men's morris is fill'd up with mud,
And the quaint mazes in the wanton green
For lack of tread are undistinguishable.
The human mortals want their winter cheer:
No night is now with hymn or carol blest.

[Act II, Scene 1, lines 88–102]

And this same progeny of evil comes
From our debate, from our dissension;
We are their parents, and original.

[Act II, Scene 1, lines 115–117]

Why is the fairy quarrel so devastating in its consequences? The fairy world represents in this play the inner world of the mind, inhabited, as Melanie Klein described, by parental figures both benign and hostile. While these powerful internal parents are at war, the hearts of the child-mortals (children in the sense that they feel small and helpless when confronted by the power of the emotions they cannot control) are disordered. Demetrius has fallen out of love with Helena, and Egeus has become a tyrannical father in the context of the quarrelling between the Fairy King and Queen. Both are under the sway of emotions lacking in love. Neither sees the damage he is doing and mistakenly pursues what he believes will satisfy him—just like the Fairy King and Queen. The nature of the "love" that has taken over is sadistic, for Egeus blind love of his patriarchal power and for Demetrius a cruelty that evokes Helena's masochistic submission, which, in turn, excites him to yet more ruthlessness:

HELENA: You draw me, you hard-hearted adamant—
    But yet you draw not iron, for my heart
    Is true as steel. Leave you your power to draw,
    And I shall have no power to follow you.
DEMETRIUS: Do I entice you? Do I speak you fair?
    Or rather do I not in plainest truth
    Tell you I do not, nor I cannot love you?

HELENA: And even for that do I love you the more.
I am your spaniel; and, Demetrius,
The more you beat me, I will fawn on you.
Use me but as your spaniel, spurn me, strike me,
Neglect me, lose me; only give me leave,
Unworthy as I am, to follow you.
What worser place can I beg in your love—
And yet a place of high respect with me—
Than to be used as you use your dog?
DEMETRIUS: Tempt not too much the hatred of my spirit;
For I am sick when I do look on thee.
HELENA: And I am sick when I look not on you.
DEMETRIUS: You do impeach your modesty too much
To leave the city and commit yourself
Into the hands of one that loves you not,
To trust the opportunity of night
And the ill counsel of a desert place
With the rich worth of your virginity.

[Act II, Scene 1, lines 194–218]

At the end of Act II, Hermia wakes from a nightmare, after Lysander has been bewitched by the love juice Puck puts on his eyes and thus believes himself to be in love with Helena. Hermia's dream of betrayal is linked to her thoughts of intercourse—the moment of intimacy in which trust is most needed, particularly by the inexperienced. (Her preoccupation is delicately suggested by disavowal, when Hermia insists that Lysander sleeps at a chaste distance from her.) This turns to fears of abandonment, and it is these anxieties that underlie the lovers' states of mind. Hermia, like Eve listening to the serpent in the Garden of Eden, has been dreaming of sexual fulfilment, and her guilt is easily preyed on in a world where God, the law, and father do not protect her vulnerability and acknowledge her right to pleasure. Oberon, the Fairy King, is waging war on his wife and the world of the women, and in the night wood Hermia thus has no access to a belief in a father who will honour her sexuality by giving her to the husband she desires.

HERMIA [starting]:   Help me, Lysander, help me! Do thy best
To pluck this crawling serpent from my breast!
Ay me, for pity! What a dream was here!
Lysander, look how I do quake with fear.

Methought a serpent ate my heart away,
And you sat smiling at his cruel prey.
Lysander! What, remov'd? Lysander! lord!
What, out of hearing? Gone? No sound, no word?
Alack, where are you? Speak, and if you hear;
Speak, of all loves! I swoon almost with fear.
No? Then I well perceive you are not nigh.
Either death or you I'll find immediately.

[Act II, Scene 2, lines 144–155]

Oberon's magical interventions, intended to bring about both good (to help the distressed Helena) and ill (to subdue his rebellious wife by mockery) lead to the exploration of the idea of love as a form of madness and, more subtly, to the idea that love exposes us to terrors that make us feel mad. In the scenes between Titania and Bottom in his donkey head, the blind idolization of doting love is displayed in comic mode and its omnipotence underscored. Beauty is in the eye of the beholder, and as Bottom sagely remarks, "Reason and love keep little company together nowadays."

TITANIA: Thou art as wise as thou art beautiful.
BOTTOM: Not so, neither; but if I had wit enough to get out of this
wood, I have enough to serve my own turn.
TITANIA: Out of this wood do not desire to go:
Thou shalt remain here, whether thou wilt or no.
I am a spirit of no common rate;
The summer still doth tend upon my state;
And I do love thee: therefore go with me.
I'll give thee fairies to attend on thee;
And they shall fetch thee jewels from the deep,
And sing, whilst thou on fresh flowers dost sleep;
And I will purge thy mortal grossness so,
That thou shalt like an airy spirit go.
Peaseblossom! Cobweb! Moth! and Mustardseed!

[Act III, Scene 1, lines 142–155]

The entrancing beauty of Titania and her fairies is counterposed to the good-hearted and friendly amazement of Bottom, their exquisite poetry and song with his bluff and unassuming prose. The encounter between the Queen and the Weaver entirely lacks the painful cruelty of the human lovers' comings and goings—it is a magical love, love that transforms, with the absurdity remaining sweet.

But elsewhere in the forest, distress and madness of a different sort have taken hold. Helena is in the hell of paranoia, believing that the two men are conspiring to humiliate her:

HELENA: O spite! O hell! I see you all are bent
          To set against me for your merriment.
          If you were civil, and knew courtesy,
          You would not do me thus much injury.
          Can you not hate me, as I know you do,
          But you must join in souls to mock me too?
          If you were men, as men you are in show,
          You would not use a gentle lady so:
          To vow, and swear, and superpraise my parts,
          When I am sure you hate me with your hearts.
          You both are rivals, and love Hermia;
          And now both rivals, to mock Helena.
          A trim exploit, a manly enterprise,
          To conjure tears up in a poor maid's eyes
          With your derision! None of noble sort
          Would so offend a virgin, and extort
          A poor soul's patience, all to make you sport.
                              [Act III, Scene 2, lines 145–161]

Later, things get even more desperate as Helena believes Hermia has joined them, and she is now surrounded by a tormenting gang:

HELENA: Lo, she is one of this confederacy!
          Now I perceive they have conjoin'd all three
          To fashion this false sport in spite of me.
          Injurious Hermia, most ungrateful maid!
          Have you conspir'd, have you with these contriv'd,
          To bait me with this foul derision?
          Is all the counsel that we two have shared,
          The sisters' vows, the hours that we have spent
          When we have chid the hasty-footed time
          For parting us—O is all forgot?
          All school-days' friendship, childhood innocence?
                              [Act III, Scene 2, lines 192–202]

These convictions of conspiracies against her gain their power from her own earlier betrayal of Hermia. Friendship is not an emotion that can be trusted in the throes of adolescence. Growing up is here revealed as an experience of losing all that is familiar—from being a cherished child, one can suddenly find oneself without any sense of support or value. The pain of adolescent self-discovery is shared between Helena and Hermia, both much more substantial characters than their male lovers, and in one night exploring a full gamut of adolescent emotion. The fragility of a sense of self is revealed: if the love object is lost, panic overwhelms. Violence and disorientation threaten the integrity of self, and this experience afflicts first one young woman then the other. Hermia's rage about the supposed slights against her relative smallness makes an audience smile but conceals adolescent desperation to assert grown-upness and a resort to primitive ferocity when made to feel little:

> HERMIA: "Puppet"! Why, so? Ay, that way goes the game!
> Now I perceive that she had made compare
> Between our statures; she hath urg'd her height;
> And with her personage, her tall personage,
> Her height, forsooth, she hath prevail'd with him.
> Are you grown so high in his esteem
> Because I am so dwarfish and so low?
> How low am I, thou painted maypole? Speak:
> How low am I? I am not yet so low
> But that my nails can reach unto thine eyes.
>
> [Act III, Scene 2, lines 289–298]

When the idealization (Shakespeare's "doting") collapses, there is murderous spite between the women, and physical aggression becomes the dominant valency for the men. The fusion of sexual and aggressive impulses described by Freud as so necessary to adult and sexual life has split apart.

But love has other dimensions than the urgent desire for possession and recognition that dominates the quartet of young Athenians. In Act IV, Titania and Oberon are reconciled, and this occurs via Titania's softening through her adoration of Bottom and its enactment in the beautiful fairy grove. The ambiguity of the scene has been much commented on by critics (Bloom, 1999; Kermode, 2000) and variously interpreted by directors, but it is indeed the ambiguity that seems the crux of the matter, not the intercourse of Fairy Queen and mortal (Kott, 1964). Titania's adoration of Bottom brings to mind the way in which a mother loves a small child, grubbiness, lack of sophistication, and all. She and her fairies provide food, skin care, and music to settle him to sleep, satisfying the longings of "his majesty the baby", Freud's description for the omnipotence of the young child. Her pleasure in this and in Bottom's grateful reception of all the marks of love is the prelude to her waking recognition that it is Oberon she loves as a husband, and that her love of Bottom and of the changeling boy were confusions, "the fierce vexation of a dream". At this moment, the preparation for the human marriages can come closer, and Theseus and Hippolyta reappear, out hunting in the woods. Oberon's magical power is used to bring Demetrius back to his old love of Helena and to judge his idolization of Hermia as a doting sickness, now "melted as the snow".

When Bottom wakes from his dream, the infantile aspects of his "rare vision" are to the fore. As he tries to recall it, his sentences founder, and Shakespeare invokes biblical language (St Paul's Letter to the Corinthians, quoted in Kermode, 2000) to convey the absolute wonder of the dreamer's experience. He sums it up thus:

> "It shall be called 'Bottom's Dream', because it hath no bottom."
>
> [Act IV, Scene 1, lines 214–215]

Despite the evident comedy of the conjunction of the divine—both biblical and fairy varieties—with Bottom's prosaic physicality, there is something profound at the heart of this speech. The dream with no bottom is the dream with no foundation in reality, the infant's dream of marrying the fairy queen, the adored mother desired by the baby. When this dream is exposed for what it is, and the fact that the Queen already has her king can be recognized, the child feels an ass. Yet the kindliness of the whole conception is what overwhelms the audience. For Bottom hopes to be able to sing his dream-ballad at the wedding-feast of the Duke. There remains a place for the child in the mind of the festive parental figures. Bottom is self-important but sweetly so, and his profound confidence in the acceptance of the mechanicals' offering is part of the inclusiveness of the world as ordered by the benign king whom Theseus represents. Shakespeare's deep attachment to the idea of kingship, explored especially in the history plays, is here linked to the personal fulfilment of the king's subjects within their identity as citizens.[7]

The containment of all these different follies belongs to Shakespeare as poet and thinker, and Theseus speaks of the writer's work at the opening of the final act:

> THESEUS: More strange than true. I never may believe
> These antique fables, nor these fairy toys.
> Lovers and madmen have such seething brains,
> Such shaping fantasies, that apprehend
> More than cool reason ever comprehends.
> The lunatic, the lover, and the poet
> Are of imagination all compact:
> One sees more devils than vast hell can hold;
> That is the madman: the lover, all as frantic,
> Sees Helen's beauty in a brow of Egypt:
> The poet's eye, in a fine frenzy rolling,
> Doth glance from heaven to earth, from earth to heaven;
> And, as imagination bodies forth
> The forms of things unknown, the poet's pen
> Turns them to shapes, and gives to airy nothing
> A local habitation and a name.
> Such tricks hath strong imagination,
> That if it would but apprehend some joy,
> It comprehends the bringer of that joy:
> Or, in the night, imagining some fear,
> How easy is a bush suppos'd a bear!
> HIPPOLYTA: But all the story of the night told over,
> And all their minds transfigur'd so together,

---

[7] One important implication of patriarchy is plainly the conception of the political world as a relationship between rulers, conceived as parents, and their dependent subjects, conceived as children. The demeaning aspects of this, both in the early struggles for equality of citizenship and in its transposed versions in the context of colonial relationships, make it difficult to think about in any remotely positive way, so much does this idea violate modern conceptions of the equality of subjects. Shakespeare's "dream narrative" enables him to explore more benign inner dimensions of this relation. These are the "positive transferences" between rulers and subjects that were also an aspect of traditional forms of authority.

> More witnesseth than fancy's images,
> And grows to something of great constancy;
> But, howsoever, strange and admirable.
>
> [Act V, Scene 1, lines 2–27]

Shakespeare's conception of the poet as giving "to airy nothing a local habitation and a name" is deeply resonant for psychoanalysts, for whom the "forms of things unknown" and the "airy nothing" stand for the rich content of the inner world, which both poetry and psychoanalysis take as their main topic for investigation.

There remains one final exploration to be made before the weddings can take place: Peter Quince's play is chosen for the celebration, and the story of the doomed illicit love-making of Pyramus and Thisbe sets before us the feared catastrophe of sexual love.[8] Ridiculous as the portrayal is, it reveals the terrors that lovers must overcome if they are to find each other. Pyramus and Thisbe are flouting the rules. Lacking external sanction, their love cannot flower. Instead, the lion "deflowers" Thisbe, and tragedy overwhelms—the belief in tenderness being overtaken by fears of sexuality as destructive and rapacious. The lion takes Thisbe's mantle, thus representing the potential confusion between the undressing of the marriage bed and a murderous attack. The display of the virgin's bloodstained garment required in traditional cultures might be seen as a culturally ordered management of these anxieties as well as the evidence of carefully guarded virginity. Teeth, claws (nails), and violent assault are dreaded, and the dagger with which Pyramus kills himself could be linked to the fear of a penis dangerous to the bride. These powerful infantile phantasies about

---

[8] The theme of what Bion described as "catastrophic change" (Bion, 1970) is important to our analysis of *A Midsummer Night's Dream* and many other plays discussed in this book. The inner and outer worlds are brought together in the various crises of these plays through the precipitation, by some dramatic conjuncture or another, of extreme anxiety. "Catastrophic change" is experienced both as a positive space in which growth and development might be possible *and* as an explosive threat of annihilation, virtually at the same time. This state of mind and feeling is important in the experience of the Macbeths, of John Gabriel Borkman and Hedda Gabler, of the lovers in *A Midsummer Night's Dream*, of Medea, of Eddie Carbone, and of Vanya, to give some examples. All of these characters come to feel driven almost to madness at certain moments.

intercourse, described so vividly by Klein, are dominant in the minds of Pyramus and Thisbe because their love is illicit. The all-important hole in the wall suggests spying, perhaps childish spying on parental intercourse in phantasy. The walls that safeguard boundaries and privacy have been breached, and what follows in unconscious logic is that the security that rules and boundaries provide is no longer reliably available. Of course, it is these rules of civility that Bottom tries to provide through Quince's prologue and his own unscripted intervention—the audience is to be reassured that these terrible imaginings are not real, to be protected from the power of the nightmare.

Perhaps these underlying anxieties are one explanation of Hippolyta's impatience with the players—after all, she was a war trophy, and the civilized marriage now about to take place conceals more primitive beginnings. Theseus is more kindly towards Quince's company than Hippolyta, as he has the confidence of his dukely power all around him and does not have to cope with the anxiety of being the outsider (the "barbarian" to the Athenian court[9]). The change of mood in Theseus from the first to the last act is quite marked. At the outset, he has reminded Hermia of the full rigours of the law that represent the assertion of patriarchal power, but at the close his more generous tone seems evident. Perhaps the wait for the wedding day has provided an opportunity for reflection, a savouring of the difference between the immediacy of rape and conquest and the time needed to woo a consenting lover.

Finally, the marriages are blessed by Titania and Oberon, who represent the parental figures of our internal world, now restored to a loving relationship. Their relationship is the background to the whole play, and it is their change of heart that makes this a happy play, one in which warmth and benevolence exceed all other forces. The hostile disarray of the fairies arose from their fighting over who can make and claim babies and the rivalry this unleashed—the very challenge the new couples will have to face as their relationship develops after the wedding. King and Queen have given way, and each acknowledged the necessity of a partner

---

[9] Hippolyta's boredom with the rustic troupe also contrasts with Titania's infatuation with Bottom and her affection for her own fairy retainers. Hippolyta, the princess captured in war, is still remote from such parental identifications.

for creativity to flourish. The final dances echo the dance of their earlier reconciliation and set the scene for the blessing of the marriages and of their fertility:

> OBERON: Now, until the break of day,
>   Through this house each fairy stray.
>   To the best bride-bed will we,
>   Which by us shall blessed be;
>   And the issue there create
>   Ever shall be fortunate.
>   So shall all the couples three
>   Ever true in loving be;
>   And the blots of Nature's hand
>   Shall not in their issue stand:
>   Never mole, hare-lip nor scar,
>   Nor mark prodigious, such as are
>   Despised in nativity,
>   Shall upon their children be.
>
>   [Act V, Scene 1, lines 387–400]

The actual wedding setting of the original production—as described by Brooks (1979)—should not divert us from the wider significance of Shakespeare's conceptions.

One of the capacities that distinguish the fairies' mode of being is the breadth of their identifications. Their wide sweep of knowledge of what is taking place and their empathy mark them out as much richer in their appreciation of the world and its possibilities than the mortals. Their language brings the scale of the universe to mind—references to distant India, to the space "between the cold moon and earth" (Oberon), Puck's delighted claim that he can "put a girdle round the earth in forty minutes"—the starting point for a learned disquisition by William Empson (1986) on Shakespeare's knowledge of astronomy!—and the importance of the seaside promontory where Titania romped with her retinue are examples of this. But the breadth of acquaintance with the physical world is matched by the detailed recollection of place and plants so characteristic of Oberon and Puck's discourse and the fairy dialogue.

> OBERON: I know a bank where the wild thyme blows,
>   Where oxlips and the nodding violet grows,
>   Quite over-canopied with luscious woodbine,
>   With sweet musk-roses, and with eglantine.

There sleeps Titania sometimes of the night,
Lull'd in those flowers with dances and delight;
And there the snake throws her enamell'd skin,
Weed wide enough to wrap a fairy in;

[Act II, Scene 1, lines 249–256]

Shakespeare the countryman is surely recollecting his Warwick-
shire childhood in the imagined flower-filled world of the fairies.
Indeed, Paul Honan (1998), author of a recent biography of Shakespeare, also links the acutely observed detail of the construction
of a wall with his boyhood memories of the wall in Church Street,
Stratford, close to his home. This fine quality of memory inspires
admiration. Honan suggests, compellingly, that Shakespeare's
huge capacity for appreciation has something to do with the special love he may have inspired in his mother as her first surviving
child, successfully reared despite the ravages wreaked on the Stratford population by the plague of 1564. His unusually solid schooling is also evident in this play, which drew on his knowledge of the
Saturnalian comedy of Aristophanes and the later plays of Terence
and Plautus and the poetry of Ovid. Also in evidence is his own
capacity for social observation; in particular his observation of
himself and his co-actors (Barber, 1959) seems a likely source for
the comedy of the mechanicals' rehearsals. Quince, like Shakespeare himself, wrote, produced and acted in his company, and the
satire is doubtless self-directed in part. Honan, in making this
point, also notes the theatricality of the lovers' behaviour, their
quick-changing feelings for each other probably a familiar event in
a troupe of actors so intensely involved with each other. Puck, the
naughty imp, delights in his boyish mischief whose mocking aim is
to spoil the pleasures of the grown-ups in the midst of this gorgeous evocation of the countryside.[10]

PUCK: Thou speak'st aright,
I am that merry wanderer of the night.
I jest to Oberon, and make him smile
When I a fat and bean-fed horse beguile,
Neighing in likeness of a filly foal;
And sometimes lurk I in a gossip's bowl

---

[10] The presence of much-loved boy actors in Shakespeare's companies may
be the origin for figures such as Puck and, later, Ariel in *The Tempest*.

In very likeness of a roasted crab,
And when she drinks, against her lips I bob,
And on her wither'd dewlap pour the ale.
The wisest aunt, telling the saddest tale,
Sometimes for three-foot stool mistaketh me;
Then slip I from her bum, down topples she,
And "tailor" cries, and falls into a cough;
And then the whole quire hold their lips and loffe
And waxen in their mirth, and neeze, and swear
A merrier hour was never wasted there.

[Act II, Scene 1, lines 43–58]

But Puck is now the servant of his master Oberon, his schoolboy impulses kept in check by their conjunction with the wisdom of greater experience of life's necessities. Titania and Oberon are both put out of joint by the impending wedding of their earthly counterparts, Hippolyta and Theseus, because of earlier entanglements, but they also manage to take responsibility for the disastrous consequences of their disunity and to restore all to their capacity for love. The love that has to be rediscovered is that which gets beyond the enchantment of the eye's doting (Kermode, 2000) and reaches for the possibility of loving with the whole mind. Insight, a quality given to them by their encounter with the fairies, tempers the mortals' blindness. Their disordered imaginations are re-ordered in the course of the play; out of painful chaos emerges a structure that may contain the confusion and complexity of their lives. The creative process has brought about a moment of rest in the tortuous rhythms of love.

CHAPTER SIX

What Ibsen knew

Ibsen and Freud

Henrik Ibsen—"our northern Henry", as Henry James called him—was born 28 years before Freud, in 1828. He completed his last play in 1900, and he died in 1906, six years after the publication of *The Interpretation of Dreams*. Whatever Ibsen knew, therefore, he discovered before Freud's writings were available to inform him.

Freud admired Ibsen. He saw in *Rosmersholm* a classical representation of the dynamics of the Oedipus complex, as Rebecca West is unconsciously compelled to repeat in the household of Rosmer and Beate the configuration that she had experienced in the home of her stepfather.[1] But Freud had many reasons for admiring the great Norwegian playwright. Ibsen, like Freud, had to struggle against conventional authority—he lived virtually in exile in Italy and Bavaria for 27 years of his life. He was, like Freud, inspired by

---

[1] Freud's discussion of *Rosmersholm* is in "Some Character Types Met with in Psychoanalytic Work: (II) Those Wrecked by Success" (Freud, 1916d). The other dramatic work discussed in this essay is *Macbeth*.

the south, in particular in Ibsen's case by its apparent freedom and sensuality, compared with the cold and authoritarian qualities of the north. Ibsen, like Freud, saw himself engaged in a lifelong struggle for enlightenment and progress, and he transformed dramatic form as deeply as Freud transformed the science of psychology. But the deepest affinity between the two men was in their commitment to self-understanding as the core of their life-work.

Freud identified with the figure of King Oedipus, as the investigator of his own tragic history. Ibsen's work represents a similar commitment to understanding, though it is usually invested in the whole of his plays, in his capacity to see his characters through to the end, rather than in characters whose singular heroism lies in their devotion to truth. Many of Ibsen's characters struggle with the truth, evading and engaging with it by turns. Some (like Ella Rentheim) long for it, but generally understanding in his plays emerges as the product of "action", as Henry James called it, which drives his characters to confront the truth of their situations. In *The Lady from the Sea*, Ibsen brings the stranger back to force Ellida and Wangel to confront the falsity of their lives. In *Rosmersholm*, the ambiguity and denial inherent in Rosmer's relationship with Rebecca West is exposed by the demand that they must choose between bourgeois convention and ideas of emancipation. Their earlier complicity in the death of Rosmer's wife makes this choice intolerable and destroys them both. In *John Gabriel Borkman*, the growing up of Erhart and the fatal illness of Ella disrupt the pathological impasse in which Borkman and his wife are living. And in *Hedda Gabler* it is an unwished-for pregnancy and the creation of a manuscript by Ejlert Lövborg with Mrs Elvsted that faces Hedda with her own depression and hatred. Ibsen repeatedly exposes the instability of untruth and falsity to self as the basis for lives. He did not, of course, propose a practice or programme for unlocking these painful conflicts; instead, he created a dramatic space in which theatre-goers and readers[2] of his day could see and learn to understand themselves.

---

[2] Many of Ibsen's plays were available as published texts long before they were performed.

We are going to draw attention to some affinities and conver-gences between Ibsen's drama and the understanding of human dilemmas deriving from psychoanalysis. "What Ibsen knew", from our point of view, will be what Ibsen knew in psychoanalytic terms: that is to say which anticipated what psychoanalysts were later—in some instances much later—to find out in their own dif-ferent ways.

Ibsen's life and work

It may be helpful to outline the major events of Ibsen's life as background in exploring the meaning of his work. For anyone tempted to look further, Michael Meyer's (1967) biography is greatly to be recommended.[3]

Ibsen was born in a small coastal trading town 100 miles south of Oslo, the second child of a merchant. His earlier paternal ances-tors had all been sea-captains. His mother, from a similar family background, brought to the marriage a considerable fortune.

Three and a half months before Henrik's birth, the first-born son died, aged 18 months, and this fact catches one's attention when one notes how many unhappy women people his plays. Perhaps Henrik the baby entered a family partly preoccupied with mourning a lost child and only partly able to welcome the new baby. The four children born subsequently all survived. The great importance of children, both actual and symbolic, in Ibsen's plays is a theme to which we shall return, but the deep ambivalence of parents towards their children is one of his disturbing insights. The horror of Hedda Gabler's suicide in the context of her pregnancy and of Little Eyolf's death as a consequence of parental preoccupa-tion and neglect are delineations of the murderous consequences of failure in the parental generation to imagine a future for their children to inhabit.

---

[3] Useful guidance to contemporary studies of Ibsen can be obtained from James McFarlane (Ed.) (1994), *The Cambridge Companion to Ibsen.*

When Henrik was seven, severe financial difficulties caused a great change both in the family's social position and in the emotional atmosphere of the home. Quarrels between the parents and a painful sense of shame pervaded family life. As eldest boy, Henrik may have been particularly exposed to the effects of this on the children, both in and outside the home. Many witnesses speak of his having the face of an old man while still in his adolescence.

Just before he was 16, Ibsen was apprenticed to an apothecary in another small coastal town. The long hours of work, tiny salary, and cramped living quarters did not impede his energetic programme of self-education, but it is also interesting to picture Ibsen as the curer of all manner of pains and as the recipient of stories of distress and anxiety. He was the main medicine-mixer in the business. During this period he fathered an illegitimate son born to the family's maid, who was ten years his senior, and he supported the child out of his meagre income.

His views on politics and society were radical and strongly voiced. He was an atheist in a repressively Protestant culture, a republican living under a monarchy, and anti-patriarchal in a society where age and gender determined access to power. His resentment and anger about both his personal circumstances and the semi-colonial status of Norway in relation to Denmark and Sweden were articulated in a great desire for political change.

In 1850 he left his apprenticeship and moved to Christiana (now Oslo), the Norwegian capital, to prepare to enter the university. This period gave him an opportunity for involvement in student politics and journalism, to spend much more time on his writing, mainly poetry in these early years, and to find his way into the theatre. An opportunity to work in the theatre in Bergen took him there from 1851 to 1857, and hence back to Christiana as a theatre director. These years of learning the craft of the theatre were frustrating and unhappy ones and created a well of bitterness towards his native land from which Ibsen found it very difficult to recover. He left Norway in 1864, aged 26, to live in Italy and later in Germany for many years before his return in 1891 for the last years of his life.

He married Suzannah Thoresen in 1858, and they had one son, Sigurd. Throughout their lives, they lived in great simplicity, in part because of Ibsen's struggle for a livelihood from his writing and in part because of his desire to invest his earnings to provide some financial security for the future. Meyer's picture of their marriage is a sympathetic one, in which Henrik's later intense involvements with several younger women are set in the context of an extraordinarily close dependence on and acknowledgement of Suzannah's love and loyalty.

The recurrent debate in Ibsen's mind about a return to Norway gives us evidence of his need to keep some distance in order to be able to think and write: the counterpoint of his terror of being trapped and immobilized inside some deathly structure. This structure is delineated in his plays recurrently: the ice channel of *Brand*, the prison and upper room in *John Gabriel Borkman*, Hedda Gabler's masochistic submission to Judge Brack. To escape from this claustrophobic catastrophe, his characters sometimes choose another death, one of their own making, so that an illusion of power over their own destiny is maintained. Many of the images Ibsen employs to explore this crazed assertion of omnipotence involve climbing up a mountain (*Brand, John Gabriel Borkman, When We Dead Awaken*) or a tower (*The Master Builder*), or sailing away across the sea (Ellida Wangel in *The Lady from the Sea*), or scaling the metaphorical mountain of overcoming one's so-called cowardice (*Hedda Gabler*). It is interesting to know that Ibsen suffered extremes of anxiety about his own physical safety, and felt himself always to be struggling with fear. On a walk in Ischia (of all places), he spoke to his companion about this as they penetrated a crevasse:

> "Where are you taking me, do you want me inside the mountain? I won't go further. It might close over us. I want to go home." [quoted in Mayer, 1967, p. 280]

Of another walk up a hill by the sea, his friend wrote:

> The last part of the way I had almost to drag Ibsen with us, for he repeatedly asserted that the cliff might fall, and when I objected that we were in proportion to the cliff as a fly to a tower, he made the curious observation that even a fly could bring down a tower if it were on the point of falling. [quoted in Mayer, 1967, p. 280]

A domestic example of his capacity for anxiety is shown by his concern for the safety of his wife and son when they were back in

Norway in 1884, while he was in Gossensass in the Tyrol. Writes Meyer:

> He warned Suzannah and Sigurd not to bathe. ("The water is cold and can easily bring on a fatal attack of cramp"), not to stand behind the horses of Trondhjem "which are well known for their habit of kicking," and, above all, to avoid anyone carrying a gun. "In almost every Norwegian newspaper I read of accidents caused by the careless use of loaded rifles. I shall be exceedingly displeased if you do not keep well away from people carrying such weapons. Should an accident happen I must be informed immediately by telegram. [Meyer, 1967, p. 552]

Meyer later reports Bergliot's description of her son's (Ibsen's grandson's) christening:

> They had him baptised by Christopher Bruun, the part-original of Brand; he wore the robe in which his grandfather had been baptised, and Suzannah carried him the font. Ibsen was very nervous lest any accident should befall the child, and as Suzannah approached the font he rose, crossed over to Bergliot, took her arm and whispered, "Do you think she'll drop him?" [Meyer, 1967, p. 744]

This state of existential terror might be linked to his continuing childish love of certain external honours, particularly the medals that are so much a part of nineteenth-century Scandinavian life— these medals, worn so proudly, perhaps assuaged some profound doubt about his right to life and provided a sense of protection from outside himself at moments when his inner security was shaken.

In his last long poem, about a sea-voyage that foundered in mid-ocean, Ibsen writes that the sailors sang *"There Is a Corpse in the Cargo."* He goes on: "I only ask. My task is not to answer." The implicit answer of his life's work is that if we are capable of going on asking, we are living our lives in a way that goes beyond the becalmed state of being dominated by our past. This relationship to his life and work must be one of the qualities which draws together so many great writers in admiration of him. On his 73rd birthday, Ibsen received a letter from the young James Joyce. Joyce wrote of

Ibsen's "inward heroism", which had inspired him. What was this heroism? We think it is located in Ibsen's inherently sceptical attitude, so linked to the questioning inherent in all psychoanalytic work.

Ibsen's exploration of the unconscious

What Ibsen was able to represent, before Freud, were characters in the grip of unconscious states of mind and feeling—unconscious, that is to say, not merely in that they are not acknowledged, but that they cannot be acknowledged without threat of internal catastrophe. The action of the late plays often revolves around the anguish of recognition of these psychic forces and the damage to which they have led. We can say therefore that Ibsen understood the unconscious, though of course as a dramatist he had neither use nor need for a theoretical language for this. His achievement is the more staggering because of the transformation he had to effect in the drama of his time to be able to create a frame adequate to these discoveries. This is the reason for the deep respect in which he was held by his great contemporaries—including Henry James, Oscar Wilde, James Joyce, Bernard Shaw, and Rainer Maria Rilke—and by successors such as Arthur Miller.

Ibsen's openness to the power of unconscious feeling both unsettles his audiences and opens them to a new depth of understanding. He has an uncanny capacity to imagine what must have been the case in the past of a character or characters to make them what they now are. He is a master of the unconscious dynamics of family history, of the unseen transmissions that take place between one generation and another. The repetition of oedipal entanglement in the life of Rebecca West, in *Rosmersholm*, is an example we have already cited. The absence of a mother in the memories of Hedda Gabler or John Gabriel Borkman, and their desperate identification instead with the violence or hardness of their fathers, is another example. In one instance, Ibsen carries forward from one play to another the inter-generational meaning of a family constellation. Hilde's loss of her mother and her resentment and jealousy of Ellida, her stepmother, depicted in *The Lady from the Sea*, becomes the unspoken emotional history of the character Hilde in *The Master Builder*. It gives meaning to her compulsive destruction of another marriage by the death of the husband. The idea that individuals and families are constrained by their pasts, and especially traumas that have proved unthinkable and indigestible, is the explicit subject of *Ghosts,* of course, and also of *Little Eyolf.*

It is interesting at this point to recall what Ibsen himself says about the construction of a play and its characters:

> Before I write one word, I must know the character through and through, I must penetrate into the last wrinkle of his soul. I always proceed from the individual; the stage setting, the dramatic ensemble, all of that comes naturally and causes me no worry, as soon as I am certain of the individual in every aspect of his humanity. But I have to have his exterior in mind too, down to the last button, how he stands and walks, how he bears himself, what his voice sounds like. Then I do not let him go until his fate is fulfilled. [Cited in Meyer, 1967, p. 580]

It seems that what Ibsen must have imagined is not merely an identity, an appearance, habits of speech, and so on, but also a life-history, the emotional constellation of a family in the previous generation.

Ibsen depicts unconscious states of mind not only as attributes of individuals, but as dynamic forces in unconscious transmission between them. For example, Borkman's wife, Gunhild, denied love as a person in herself by John Gabriel, is instead compelled to identify totally with him and to take on his narcissistic life project as her own, as a means of psychic survival. When this structure collapses in Borkman's life, she can only hold herself together by the idea that she can retain and pass on intact to her son this messianic project, which becomes a toxic mission whose main object is to discharge her own resentment towards Borkman for all that he has destroyed in her.

MRS BORKMAN: I will set up the monument over the grave.

BORKMAN: The pillar of shame, perhaps you mean?

MRS BORKMAN [*in rising emotion*]:   Oh, no, it won't be a tablet in stone or metal. And no-one shall be allowed to carve a scornful inscription on the tablet I set up. It shall be as though a ring, a living hedge of trees and bushes, were planted thick, thick

round your buried life. All the dark things that once were shall
be covered over. They shall hide John Gabriel Borkman in ob-
livion from men's eyes.

BORKMAN [*hoarsely and cuttingly*]:   And this work of love, *you* will
perform?

MRS BORKMAN: Not in my own strength. I wouldn't dream of thinking that. But I've bred up a helper to dedicate his life to this one
aim. *He* shall live a life so pure and lofty and radiant that your
own life underground shall be obliterated here on earth.

BORKMAN [*gloomy and threatening*]:   If it's Erhart you mean, say so at
once!

[*John Gabriel Borkman*, Act 3, pp. 345–346][4]

Shortly after this, when Erhart, their son, has left with his lover,
Mrs Wilton, Borkman goes outside into the cold and climbs the hill
on which he dies.

It is because Erhart has enjoyed a loving childhood with Ella
Rentheim, who is attached to him as the child of Borkman and her
twin sister—an attachment that overrides her jealousy—that he can
refuse this poisonous inheritance. He has sought to make reparation for his father's crimes to the daughter of his most loyal victim,
Frida Foldal, recreating in the new generation some of the hope
that has been destroyed for the old. Erhart's choice of the divorced
but life-loving woman, Fanny Wilton, seems also to be an unconscious repetition of his earlier experience, since Ella had also been
abandoned, was also capable of love, and indeed lived, if not in the
south, at least in the warmer westerly part of Norway. Meticulous
as Ibsen was in his work, one thinks that some of these extraordinarily apposite determinations in his plays must have come from
his unconscious rather than his conscious understanding.

Ibsen and marriage

Ibsen's perspective on marriage is a deeply gloomy one. His plays
explore a series of bad if not disastrous marriages—in *The Doll's*

---

[4] Extracts from *John Gabriel Borkman* are taken from *Henrik Ibsen: The Master
Builder and Other Plays*, translated by Una Ellis-Fermor (Harmondsworth: Penguin, 1958).

House, Ghosts, Hedda Gabler, Rosmersholm, Little Eyolf, and *John Gabriel Borkman,* for example. His insight into these tragedies comes in particular from his understanding of, interest in, and empathy with the experience of their women characters. He was, in his own temperament and mode of life, a somewhat unlikely hero of feminism, yet he depicted in a most profound way the almost-absolute block on women's opportunities for independence, self-expression, and intimacy that the bourgeois marriages of his day presented.

Raymond Williams, writing about Ibsen, describes the dominant structure of feeling of his plays as one in which the aspiration towards living social relationships with others is repeatedly blocked by an intractable sense of isolated individual selfhood. Williams thought that the liberal ideal of self-realization was represented in Ibsen's characters in all its self-contradictoriness, since the more they asserted their own identities, the more they cut themselves off from the relationships with others that are necessary to give identities meaning.[5] Ibsen thus created the form, according to Williams, of "liberal tragedy", which represented the impasse of liberal individualism as well as its element of authentic hope. This argument plainly has force and can be seen as a sociological description of the various forms of narcissistic character-structure that we see elaborated in the plays.

> All we can say, reflecting on Ibsen's tragedy, is that the deadlock reached there, the heroic deadlock in which men die still struggling to climb, was indeed necessary. For there is no way out, there is only an inevitable tragic consciousness, while desire is seen as essentially individual. We have to push past Ibsen's undoubted social consciousness to discover, at its roots, this same individual consciousness. Certainly there is to be reform, the "sick earth" is to be "made whole", but this is to happen, always, by an individual act: the liberal conscience, *against* society. Change is never to be *with* people; if others come, they can at most be led. But also change, significantly often, is against people; it is against their wills that the liberator is thrown, and disillusion is then rapid. He speaks for human

---

[5]Raymond Williams's argument is briefly presented in *Modern Tragedy* (1966), pp 95–103.

desire, as a general fact, but he knows this only as individual fulfilment. The self then makes its most terrible discovery: that there is not only a world outside it, resisting it, but other selves, capable of similar suffering and desire. It is possible then for fulfilment to be re-defined; a getting away from the world and from others: the loneliness of the high mountains. But desire had included the joy of life; the life of earth, and of men and women, which the hero is still governed by, even while he drives himself to reject it. The conflict is then indeed internal: a desire for relationship when all that is known of relationship is restricting; desire narrowing to an image in the mind, until it is realised that the search for warmth and light has ended in cold and darkness. Every move towards relationship ends in guilt. [pp. 100–101]

But just as central a theme of the plays as this emerging crisis of bourgeois individualism (Ibsen's main characters are distinctively bourgeois, of course) is a pervasive crisis in gender-relations— that is, in the dominant structures of patriarchy. The heroines of the nineteenth-century novels of Jane Austen, Charlotte Brontë, George Eliot, and many others go on seeking their destiny in a good marriage (sometimes successfully, one way or another), but Ibsen's heroines have invariably been disappointed. They are shown, like Hedda Gabler, to have married only because there is no other feasible option in life. Or to have not married, like Ella Rentheim, because for their chosen man there was an interest more vital than marriage for love. Or to have married, like Gunhild Borkman, and found that survival depended on their complete identification with their husband's megalomaniac ambitions. Or to find in their marriage to a safe and good man, like Ellida Wangel in *The Lady from the Sea*, that the most passionate and independent part of themselves has been shut out.

Ibsen must have learned much about these matters from his own inner experience. The twin sisters in *John Gabriel Borkman* may be understood as different aspects of the same woman or love-object. The sense of this play as the drama of a state of mind is made clear by the description of the eight years during which Borkman has lived in the ballroom above Gunhild's living-room, pacing about, as Mrs Borkman puts it, like a sick wolf. These eight years represent in dramatic form the timelessness of an unconscious structure of mind that prevents all thought, growth, and change. This mental prison is in fact unlocked by Ella's continuing love for Borkman, and her wish to communicate with him, and to understand before she dies why their lives had been destroyed.

We do not want to idealize Ibsen in this respect. Ibsen fully confronts the sufferings brought on both sexes by the structures of patriarchal power, but he does not know how these are to be overcome. This is the sense in which Raymond Williams was right about the social impasse that Ibsen's work reflects. He also remained somewhat caught up in these structures himself, in both his life and in his work. In two plays, for example, he portrays younger women—Hilde in *The Master Builder* and Rebecca West in *Rosmersholm*—seemingly intruding into established marriages and in both of these the husbands are rendered as partially passive figures, led astray by the women's compulsive manipulations. This pattern was quite different from Ibsen's own personal experience, where it seems unlikely that Ibsen was merely an unwitting victim of intrigues by women. Emilie Bardach, the first of a series of young women with whom Ibsen fell in love (and with whom in this case he then broke off relations), was wounded by the suggestion, which Ibsen seems to have allowed to stand, that she was in some way the real-life model for the character of Hilde.

The Lady from the Sea.   Here Ibsen tells a story whose meaning is the necessity of freedom to both partners in a marriage. Wangel comes painfully to the recognition that his wife will never come back to him unless she is left free to make her choice, which will be to leave with her lover of many years past, or not. Both his courage, and Ellida's decision to stay with her husband when the choice is made, are convincing and moving. But Ibsen has nevertheless structured this situation in a way that covertly upholds the claims of marriage over what might have been constructed as its more authentic and passionate alternatives for Ellida. He loads the dice against the extra-marital alternative by giving Ellida's stranger, to whom she made a vow many years before, the character of a murderer. He is also considerably more possessive and self-centred than the husband who has imprisoned her in a rather empty kindness, while his emotional life remains caught up with his daughters. Ibsen thus chooses to locate the most potent forces of darkness outside the marriage, not within it, and the marriage, rarely enough in Ibsen, is shown to be capable of renewal, indeed of a first real beginning through mutual understanding.

John Gabriel Borkman.   But if *The Lady from the Sea* is structured somewhat one-sidedly, there is something wonderfully reparative towards Ibsen's own internal love objects in *John Gabriel Borkman*. We think that the monomaniac, self-willed character of Borkman, like Ibsen's other self-made heroes (e.g. *Brand, The Master Builder*) must be drawn in part from within. There is a similarity between Borkman's state of mind—his plans of redemption for the entire world—and the state of epistemic narcissism described by Ron Britton in his writing about William Blake (Britton, 1998, chapter 14). Ibsen's own life's work as a dramatist, through the decades of struggle to his final enjoyment of celebrity, involved the subordination of virtually everything to the project of his writing, since he experienced his work as a kind of destiny not so far different from the dreams of some of his characters. ("He was always occupied in his work", wrote his daughter-in-law Bergliot). His character, Borkman, had a crushing way with the truth,

> FOLDAL: . . . But is it quite certain they've already gone away with her?
> BORKMAN: They went away with her in the sledge that ran you over in the road.
>
> [Act 4, p. 363]

There may be an echo here of the lofty attitude Ibsen could from time to time take to those who crossed him. Meyer describes an occasion when Ibsen had been insulted by a guest speaker the worse for drink, who came to apologize the next day. "Young man, the secret of drinking", Meyer reports him saying, "is never to drink less the day after" (Meyer, p. 754).

The twin sisters in *John Gabriel Borkman* represent alternate ways in which a figure like Borkman (which is to say in part a figure like himself) treated his loved women: on the one hand, subordinating them ruthlessly to his own will; on the other hand, abandoning them, in his mind at least, when the demands of his relentless narcissism required it. What is remarkable in the portrait

of Ella Rentheim is that she is shown as having survived to remain
capable of love (contrary to what she herself says), and especially
of love for Erhart, in part because he *is* Borkman's son.[6] Ibsen
surely represents in this play—not in Borkman the character, but in
the whole ensemble of the action—reparation for the psychic damage inflicted on the women whose lives had revolved around a
dominating male ego such as his own.

Hedda Gabler.   Another text in which one can explore the depth
of Ibsen's exploration of the inner lives of his characters is *Hedda
Gabler*. The play opens as Hedda and her husband, Jorgen Tesman,
return home from their European honeymoon. Heavy in the air is
the matter of what is happening in their sexual relationship. The
observers of the marriage intrusively concern themselves with
Hedda's body, which should, they think, be showing the signs of
pregnancy. Tesman rather smugly surveys his beautiful property,
while being completely out of touch with her feelings. Hedda conveys her horror at the idea of a child growing within her. Just as she
speaks to Judge Brack of the awful boredom of "everlastingly having to be with the self-same person" on her honeymoon, so one
senses her terror of being imprisoned by a child who, she feels,
would prevent her getting away from herself. There is a frightening reversal in Hedda's mind—what she seeks is to control the
lives of others, but what her sexual destiny faces her with is the fear
of being controlled in her turn.

The oppressive atmosphere of repressed sexuality is present in
many of Ibsen's plays. In *Hedda Gabler*, we are shown a variety of
ways in which the development of character is distorted as a consequence of the failure of sexual expressiveness. In Tesman, and in
the pretty but dangerously innocent Mrs Elvsted, we see characters
stuck in a denial of the reality and power of sexual feelings. They
share the belief that if one chooses not to notice disturbing things,

------

[6] One of the fine qualities of Vanessa Redgrave's portrayal of Ella Rentheim
in the 1996 Richard Eyre production at the National Theatre was her ability to
express several different and contradictory feelings at the same moment, denying the capacity to love in words, while expressing it in her attention, giving with
a kiss what she could or would not say.

then the experience of being disturbed will be evaded. When Lövborg reappears after his disastrous night on the tiles, he says:

LÖVBORG: Everything's too late now. It's all up with me.

Thea responds:

MRS ELVSTED: Oh, no! Don't say that!
LÖVBORG: You'll say so yourself when you hear . . .
MRS ELVSTED: I won't hear anything.

[Act 3, p. 340][7]

This deadly innocence is acted out between Mrs Elvsted and Tesman in the final scene, where they are busily working together on reconstructing Lövborg's manuscript and ignore the auguries of Hedda's despair, leaving her to shoot herself in the next room. Not knowing about sexual desire is thus linked to a broader theme of not knowing, a phenomenon that ranges from "turning a blind eye" to a pervasive refusal of development. Such failures to engage with emotional reality involve a profound threat to life (this idea is explored in Steiner, 1985, 1993).

Ejlert Lövborg's divided consciousness derives from a different response to sexual repression. For him, there is a split in relation to women, care and tenderness being located in Mrs Elvsted and violence and sexual excitement in Hedda Gabler and Mademoiselle Danielle, the red-haired lady of the night who represents to all the characters the dangerous degradation inherent in the acknowledgement of female sexuality. The instability of this psychic organization is represented in the play by the power of alcohol to transform Lövborg from prospective intellectual star to degenerate and social outcast in less than 24 hours.

Judge Brack and Hedda occupy a third position. Each of them is appalled by their shared image of a repressive bourgeois marriage. Brack's solution is to insert himself between man and wife and create a triangle which, he remarks to Hedda, is "really highly convenient for all concerned". She is tempted by the arrangement he offers her, of an ongoing flirtation conducted beneath Tesman's

---

[7] Extracts from *Hedda Gabler* are taken from *Henrik Ibsen: Hedda Gabler and Other Plays*, translated by Una Elis-Fermor (Harmondsworth: Penguin, 1961).

nose, until she perceives that the underlying desire in Judge Brack is to have her in his power. Their mutual excitement is profoundly voyeuristic, and the many references to Brack's entering the house through the back door refer not only to his sexual invitation to Hedda, but also to his pleasure in spying on the intimate lives of others and the refusal to acknowledge any boundaries that could exclude him. His title of judge, and the proximity to the police that this affords him, adds to his opportunities for prurient intrusion, as we see when he reports Lövborg's fate. Their gossipy exchanges are rooted in their shared inability to expose themselves to real engagement with other people and their preference for watching others struggle with emotion. Hedda puts this into words as the others leave for Brack's party:

> BRACK: And so the procession starts, gentlemen. I hope we shall have a gay time, as a certain charming lady puts it.
> HEDDA: If only that lovely lady could be there, invisible.—
> BRACK: Why invisible?
> HEDDA: So as to hear a little of your gaiety—uncensored, Mr Brack.
> BRACK [LAUGHING]:   I shouldn't advise the charming lady to try!
>
> [Act 2, p. 323]

After the men have departed, Hedda says to Mrs Elvsted:

> HEDDA: I want, for once in my life, to have power over a human being's fate.
> MRS ELVSTED: But haven't you got that?
> HEDDA: I have not. And never have had.
> MRS ELVSTED: Not over your husband?
> HEDDA: That *would* be worth having, wouldn't it! Ah, if only you could realise how poor I am. And here you are, offered such riches! [*Throwing her arms passionately around her.*] I think I shall burn your hair off, after all.
>
> [Act 2, p. 324]

This sequence takes us directly to the matter of Hedda's envy and jealousy and to the torment she experiences when these emotions are aroused in her. The hatred of anything new or lovely that is not her possession drives her mad. Other characters are touched by this too. Brack cannot stand the idea of Lövborg's recovery from alcoholic collapse, Tesman cannot stand the idea that Lövborg's book and ideas may be more valuable than his own, but it is Hedda who is completely overwhelmed. She burns Lövborg's manuscript, because she knows it is the outcome of a creative link between Lövborg and Mrs Elvsted. She wishes to deny (that is, murder in thought) or destroy in some other way her own pregnancy. Even Aunt Julle's new hat, bought in honour of Hedda's return, is stripped of its appeal by her icy mockery.

The threat posed by anything new whose existence is entwined with elements of love (Mrs Elvsted's love for Lövborg, Aunt Julle's love for Tesman, and so on) is unendurable. The pain of recognizing in others the capacity for love that one lacks oneself is too great, and the impulse to spoil is given free rein. Mrs Elvsted's exit after the supposed loss of the manuscript captures the devastating grief Hedda would experience if she did not hurl it into others.

> MRS ELVSTED: Oh I don't know myself what I'm going to do. Everything is dark ahead of me now.
>
> [Act 3, p. 342]

Hedda goes on to accuse Lövborg of callous behaviour.

> HEDDA: To go and destroy what has filled her soul for all this long, long time! You don't call that callous?
>
> [Act 3, pp. 342–343]

A momentary contact with her own guilt as the destroyer of both the manuscript and the relationship between Mrs Elvsted and Lövborg is instantaneously transformed into an accusation intended to pierce Lövborg's conscience. She succeeds to devastating effect as Lövborg speaks of the terrible thing he has done "just losing" the child-manuscript that contained Thea's soul, and his intention to "put an end to it all". He cannot bear the guilt any more than can Hedda, and he becomes the recipient of her suicidal despair.

The absence of fulfilling sexuality is paralleled by the absence of meaningful activity for Hedda. The decoration of the house is complete, her imagined career as a hostess is blocked by financial constraints, and she finds herself immured with her dangerous boredom, relieved only by such visitors as arrive or by her pistol-practice. How clearly Ibsen displays the human necessity for meaningful work—a theme also dear to Freud's heart: both men understood that aggressive impulses need some ordering structures within which they can be constructively deployed. The general's daughter, whose mother never rates a mention, has an identity formed by aggressive self-assertion but has painfully little opportunity to struggle with the external world's realities. She fantasizes a future in politics for the ill-suited Tesman, which would provide her with a public role more suited to her personality. The intensity of her boredom with its overtones of incipient despair is all that is left to her when her pseudo-living breaks down. One such moment is painfully realized in a conversation with Lövborg reviewing their earlier intimacy:

> LÖVBORG: It was you who broke it off.
> HEDDA: Yes, when there was imminent danger of our relationship becoming serious. You ought to be ashamed of yourself, Ejlert Lövborg. How could you take advantage of your unsuspecting comrade!
> LÖVBORG [clenching his hands]:   Oh, why didn't you make a job of it? Why didn't you shoot me down when you threatened to?
> HEDDA: Yes . . . I'm as terrified of scandal as all that.
> LÖVBORG: Yes, Hedda. You are a coward at bottom.
> HEDDA: An awful coward. [Changing her tone.] But it was lucky enough for you. But now you have consoled yourself so delightfully up at the Elvsteds . . .

She goes on seductively:

> HEDDA: . . . But now I will confess something to you.
> LÖVBORG [eagerly]:   Well?
> HEDDA: That my not daring to shoot you down—
> LÖVBORG: Yes?
> HEDDA: That wasn't my worst piece of cowardice that night.
>
> [Act 2, pp. 317–318]

This is Hedda's confession of sexual desire, fatally confused with phantasies of violence. But no sooner has Lövborg understood what she said, than she drives him off again:

> HEDDA [Quietly, with a sharp angry glance]:   Take care! Don't assume anything like that!
>
> [Act 2, pp. 317-318]

The anxieties underlying the restless search for release from her self-disgust are perhaps touched on when Tesman asks if she will accompany him in visiting his dying aunt. Hedda's response demonstrates her painful fragility:

> HEDDA: No, don't ask me to do things like that. I don't want to think of sickness or death. You mustn't ask me to have anything to do with ugly things.
>
> [Act 3, p. 333]

Most frightening of all to her, and defended against by the alternative of an aestheticized consciousness, would be this encounter with loss. How ugly it would be to be reduced to helplessness in the face of death. Perhaps this is a hint that Hedda's glittering carapace has developed in response to an overwhelming loss—the early loss of her mother, one is tempted to imagine.

The relationship to dependence is a difficulty for all the characters in the play. Hedda hates it because it is for her imbued with humiliation, an exposure to cruelty and contempt. Judge Brack agrees with her. Tesman seems to have enjoyed a prolonged narcissistic dependence on the aunts who replaced his idealized lost parents, and there seem few signs of adolescent stirrings towards separateness and independence in his character. The return from his honeymoon is a return to his cherished carpet slippers—he seems to be passing from childhood directly into a premature old age. Mrs Elvsted, a painfully deprived child at heart, tries to care for herself through her care for Lövborg, and a similar constellation is manifest in Aunt Juliana, whose only way of living is to care for needy dependents.

There is very little opposition to the destructiveness let loose as the story unfolds, and this leaves us, the audience, as the witnesses whose response to the play is left to be the only source of hopefulness. There is no recognition of the meaning of what is happening among the play's characters and barely any capacity to acknowledge the reality of it. Tesman's and Brack's responses to Hedda's suicide are like clichés from poor-quality literature indicating how out of touch they are:

> TESMAN [shrieking to Brack]:   Shot herself. Shot herself in the temple! Think of it!
>
> BRACK [Half collapsed in the easy chair]:   But merciful God! One doesn't do that kind of thing.
>
> [Act 4, p. 364]

Ibsen knowingly leaves us deeply shocked, facing deaths in a stage-world where mourning is unlikely to be possible.

John Gabriel Borkman. By the time Ibsen wrote *John Gabriel Borkman*, he has become able to integrate a response to tragic death within the drama itself, and the impact on the audience is therefore a very different one. The artist Edvard Munch described this later play as "the most powerful winter landscape in Scandinavian art", and its consummation, when John Gabriel dies in a snowstorm on the mountain, conveys the meaning of a frozen heart bursting under the impact of released human feelings, in contrast to the cold despair of a suicide whose meaning is denied. Ella Rentheim and her sister Gunhild do fully come together over the dead body of Borkman:

> MRS BORKMAN: . . . And so we two can take each other's hands, Ella.
> ELLA RENTHEIM: I think we can now.
> MRS BORKMAN: We two twin sisters—over the man we both loved.
> ELLA RENTHEIM: We two shadows—over the dead man.
>
> [Act 3, p. 370]

Ibsen's capacity for learning from the experience of his life, his enjoyment of his son's gifts, his daughter-in-law's gaiety, and the birth of his and Suzannah's grandchildren seems to be the familial counterpart to the long struggle to overcome pessimism in his art.

The child's perspective

It is ironic that the courage that Ibsen berated himself for lacking is what others most revere in his work. Henry James, to whose novel our title refers, was energized to complete his becalmed draft of *What Maisie Knew* after he had read a proof of *John Gabriel Borkman*, which showed him the writer's task: "The march of an action is the thing for me to, more and more, attach myself to." This sense of having to follow where the characters are leading is awe-inspiring when this means facing up to the kinds of psychic damage that James and Ibsen were able to contemplate.

James's Maisie, if she was to survive as a person, had to know more than her elders about their motivations and to understand that she was a person of but little account to them. She lived in a world of parental figures who were almost totally dominated by narcissistic manoeuvres. She was dependent on adults to engage in links which could benefit her as a child, but she was in fact squeezed out by the perverse coupling around her. She is the voice of the children born of failed parental relationships miraculously saved by her intelligence and capacity to benefit from the very limited sustenance she received, and thus able to record the pain involved in what she came to know.

Ibsen too understood the costs of the self-absorption of his characters. This goes as far as the death or death-in-life of children perceived as threatening the project of his fearful heroes and heroines. Maisie, as a child whose nature helps her not to betray herself through self-deception, came to know the qualities of her world without being able to put into words what she knew. James found in Ibsen a writer who enabled him, and now us, to see what happens when the truth is thought and spoken—there is a terrible pain to bear, but the action is going forward: not impasse, but engagement with life's tragedies.

Ibsen and psychoanalysis

In conclusion, we would like to identify some of the parallels that can be drawn between Ibsen's and Freud's achievements.

Ibsen worked out how to put unvarnished life on to the stage, in realistic mode. This was in part because of his great capacity for close observation and for imagining from observation the full meaning of a life. This listening for detail, like Freud's, is related to his capacity to catch the underlying unspoken communication, the evidence that Freud came to investigate as the repressed unconscious.

Ibsen was, of course, deeply aware of the powers of both sexuality and destructiveness, the two major drives of Freudian theory. Ibsen portrayed on the stage lives blocked by the repression of these desires and by the crises to which their repression and nonrecognition gave rise. He understood, too, the fundamental difference between narcissistic structures (omnipotence, denial of dependence, mania, self-idealization, etc.) and relationships based on these, and dependent object relationships, which allow for separateness, interdependence, and difference. He was particularly aware of gender as the basis for acute forms of splitting and projection, as in *The Doll's House*—the first play that made him really famous.

He understood the phenomenon described by W. R. Bion of the resistance to becoming aware of emotional reality (that is, the refusal of understanding), because he understood the catastrophic change that could be required within characters where there had been massive denial. For example, Hedda, faced with hated dependence, would rather die. Ibsen understood the intense difficulty of change, and the power of the impulse to repeat. He was thus able to explore searchingly in his work what is destroyed if the truth cannot be tolerated.

Finally, there is Ibsen's devotion to the work of writing and to the psychic burden that this entailed. Just as psychoanalysts must be able to tolerate pain through exposure to the minds of their patients, so in the work of a writer like Ibsen—and no doubt, too, of the actors who take on his characters—there is need to bear the exploration of the most inaccessible and painful aspects of the self. Ibsen was able to go on doing this throughout a long life, bearing the loneliness that this entailed. Arthur Miller, in writing of the broad sweep of Western dramatic art, feared that the stoicism of Ibsen, whose tragedies rest on the idea of the spiritual power of the truth and the idea of a human impulse towards it, had been displaced by Strindbergian despair. Continuing fresh productions of Ibsen's plays indicate, however, that many continue to respond to his truth-seeking dramatic voice.

CHAPTER SEVEN

Chekhov:
the pain of intimate relationships

C hekhov was a doctor, in what we would now call general practice,[1] before he became a playwright, and he is like a good doctor, even a psychoanalyst, in his almost unvarying refusal to blame or judge his subjects.[2] Instead, his interest is in understanding his characters as they are. He wishes us to recognize their suffering, to understand that its origins lie outside themselves, but also to see the cruel way in which they cannot help but pass on their mental pain to others—including, most often, those whom they most love. The characters in his great plays are linked by and trapped within these circuits of suffering. Chekhov provides an anatomy of the different ways there are of coping or not

---

[1] Much valuable information is provided in Donald Rayfield's recent meticulous biography, *Anton Chekhov: A Life* (1997). A broader introduction to contemporary Chekhov studies is given by Vera Gottlieb and Paul Allain (Eds.), *The Cambridge Companion to Chekhov* (2000).

[2] There are few exceptions in Chekhov's plays, and perhaps even those that seem so (such as Natasha in *Three Sisters)* could be portrayed with sympathy on the stage.

coping with such pain, including the extremes of killing and suicide, of self-distancing by abandonment, and of narcissistic complacency—and also, at the opposite pole, in representations of a
capacity for "depressive pain" suffered on behalf of loved others, of
the highest order. It is the representation of such willingly shared
suffering, for example at the end of *Three Sisters* and *Uncle Vanya*,
that often moves their audiences to tears of sympathy.

The capacity for depressive anxiety is the contrary of the splitting of good and bad, of the projection of love into one object and
hate into another. It can be a quality of writing, as well as a represented attribute of those constructed imaginatively in writing.
Chekhov's dramatic writing is distinguished by this quality, by his
ability to hold in mind, and represent on the page, qualities in the
same characters which evoke both hate and love for them—or, to
put this another way, which enable us to go on feeling love and
sympathy for characters who are nevertheless perpetrating great
damage to those around them. Thus we feel for the suffering of
Yeliena as well as for Sonya in *Uncle Vanya*, and for Arkadina in
The Seagull and Ranyevskaia in *The Cherry Orchard*, even as they
each ruin the lives of their own children. It is this capacity to
maintain a sympathetic understanding attention to the person,
with a continuing love for them, whatever destructiveness that
person is gripped by, that links Chekhov's writing to the work of
psychoanalysis.

In this chapter we discuss three of Chekhov's plays, in order of
their composition: *Uncle Vanya, Three Sisters,* and *The Cherry Orchard*. Our contention is that these family tragedies function at
three levels: the widest is the social structure of Russian society, of
whose power and inertia we are often reminded; the middle stratum is the family structure itself and relationships in the family,
which extend to include servants and hangers-on of various kinds;
the third level is the interior of the characters, their hearts, minds,
and souls. We the audience are aroused at all these levels.

The social structure is represented for us by particular family
constellations in crisis. Chekhov shows us that when a social order
is breaking down or failing, adults are unable to take proper responsibility for their children, and as a consequence a new generation cannot be formed to allow the family to live on in the future.
Something is coming to an end.

Uncle Vanya

In *Uncle Vanya*, Chekhov explores with tenderness the wounds of the soul. Sonya is the embodiment of the truth-seeker, whose searching is characterized by delicacy and kindness as well as painful realism. She is someone who can love despite a failure to be loved in her turn. Both her father and Astrov fail to recognize her qualities, but in her final speeches we hear that in the midst of her immense sadness she is still sustained by a belief in being loveable. This is cast in religious terms, but can also plausibly be linked to her relationship with her dead mother, pictured as still loving her in the heaven Sonya is describing to Vanya. She is thus able to bear even great pain, in contrast with the self-pity in which Vanya fears he will drown. The audience's response represents, in a good performance, Sonya's deep conviction that she can be heard, understood, and loved for herself. Before us, was Chekhov.

At the start of the play we meet Astrov, the cultivated but narcissistic country doctor who seeks Nanny's care and containment. She offers him a glass of vodka, aware of his weakness. He himself is aware that something within is amiss.

> ASTROV: My brains are still functioning all right, but my feelings are somewhat duller. . . . I don't love anybody. Except you perhaps.
>
> [Act I, p. 188][3]

His admission to this elderly maternal figure whose sensitivity and solidity is a support to many in the family, is a first statement of the sense of neediness and primary deprivation that many of the characters share. We learn that a disabling sense of guilt about the death of a patient on whom he was operating is part of his uneasiness. Nanny comforts him, but she is a character who can understand but not challenge—the too-soft mother who allows the men to fail to grow up and to continue to expect from the women forgiveness and unquestioning tolerance of their selfishness. A society that delegates mothering to nannies is built on disabling splits in both male and female identities.

What Astrov has been devoting himself to is the restoration and care of the Russian forests, which are under attack. The destruction

---

[3] Extracts from *Uncle Vanya* are taken from *Anton Chekhov: Plays*, translated by Elisaveta Fen (Harmondsworth: Penguin, 1959).

of the forests (as of the cherry orchard in another of Chekhov's plays) is an image of great complexity. Astrov speaks as the conservationist of the landscape and works with intensity at his project of reclamation and mapping. His passion for regeneration is rooted in his unconscious awareness of the devastation of his inner world and his wish to restore that. But the clearing of forests is probably not only a consequence of lazy thoughtlessness, as he claims; it is also an emblem of change and development. It is the refusal of change that is one theme of this play. The fears aroused by the prospect of the unknown are so catastrophic in their intensity that Vanya attempts murder, and the play's ending describes the reconstruction of the lives of its characters in exactly the form they had prior to the events of the drama. As Vanya says to Serebriakov:

VANYA: Everything shall be as it was before.

[Act IV, p. 241]

This intolerance of change makes the passing of the years a terrible problem. Serebriakov, an extreme case of hypochondria, summarizes his quandary thus:

SEREBRIAKOV: This damnable disgusting old age! The devil take it! Since I've aged, I've become revolting even to myself. And you must find it revolting to look at me . . . all of you.

[Act II, p. 201]

Vanya, too, is tortured by his ageing, and the lost opportunities for love, marriage, and independent life, that Yeliena's appearance forces him to confront. When his mother insists on telling him how he has changed in the past year or so, from "someone who used to be a man with definite convictions, an inspiring personality", Vanya angrily replies

VANYA: Oh yes, I used to be an inspiring personality who never inspired anybody! . . . [Pause.] I used to be an inspiring personality! You could hardly have made a more wounding joke. I'm forty-seven now. . . .

[Act I, p. 194]

and he goes on:

VANYA: But now, if you only knew! I lie awake at night, in sheer vexation and anger—that I let time slip by so stupidly during the years when I could have had all the things from which my age now cuts me off.

[Act I, pp. 194–195]

The pain of this mid-life crisis is so great that he feels driven out of his mind. Astrov's deterioration is also linked with the loss of youthful hopes; both these two turn to vodka to protect themselves from awareness of their self-destructive emotional state and thus further undermine the possibility of self-understanding as a source of growth. (Addiction to alcohol has remained a flagrant symptom of the stresses of Russian life to this day.) Yeliena reproaches Vanya for drinking again, and he responds:

VANYA: At least it gives the illusion of life . . . don't prevent me.

[Act II, p. 206]

The need for illusion, on which all the characters except Sonya depend for much of the time, is linked to the depth of pain they would face without its comforts. For Vanya, this is entwined with his feeling for his dead sister, Sonya's mother.

SONYA: Uncle Vanya, so you got drunk again with the doctor? You're a fine pair! It's not becoming at your age.
VANYA: Age has nothing to do with it. When people have no real life, they live on their illusions. Anyway it's better than nothing.
SONYA: All the hay has been cut, it rains every day, everything is rotting, and you are living on illusions! You've been utterly neglecting the estate. . . . I've had to work alone, I'm quite worn out. . . . Uncle, there are tears in your eyes.
VANYA: Tears? It's nothing . . . nonsense! You looked at me then as your dear mother used to . . . my sister . . . my dear sister . . . if only she knew.

[Act II, p. 209]

Vanya's uncompleted mourning and failure to protect his sister's vulnerable daughter leaves him crippled with guilt. A similar situation deprives Sonya of Astrov's real attention—his preoccupation dulls his capacity to hear her declaration of love. The pain of guilt for destructive impulses not owned is too much for each of these men, and Sonya's shrewd eyes, commented on by Yeliena when they become friends, persecute them because of their honesty.

The two young women are also deeply unhappy. For both, Astrov is an object of attention and fascination. Sonya is in love with him, and Yeliena finds him attractive in the intense boredom and frustration of country life. The storm that takes place outside during the play has its equivalent on the stage, as these sexual attractions are admitted.

Act II has a brilliant and terrible conclusion when Sonya goes to ask her father if Yeliena can play the piano for her—she was a musician in St Petersburg—and comes back to say, "We mustn't". The music that isn't heard—Yeliena says playing would have made her "cry like a foolish girl"—resonates in the audience's mind as the possibility for growth and love that is crushed in these women.

There is a link between the absence of focus and meaningful work in the external world and the state of boredom and narcissistic self-preoccupation that weighs so heavily. Yeliena's indolence is infectious, as Sonya and later Astrov note ruefully. Sonya's suggestion to Yeliena that she might like to involve herself in the work of the estate could hardly be more unsuitable: Yeliena's own neediness makes her unable to imagine the lot of others. The difficulty about adult work is that it involves shouldering responsibility and being able to look after the needy parts of ourselves without projection.

Because everyone in this society is dependent on hierarchy, hopes have to be projected upwards, on to a mythical Moscow in *Three Sisters* when potent parents still existed, or to an unattainable professorship in *Vanya*. This situation depletes everyone's capacities. In this vertically dependent world, when the top of the family fails (through bereavements, bad marriages, or unfortunate second marriages), opportunities for the children are blighted. Chekhov, for reasons of dramatic condensation, heightens and over-determines these situations, but in doing so he reveals both the predicaments of a particular historical moment and the more universal problems of dependency within families.

Vanya struggles with his pained awareness of his self-deceit. He rages at the feeling that his life has been stolen from him, but he is also sadly conscious of how much the grandiosity projected into the professor's supposed importance also represents his collusion with a deadly force within himself. His idea that he could have been a Dostoevsky masks his hopeless sense of impotence (tragicomically evoked by the failed murderous assault on the professor). Inner obstacles have held him back: the little boy dependent on nanny's comfort, the madman of the family to be treated more-or-less as a patient because of his fragility. The shame he feels when faced with a picture of himself which he recognizes—the "normal crank" Astrov speak of—is devastating and leads to a suicidal gesture that is attention-seeking, yet also authentic in its despair.

Chekhov's compassion for all his characters, and his refusal to judge them, is particularly clear in the scene in which the whole family is gathered. Although it is easy to identify with Vanya and Sonya and to see Serebriakov's proposal to sell the estate as wholly selfish and insensitive, his plan does, in reality, contain some possible benefit for everyone, although Vanya and Sonya are terrified by the idea of any change in their lives.

The continuing dependence of grown-up children on their parents is represented as extreme in Chekhov's patriarchal world. To marry in a way that is socially acceptable, daughters need to have dowries and sons need to have estates, or alternatively a successful professional or official career. There are chronically not enough of these to go round, in what is represented as the stagnating agricultural economy of Russia. In each of his plays Chekhov heightens the intensity of this general social condition by introducing a bereavement, critically wounding, both internally and externally, the capacities of these families to support their children in taking up adult roles as heads of families and parents in their own generation.

In *Uncle Vanya* Sonya and Vanya seem to have been able to bear the sacrifice of being left behind by the parent-members of their family, so long as the parenting couple were both alive. They slaved to support Serebriakov and his wife in Moscow, Vanya and his mother also working without payment as his translators and scribes to assist his academic career. But their hostility towards Serebriakov's young second wife, and her parasitic way of life, perhaps contains some repressed resentment of the dead mother and sister too.

The shadow of Serebriakov's bereavement and loss also falls over the play. The earlier admiration of him, by the entire family back on the estate, is not to be understood as entirely a delusion. It is important that the retired professor is also shown to be deeply unhappy, aware that he no longer feels loved or respected. His pain at night keeps him out of Yeliena's bed, and his infirmity has to be nursed as a substitute for the child he and Yeliena will never have.

Most of the characters in this play are struggling with the fact of not having found an appropriate place within the normal generational life-cycle. The society depicted by Chekhov is one in which hierarchical and vertical dependencies are much stronger than horizontal bonds to individuals and families of a similar social status. The countryside leaves these families isolated, and even in small towns such as that of *Three Sisters* there seem to be few who are counted as social equals. There are no country houses, friendships, effective extended families, to secure marriage partners and generational continuity. There is none of the ritualized and intricate social exchange we find in Jane Austen's rural world of eighteenth-century England, in which an elaborate market in marriage and settled property operates and in which there are also some independent opportunities for young men. The social explanation of this situation is the legacy of feudalism in Russia, still alive in everyone's memory, when all social relations were framed within unbreakable hierarchies of birth.[4] In this respect Chekhov is the poet of a dying social milieu.

A source of pain for Vanya, Astrov, Yeliena, Sonya, even Serebriakov, is that they are in touch with the reality of what they do not have and become more so as the action proceeds. They continue to love the good, even as it is passing beyond their grasp. This is true also for the sisters, and for Baron Toozenbach, in *Three Sisters*, and, in *The Cherry Orchard*, for Ranyevskaia, Lopahin, and Varya. Like almost everything else in Chekhov, the good and the beautiful, which his characters are denied but for which they retain a longing, has both a social and an emotional meaning. At a social level, it is a lost style of life, a memory of Moscow, material im-

---

[4] It is possible that clientelist societies, where opportunities are in scarce supply and where preferment depends on favours from above, generate analogous kinds of social blockage and suffering.

provement, the preservation of the vanishing forests, real intellectual achievement. The characters of these plays mourn and anguish
over the absence of qualities of energy, cultivation, worldly success, moral commitment, beauty, which should give their lives
meaning. Often they try to project this lack outside themselves,
complaining of the dull people around them and the depressing
state of Russian society. But they know, or come to recognize, that
it is also within them, and this knowledge often brings them to
despair.

At an emotionally intimate level, the principal object of painful
loss is access to good internal parents. The dead Vera in *Uncle
Vanya*, reincarnated in an unwelcome form in the beautiful Yeliena,
and the long-dead mother and recently dead father in *Three Sisters*
are the emotional objects that arouse the most passion and despair.

The character of Yeliena, in *Uncle Vanya*, condenses both the
social and the emotional aspects of this situation. She is lazy, narcissistic, and yet emotionally sophisticated. She understands what
Sonya, Astrov, and Vanya are feeling, but she seems to have no
deep feelings of her own. She brings destruction wherever she
goes, as Astrov points out to her, because she is a magnet for the
passions of others that she cannot return.

But Yeliena is also a representative of the beautiful sexual mothers, now dead, abandoning, or neglectful, who haunt these plays.
Her beauty is a source of torment rather than pleasure to those
around her, because she is out of reach, arousing admiration and
desire that she is unable or unwilling to satisfy.[5]

She perhaps represents, as do Arkadina in *The Seagull* and
Ranyevskaia in *The Cherry Orchard*, the other side of the situation,
where it is nannies who are assigned the real mothering roles. It is
no wonder that the young people in these plays find it so difficult
to make emotional and sexual choices when the internal objects
who correspond to those choices have been experienced as seductive but at the same time abandoning.

---

[5] Yet we also feel for this beautiful woman stifled in the country, a musician
who is forbidden by her husband to play. She also represents a vision of the
cultured and "modern" city life that many of Chekhov's characters hold up as
their ideal.

Serebriakov may also carry the feelings projected into fathers in this family constellation—not, that is, as a giver of love and care, but as someone who has monopolized and stolen the mother's capacity for love from the children. Sonya, at the end of *Uncle Vanya*, appeals to her father to show charity to his family. She does not appeal to his love for her, instead seeking comfort from her old nanny.

Richard Gilman (1995), in his excellent study, points out that in all three of these last plays a family house is shown to be at risk. Natasha is stealing the sisters' house from them in *Three Sisters*, the house of the *Cherry Orchard* is sold up, and Serebriakov tries to dispose of the family estate in *Uncle Vanya*. These houses are representations of a longed-for protected space, safeguarded by benign internal parents, and their loss is a tragic inheritance.

Three Sisters

Perhaps the best-known of all Chekhov's dramatic images is the poignant longing of the three sisters to return to Moscow. The opening speech by Olga, the oldest of them, takes us straight to the centre of their distress: while Irena's saint's day should be an occasion for celebration, it is also the anniversary of their father's death. The sisters are living in a world overshadowed by perpetual mourning for their dead parents and their past hopes of life, and events in the present cannot be freed from this mood of sadness. Melancholy, indeed.

> OLGA: It's so warm today that we can keep the windows wide open, and yet there aren't any leaves showing on the birch trees. . . . Everything in Moscow was in blossom by now, everything was soaked in sunlight and warmth.
>
> [Act I, p. 249][6]

The beloved birches of the Russian landscape seem rendered barren for these three young women whose inner landscape does not contain an image of a flourishing parental couple. Behind the loss

---

[6] Extracts from *Three Sisters* are taken from *Anton Chekhov: Plays*, translated by Elisaveta Fen (Harmondsworth: Penguin, 1959).

of father is the earlier one of mother. The double bereavement is almost more than they can bear, though when Irena, the youngest, speaks sweetly of memories of the time that mother was still alive, Olga's appreciation of life is revived.

In fact, the atmosphere of the household combines and confuses birthday and wake. The house seems to be open to everyone to come and go—the officers hang around as they please, rather as if the funeral of the dead father had drifted on for a whole year. The loss, first of mother, then later of father, has left the four children bereft and needy. Masha has married Koolyghin, a schoolteacher, and is unhappy. As Irena explains, with the candour of the youngest child of the family,

> IRENA: Masha's a bit out of humour today. You know, she got married when she was eighteen, and then her husband seemed the cleverest man in the world to her. It's different now. He's the kindest of men, but not the cleverest.
>
> [Act I, p. 267]

Their father, a soldier, had wanted them to become educated. As Andrey says,

> ANDREY: Yes, my father—God bless his memory—used to simply wear us out with learning. . . . Yes, thanks to Father, my sisters and I know French and German and English, and Irena here knows Italian too. But what an effort it cost us!
>
> MASHA: Knowing three languages in a town like this is an unnecessary luxury. In fact, not even a luxury, but a sort of useless encumbrance . . .
>
> [Act I, pp. 262–263]

Andrey hopes to be a professor at Moscow University. The sisters dream that his success will take them all back to Moscow. We get a picture of their father having kept them going, in his own loneliness, by imposing discipline and self-improving hard work upon them. Chekhov, with a characteristic touch, hints at their father's own plight:

> OLGA: And yet there weren't many people at his funeral.
>
> [Act I, p. 249]

And then, both recalling the bleakness of the day and protecting her memory of him,

OLGA: Of course, it was raining hard, raining and snowing.

[Act I, p. 249]

It is too much for them to sustain their father's hopes for them when he is no longer there. Andrey has become lazy and rushes into marriage to the ambitious Natasha, for whose gaucheness he feels sorry. He is fleeing from his sisters' high expectations and implicit demands of him, as the surviving man in this family. Masha has mistaken Koolyghin for the intellectual her father would have wanted for her. He is kind, but an archetype of a pedantic schoolteacher whose phrases, awarding bad marks and so on, continually remind everyone of the schoolroom. Olga works, as she has learned to do as her father's eldest daughter in this be-reaved household, but she is nearly exhausted from the burden she carries of looking after others, both at her school and at home. Irena, the youngest, is the remaining focus of the family's hope.

Characters are trapped by the past, even as they struggle to escape from it. Vershinin, unhappily married, with a suicidal wife, and remembering his younger days in Moscow, when he was per-haps in love with Masha's mother, falls for Masha, who is, like him, unhappy in her marriage. Vershinin seems to bring Masha's father back to life for her—he recalls him in certain ways, with a wife seeming to be on the brink of death if not yet dead and with two if not three nearly orphaned little girls. This affair is a repetition compulsion, Masha in projective identification with a mother she can scarcely remember, Vershinin repeating with the second gen-eration of this family a love affair that he may already have at least imagined with the first. "I knew your mother", he tells Masha.

This family is defenceless against the needy, greedy, and envi-ous projections from those drawn to it. This is because of the ab-sence of functioning parents, able to regulate and guide their children's future, and to take responsibility for the perpetuation or reproduction of the family's social, cultural, and material capital—that is, their social position, their aspirations to education and culture, and their estate. But also because of what Chekhov shows to be the essentially parasitic relationship of the officer class of this society to the landed families of the provinces. These officers seem able to expect endless hospitality, as representatives of a social class otherwise in scarce supply in a small town that seems far from

Moscow and St Petersburg. These soldiers perpetually move on and expect never again to meet those they have lived among. When the battery is given another posting, Vershinin abandons Masha.

Masha's marriage is the first representation of a marriage that does not sustain its members. Later comes Andrey's disastrous union with Natasha, and the final tragedy of the play concerns Irena's loveless engagement to Baron Toozenbach and his suicidal involvement in a duel, which, we understand, is a consequence of his pained awareness of her inability to love him. Being unloved is, in fact, an experience of many of the characters: the marriages link one who loves with one who does not. We are left wondering about the idealized picture of the marriage of the earlier generation: perhaps it remains in so rosy a glow in the sisters' minds because they have been unable to think more profoundly about their parents' lives. There are the hints of Chebutykin's long involvement with their mother, an awareness of their father's unsatisfying years of loneliness, and evidence of difficulty in fully facing the facts about Andrey's deterioration and Natasha's betrayal. There is awareness of what is wrong, but a simultaneous evasion of the full implications. Chekhov writes about idealization and its consequences explicitly in the middle part of the play, which documents the widening collapse of the family.

> VERSHININ: We Russians are capable of such elevated thoughts— then why do we have such low ideals in practical life?
>
> [Act II, p. 276]

Speaking of his own unhappy domestic life, he adds,

> VERSHININ: Yes, why does his wife wear him out, why do his children wear him out? And what about him wearing out his wife and children?
>
> [Act II, p. 277]

This moment of painful insight is quickly turned into a self-pitying appeal to Masha to be understood. Persecution dominates and pushes out reflectiveness.

> VERSHININ: When the children are ill, I get so worried. I feel utterly conscience-stricken at having given them a mother like theirs. What a despicable woman! We started quarrelling at seven

o'clock, and at nine I just walked out and slammed the door. . . .
Don't be angry with me. I've nobody but you.

[Act II, p. 277]

Masha seems aware that there is something deadly in this appeal
when she replies:

MASHA: What a noise the wind is making in the stove. Just before
father died the wind howled in the chimney, just like that.

[Act II, p. 277]

But her intuitive grasp gives way under the pressure of her longing
for the more sophisticated emotional attention that Vershinin offers her. She recognizes that the passionate longings to which she
has been opened up by her deep deprivation are linked to the
death of her capacity for good judgement.

Irena, wooed by the faithful Baron, is troubled by her unkind-
ness, but she too cannot quite bear to think about herself for long.

TOOZENBACH: I'll go on fetching you from the post office, and bringing you home every evening for the next twenty years . . . unless
you send me away.

IRENA: A woman came into the post office just before I left. She
wanted to send a wire to her brother in Saratov to tell him her
son had just died, but she couldn't remember the address. So
we had to send a wire without an address, just to Saratov. She
was crying, and I was rude to her, for no reason at all. "I've no
time to waste," I told her. So stupid of me. We're having the
carnival crowd today, aren't we? . . . How nice it is to rest.

[Act II, p. 278]

The image of a telegram about a child's death sent without an
address conveys brilliantly the problem of unbearable pain that
has nowhere to put itself, no containment. Of course, poor Irena
could not stand it. She has no space in her mind for any more
losses, and this is why she later ignores the evident threat to
Toozenbach's life from the murderous Soliony.

The great difficulty in thinking and in finding meaning in their
lives is something the characters struggle with immensely. Masha's
contribution to a long debate makes a profound point:

MASHA: I think a human being has got to have some faith, or at
least got to seek faith. Otherwise his life will be empty. . . . How

can you live and not know why the cranes fly, why children are born, why the stars shine in the sky! You must either know why you live, or else . . . nothing matters . . . everything's just wild grass.

[Act II, p. 282]

The three sisters attempt to hold on to a picture of themselves as children born out of parental love, but they are struggling in an external world that offers little protection to young women without a father. Their longing for sexual fulfilment and their terrible disappointment in the men they are surrounded by corrodes their inner hopefulness. The external deprivations of provincial Russian life thus leave unmodified the idealized picture of Moscow as the place where they could have had fuller lives.

Olga's longer schooling in suffering and her greater capacity for sympathy—perhaps she was a bit more ready for the loss of her mother than the younger ones, though the tragedy of her present state of mourning is made manifest—creates an emotional envelope for the desperation of Masha who is so angry and so despairing, and for Irena, who feels her mind is breaking up.

IRENA: I can't stand it any more. Where has it all gone to? Where is it? Oh God, I've forgotten. . . . I've forgotten everything . . . there's nothing but a muddle in my head. I don't remember what the Italian for window is, or for ceiling . . . Every day I'm forgetting more and more, and life's slipping by and it will never never come back . . . We shall never go to Moscow . . . I can see that we shall never go . . .

[Act III, pp. 304–305]

Chekhov's writing

There are moments in Chekhov when an aspect of a character emerges in bold terms—for example, when Natasha shouts at Anfisa for sitting down in her presence. But there are many more subtle moments in which narcissism, or idealization, or self-centredness are revealed merely by an unexpected sequence of remarks, in conversations that seem momentarily thrown off their normal course by unintended revelations of self. While Chekhov's dialogue seems so ordinary and natural, his characters continually say more than they know or intend about their feelings and self-preoccupations. It is a striking affinity between Chekhov and psychoanalysis that his characters are so multi-dimensional, and that we have to read and listen for different levels of meaning in what they say. For example:

MASHA: Perhaps it's different in other places but in this town the military certainly do seem to be the nicest and most generous and best-mannered people.

VERSHININ: I'm thirsty. I could do with a nice glass of tea.

[Act II, p. 276]

As Masha and Vershinin describe their unhappy lives to each other, Vershinin returns to his neediness:

MASHA: You're a bit low-spirited today, aren't you?

VERSHININ: Perhaps. I haven't had any dinner today. I've had nothing to eat since morning. One of my daughters is ill, and when the children are ill, I get so worried. I feel utterly conscience-stricken at having given them a mother like theirs. Oh, if only you could have seen her this morning! What a despicable woman! We started quarrelling at seven o'clock and at nine I just walked out and slammed the door. [*Pause.*] I never talk about these things in the ordinary way. It's a strange thing, but you're the only person I feel I dare complain to. [*Kisses her hand.*] Don't be angry with me. I've nobody, nobody but you ...

[Act II, p. 277]

Thus this self-pitying unhappy husband makes his appeal for understanding and love to Masha.

Later in this scene, the two younger officers come in, and we see that even they, who are relatively sweet-natured, cannot forget their own neediness:

FEDOTIK [*to Irena*]:   I've got you some coloured crayons at Pyzihkov's, in Moscow Street. And this little penknife too. . . .

IRENA: You still treat me as if I were a little girl. I wish you'd remember I'm grown up now. [*Takes the crayons and the penknife, joyfully.*] They're awfully nice.

[Act II, p. 283]

But Fedotik can't bear to let her have all the pleasure:

FEDOTIK: Look, I bought a knife for myself too. You see, it's got another blade here, and then another. . . . This thing is for cleaning your ears, and these are nail-scissors, and these are for cleaning your nails. . . .

[Act II, p. 283]

Fedotik's Rodé then finds this too much for him

RODÉ [*in a loud voice*]:   Doctor, how old are you?
CHEBUTYKIN: I? Thirty-two. [*Laughter.*]

[Act II, p. 283]

How old is anyone here, one might ask? But in case one hadn't quite noticed, the covert spoiling relentlessly goes on.

IRENA [*playing patience*]:   It's coming out. We'll get to Moscow!
FEDOTIK: No, it's not coming out. You see, the eight has to go on the two of spades. [*Laughs.*] You see, that means you won't go to Moscow.
CHEBUTYKIN [*reads the paper*]:   Tzitzikar. Smallpox is raging.

[Act II, p. 283]

Anfisa, who does attend to the needs of others, brings in the tea, and Masha and Irena both demand her attention, like small children.

MASHA: Bring it here Nanny, I'm not coming over there.
IRENA: Nanny!
ANFISA: Comi–ing!

[Act II, p. 284]

Provoked by this demonstration, Natasha turns to Soliony and starts to babble on about Bobik, her "extraordinary child". Soliony then in turn responds to this provocation of infantile need:

SOLIONY: If that child were mine, I'd cook him up in a frying pan and eat him.

[Act II, p. 284]

This is a most subtle delineation of a scene of acute emotional need and the hostility and competitiveness that this brings out. In the absence of the dead parents of this household, there is simply not enough of anything for anybody, and when anyone seems to feel satisfied even for a moment, they are promptly attacked by those around them. Masha, wearing black while Irena is wearing white on her birthday, cannot contain her depression at the prospect of this party and is about to leave for home, explaining how much more fun parties were when Father was alive and when there were so many officers. But she tries to protect her sisters from her bad feelings, and Olga says to her, tearfully, "I understand you, Masha". We are reminded that Olga has said at the beginning the play, before the various unhappy marriages and love affairs have been revealed to the audience,

> OLGA: I suppose that everything God wills must be right and good, but I can't help thinking sometimes that if I'd got married and stayed at home, it would have been a better thing for me. [*Pause.*] I would have been very fond of my husband.
>
> [Act I, p. 251]

The end of the play

The emotional bonds that survive the various catastrophes of this play are those between the three sisters, the kindness and affection of Koolyghin for all of them, and their fondness for Anfisa, their old nurse. (At the close, Anfisa goes to live in the school-house with Olga; she at least can say she has found happiness.) The members of the family are all on stage at the end, even Chebutykin, whom they have not rejected, and Andrey, pushing his son Bobik's pram. When Andrey has been half-destroyed by his marriage, Baron Toozenbach has been killed, and Vershinin has left, abandoning Masha, it is Olga who puts her arms round her two sisters and comforts them as best she can:

> OLGA: No, my dear sisters, life isn't finished for us yet! We're going to live! The band is playing so cheerfully and joyfully—maybe if we wait a little longer we shall find out why we live, why we suffer. . . . Oh, if only we knew, if only we knew!
>
> [Act IV, p. 329]

The audience does now know more than it did before the play about the sustaining power of depressive capacities to contain suffering and generate hope.

The Cherry Orchard

The action of *The Cherry Orchard* represents a crucial late stage of the failure of an upper-class landed family successfully to reproduce itself and its way of life. The play begins as Ranyevskaia returns to her estate from Paris, to learn that she must sell her beautiful cherry orchard as building land for holiday villas and demolish the family house, or face complete ruin. The estate has been decaying, in the absence of its owner in Paris. Varia, Ranyevskaia's adopted daughter, who has been left in charge of the house, has difficulty in maintaining authority over the few remaining servants and has hardly any money to feed them. Ranyevskaia feels shamed by rumours that Varia can only provide dried peas for the servants to eat. When a Jewish band is hired for a dance, Feers, the old servant, comments "that we used to have generals, barons and admirals dancing at our balls, but now we send for the post-office clerk and the station-master, and even they don't come too willingly".

Lopahin, the son of a peasant who has become a successful businessman, has the energy and determination that Ranyevskaia and her brother Gayev entirely lack. Gayev, whose meanderings are an embarrassment to everyone, is reduced to hoping for a miraculous rescuing gift from their richer relatives, who have, however, long since abandoned this failing branch of the family. Trofimov, the perpetual student, has in effect opted out of life, preferring poverty and empty philosophizing (which he nevertheless criticizes as a vice of contemporary Russia) to facing the world. Yasha, Ranyevskaia's manservant, has been corrupted by his service with her in Paris and seems to have adopted his mistress's rapacious lover (who has spent all her money and then abandoned her for another woman) as his role-model. The modern world of commercial development and more widely dispersed wealth appears merely as a vulgar threat to this family, though Lopahin points out to them that if they could come to terms with it by selling off some land, it would enable them to save themselves. The twice-repeated sound of what Lopahin says is a breaking cable in a distant mine-shaft symbolizes the violence and danger of industrial modernization for this whole society.

Yet important as these social dimensions are, *The Cherry Orchard* is more than the representation of a social class in terminal decline. Set within this social context is a crisis of family relationships, of the non-fulfilment of the responsibilities of one generation for another. This pattern—of an interweaving of a crisis of an entire social stratum of Russian society with a crisis of family—is, as we have noted, the common theme of the major plays of Chekhov.

Chekhov described *The Cherry Orchard* as a "comedy", but its audiences face tormented characters whose painful passions are expressed in destructive and self-destructive action. How can we understand the play as comedy?[7] In this play, there are no virtuous characters or vicious ones. Misunderstandings between persons, which can and should be represented with humour, occur throughout. But mostly this humour does not represent shafts of deliberate malice, concealed in the form of wit; rather, it enacts the incidental emotional damage that the characters are continually but unconsciously inflicting upon one another. What the audience finds itself reluctantly smiling at is the recognition of the fact that such everyday conversational wounds are indeed regularly inflicted in social life, through the complacency and self-boundedness of the characters, which is recognizable as little greater than one might observe anywhere. The dispersal and distribution of these misunderstandings and hurts throughout the dialogue of the play, and the everyday quality of its actual moments of intense

---

[7] Richard Gilman (1995, pp. 200–201) discusses the puzzling designations of these plays as "comedy" or "drama". Chekhov described *The Seagull* and *The Cherry Orchard* as comedies, he sub-titled *Three Sisters* as "a drama", and *Uncle Vanya* as "scenes from *Country Life*". In fact, the conventional categories of comedy and tragedy do not seem to fit his work, as he may have recognized himself. The common pattern of tragedy culminates in the catastrophe or death of a particular individual, in whom have been lodged exceptional qualities. Comedies usually represent a more everyday world, and both its better and worse characters usually survive the action of their plays. Chekhov's plays convey a depth and evenness of sympathy unusual in comedy, but rather than assigning catastrophic ends to individual heroes and heroines, as tragedies do, Chekhov represents loss and pain as experiences shared by nearly all those he has placed on his stage. This was to create a new genre and sensibility, a deeply democratic way of responding to the world, which we see as a shaping influence on later dramatists such as Beckett.

crisis, reflects Chekhov's evenness of attention and sympathy, his wish to locate the pain in the whole situation of a family, a larger household, and as indeed the representatives of a social class, and not in particular evil people within them. This is why, in this and in Chekhov's other great plays, the most terrible things (a suicide, a desertion, the failure of a relationship) seem just to happen, as everyday events; they resist or undermine their depiction as dramatic crises. Even when a murder is attempted, as in *Uncle Vanya*, its execution is both farcical and unsuccessful, leaving everyone to have to cope with the pain and misery that are the real issue at stake.

Ranyevskaia's failure to nurture and protect her children and the dependents of her household is shown to be the outcome of her own neediness and her guilt. She has, in the past, married beneath her, a solicitor instead of a nobleman, and her husband was a drinker. Her seven-year-old son Grisha drowned one month after her husband's death. She has never got over these disasters, and the guilt brought about by them (and the consequent failure to mourn) also seems to have emotionally crippled Pyetia (Trofimov), who was at the time the boy's tutor. Ranyevskaia's boundless guilt expresses itself in her compulsion to give away all her money, even to strangers, even while her estate sinks into debt.

Her imminent return from abroad at the start of the play reveals a household transfixed by idealized memories. Lopahin remembers Ranyevskaia, as the great lady of the house, tending him as a boy, when he had a bleeding nose caused by a blow from his father. He remembers her saying to him: "Don't cry, little peasant." He thinks to himself, I am now rich, but I am still a peasant, imagining himself through Ranyevskaia's eyes. Dooniasha, the parlourmaid, cannot wait for her young mistress Ania to return from her visit to Paris—she is bursting to tell her of the proposal she has just had. Trofimov has come to meet them on their arrival, and this is plainly an important event for him too.

But when Ranyevskaia arrives, her thoughts are all for herself and her own sentimental and idealized memories:

RANYEVSKAIA: The nursery, my dear, my beautiful room! I used to sleep here when I was little. . . . [*Cries.*] And now I feel as if I were little again. [*She kisses her brother, then Varia, then her brother again.*] And Varia is just the same as ever, looking like a nun. I recognised Dooniasha, too. [*Kisses Dooniasha.*]

[Act I, p. 336][8]

The audience may only just notice the incidental humiliation of Ranyevskaia announcing that she recognizes Dooniasha, who has been almost overcome at the prospect of this reunion, and of her remark, in Varia's hearing, that she still looks like a nun.

The subtle diminution of all whom Ranyevskaia encounters in her self-regarding state of mind is reinforced by Ania, who seems much identified with her mother. Dooniasha tells Ania

DOONIASHA: We've waited and waited for you. . . .
[*Helps Ania to take off her hat and coat.*]

[Act I, p. 336]

But Ania's thoughts are only for herself:

ANIA: I haven't slept for four nights. . . . I'm frozen.
DOONIASHA: You went away during Lent, and it was snowing and freezing then, but now its spring-time. Darling! [*She laughs and kisses her.*] I could hardly bear waiting for you, my pet, my precious. . . . But I must tell you at once, I can't wait a minute longer. . . .
ANIA [*without enthusiasm*]:   What is it this time?
DOONIASHA: Yepihodov, the clerk, proposed to me just after Easter.
ANIA: You never talk about anything else. . . . [*Tidies her hair*] I've lost all my hairpins.

[Act I, pp. 336–337]

Ania is little more responsive to her half-sister Varia's affectionate welcome:

VARIA: Thank God you've arrived. You're home again. [*Embracing her*] My darling's come back. My precious!
ANIA: If only you knew the things I had to put up with!
VARIA: I can just imagine it.
ANIA: I left just before Easter: it was cold then. Charlotta never stopped talking, never left off doing her silly conjuring tricks all the way. Why did you make me take Charlotta?

---

[8]Extracts from *Three Sisters* are taken from *Anton Chekhov: Plays*, translated by Elisaveta Fen (Harmondsworth: Penguin, 1959).

VARIA: But how could you go alone, darling? At seventeen!
[Act I, p. 337]

Ranyevskaia and Ania are exhausted from their long journey, and it *is* the middle of the night. Thus their self-preoccupation is normalized, seemingly excused. But these casually inflicted injuries to those who love them reveal their deep incapacities to attend to and respect others. Ranyevskaia is unable to listen to Lopahin, who remains to her, as to her brother Gayev, a peasant, an inferior unworthy of full respect. It is her disrespect for both Lopahin and Varia that dooms their long-awaited marriage. Varia, compelled to house-keep for her adoptive mother in her absence, has all but foregone hopes of a marriage of her own, and although Ranyevskaia seems to want to arrange her partnership to Lopahin, this appears to engage little of her attention or feelings. Lopahin, pushed aside by Ranyevskaia and Gayev when they reject his offer to save them by selling the cherry orchard, chooses to triumph over them by buying them out rather than entering into the alliance through marriage, which their contempt for him and their consequent ruin has now devalued. Ranyevskaia breaks up Ania and Trofimov's affectionate friendship and incipient romance too, condemning Trofimov for his worldly failure. Her own failed partnerships make her incapable of identification with sexual partnerships for her daughters, and perhaps unconsciously envious of them.

At one level, this can be seen as a failure of social transmission, the economic ruin of the family leaving them without the means to provide for and marry off its daughters. The flight to fantasies of lives of metropolitan glamour (which in reality seem to amount more to a rootless and penurious form of exile), which possess Ranyevskaia and Ania and, in disastrous identification with them, their servants Dooniasha and Yasha, do not provide a real alternative. Indeed, Dooniasha, her attainable possibility of marriage to Yepihodov having been destroyed by Yasha's cynical seduction, is immediately abandoned by him.

But the failure is more than a social one. It is Ranyevskaia's image of herself as someone who has squandered her parents' inheritance on a drunkard, and of her painful sense of having allowed her seven-year-old son to be drowned, that lies at the heart of her inability to protect her own life or the lives and futures of those she loves.

The failure of emotional containment, we might say, is comprehensive in this play. Chekhov seems to believe that aristocracies based on descent must fail in this respect, because of the contempt and disregard in which "inferiors" are held. This contempt, as Hegel pointed out in his parable of the master and slave, then leaves the superiors also devoid of social recognition. In this play, we hear of the family being in turn despised by its grander relations. In *The Cherry Orchard* this deep disparagement is damaging in its effects in both directions. Ranyevskaia and Gayev are unable to accept the good advice and help of Lopahin. Lopahin is denied the respect that might have enabled him to save the family and reproduce it with Varia in another generation. Dooniasha, Yasha, Yepihodov, and Trofimov are led into a social no-man's-land where what they could have is demeaned as worthless and what they come to feel they want is unattainable and delusory. In the process the worst of them, Yasha, treats even his own mother with contempt and abandons her without a word. The old servant, Feers, who is faithful to the mutual obligations of the old order and who has cared with affection for his master, Gayev, is forgotten and left to die in the abandoned house. This is a shocking moment, far from any conventional conception of the comic, and emblematic of the disastrous collapse of family that shadows the action.

But while the sources of this general family tragedy, for it is such, lie in the social structure that is represented for us, the experience of this is lived out in the medium of family relationships. What happens when a social order breaks down or fails, Chekhov shows us, is that adults are unable to take proper responsibility for their children, and as a consequence a new generation cannot be formed to reproduce the lives of its parents.

Conclusion

It is essential, in our view of these plays, that one recognizes that they are at the same time the representations of states of feeling and the descriptions of a structure of social relationships, in a historical context that gives these feelings their particular forms. The context, not least in Russia, has been a recurrent one. Chekhov shows a social world where the main necessity is to endure in a spirit of love a situation in which there seems to be little hope for the future. Some see these plays as anticipations of a revolutionary catastrophe to come.[9] But in view of the sufferings experienced by Russians after the 1917 revolution,[10] and then again after its ultimate collapse in the 1990s, perhaps continuing pain and the difficulties of psychological survival is its more universal theme.

The "structures of feeling" represented in these plays can, we suggest, be illuminated through the vertices of both psychoanalytic and sociological thought. In drama and fiction, representations take the form of imagined particulars, including characters, patterns of interaction, and narrative sequences of events. But these particular "stories" can also be seen as instances of ideal-typical patterns, which in the discourses of social science or psychoanalysis are described in more generalized and theoretical terms. We have tried here to suggest, in interpretation of these plays, what some of these terms might be. One way of recognizing the genius of Chekhov's dramatic work is to show how vast a social and psychological reality he has been able to understand and represent in the form of drama.

<hr />

[9] The descriptions of the *ancien régime* of pre-revolutionary Russia, in Orlando Figes' outstanding *A People's Tragedy: The Russian Revolution 1981–1924* (1996), and the small possibilities he identified of a less catastrophic modernization than took place, indirectly illuminate the world represented in Chekhov's plays.

[10] Daniel Bertaux's life-history interviews with members of families expropriated after the 1917 revolution, about their subsequent struggles to maintain the integrity and continuity of their families, provide insight into this later history, in moving individual terms. (See Bertaux & Thompson, 1997.)

CHAPTER EIGHT

Oscar Wilde's glittering surface

W ilde's plays are probably second in the British public's affection only to Shakespeare's—both the regularity of prestigious West End theatre productions and their great popularity in regional theatre as well as in the substantial world of amateur theatre attest to this fact. This is perhaps a good reason in itself for attempting to explore where their fascination lies. But there is also the very particular feature of Wilde's writing, and indeed of his conversational feats, that the admiration of his verbal brilliance that is continually pulled out of us is so frequently tinged with paradox, an awareness that the comedy both conceals and evokes something other than the surface wit. The fact that Wilde's own life was lived in such a theatrical fashion and that the unprotected, ever-innocent, childish impulse to display in public what is ordinarily more private was the source of such tragedy for him heightens our response to his writing. It is the record of something brilliant and gorgeous, but also damaged and vulnerable, and all of this consciously so. It is especially extraordinary when one keeps in mind that the period of his outstanding success in the theatre (1892–95) immediately preceded his disastrous series of court appearances and imprisonment, from which he never recovered.

Wilde's first really successful play was *Lady Windermere's Fan* which was first produced in 1892 (and published in 1893). It is instructive to keep in mind some of the other major work being produced in the theatre of that time. Ibsen was gradually becoming well known, and Bernard Shaw, an admirer of Ibsen, as Wilde was himself (Ellmann 1987, p. 315), had written his essay on "The Quintessence of Ibsenism" in 1891. Wilde as a writer is working along very different lines, avoiding the realistic presentation of life pioneered by Ibsen and most interested in producing dialogue as brilliant and gem-like as possible. It is striking when one reads Wilde's plays to discover just how many extremely penetrating and oft-quoted phrases he has bequeathed to the language, and to see these familiar jewels in their original setting.[1] We shall try to draw attention in our discussion of two of his plays to the deeper issues and feelings that are to be found not far beneath their surface glitter.

Lady Windermere's Fan

The story of the play—all the action of which is packed into 24 hours—is simple. It is the morning of Lady Windermere's 21st birthday. She is at home arranging flowers, ready for the dance that she and her husband have arranged for the evening. A fan, her husband's gift, is visible on the table. Lord Darlington calls. Although he is a society smoothie, he is shown as having genuine feeling for her, and he believes Lord Windermere to be having an affair with Mrs Erlynne, a newly arrived mysterious figure at the edges of London society. He hints at Lady Windermere's vulnerability, offering his friendship/love in the belief that she might be tempted by him in this situation. She, however, is very much the "Puritan" and will have nothing to do with him on these terms. Their conversation is interrupted by the arrival of Lady Berwick,

---

[1] Ellmann (1987) discusses the contrast between platitude and epigram as central to Wilde's linguistic interest.

who reveals the current gossip about Lord Windermere to his wife in the guise of sympathetic concern. Lady Windermere, at first disbelieving, is deeply shocked. Her fears are confirmed when her husband asks her to invite Mrs Erlynne to the party, which she refuses to do. He invites her himself, and we understand that whatever the details, his primary interest in her is not a sexual one.

At the party, all varieties of "society" are present and display their motives, good and (mostly) bad. Mrs Erlynne reveals herself to the audience as Lady Windermere's mother—Lady Windermere believes that her mother had died when she was an infant. Lady Windermere, profoundly offended by her husband's betrayal, as she understands his insistence on Mrs Erlynne's presence, has decided to leave their home and accept Lord Darlington's offer. She goes secretly to his rooms. Mrs Erlynne is determined to protect her daughter from a repetition of her own sad history of abandoning her husband and child for another man, and she skilfully saves the day. The fan becomes crucial evidence of Lady Windermere's presence in Lord Darlington's rooms, but Mrs Erlynne claims that she has mistakenly picked it up at Lady Windermere's party. The two women—mother and daughter—share the name inscribed on the fan. Meanwhile Lady Windermere, her honour saved by Mrs Erlynne's ingenuity, kindness, and determination, is back home, only to be confronted by her husband's denunciation of Mrs Erlynne as a "wretched woman", "as bad as a woman can be"—a fact proven in his mind by her presence in a man's room, unaccompanied. The tables are turned, as Lady Windermere now sees things very differently. Mrs Erlynne arrives to return the fan and announce her departure from London. She has in the meantime cleverly talked her way into acquiring a rich husband willing to leave with her—the foolish Lord Augustus. Catastrophe is thus averted.

Wilde's subtitle to the play is "A Play about a Good Woman", and it is evident that Mrs Erlynne's goodness is one dimension, and that Lady Windermere becomes better by being less constrained by what she had previously believed was required of a good woman. Both women end up better off than they were at the start—one has got the husband she wants, the other has acquired some wisdom and generosity of spirit. The loser is very obviously "society", held up to ridicule on many levels. Its male figures—

Lords Darlington, Windermere, and Augustus—are all outwitted in one way or another.

Questions of morality

The play moves us despite its apparent devotion to the trivialities of society life and familiar tricks of plot, as signalled by its title. Why is this so?

One powerful theme is immediately placed before us in the Windermeres' quarrel about whether Mrs Erlynne is to receive an invitation and thus be enabled to re-enter "good society". Excluded and desperate to regain acceptance, she describes the experience of social exclusion, in trying to persuade Lady Windermere to return home from Lord Darlington's rooms:

> MRS ERLYNNE: You don't know what may be in store for you, unless you leave this house at once. You don't know what it is to fall into the pit, to be despised, mocked, abandoned, sneered at—to be an outcast! To find the door shut against one, to have to creep in by hideous byways, afraid every moment lest the mask should be stripped from one's face, and all the while to hear the laughter, the horrible laughter of the world, a thing more tragic than all the tears the world has ever shed. You don't know what it is. One pays for one's sin, and then one pays again, and all one's life one pays. . . . You couldn't stand dishonour. No! Go back, Lady Windermere. . . . Your place is with your child.
>
> [Act III, lines 141–188][2]

There are extraordinary resonances for us in listening to this—literary ones, in other explorations of responses to loss and exclusion (think of Medea's intolerance of mockery), and at the level of real events, our awareness that Wilde is writing about what his own life will become after his disgrace. The account in Ellmann's biography of his last years (Ellmann, 1987) is full of instances of just such social rejection and loneliness.[3]

---

[2] Extracts from *Lady Windermere's Fan* are taken from *Oscar Wilde, The Importance of Being Earnest and Other Plays* (Oxford: Oxford University Press, 1995).

[3] For useful commentary on Wilde and his work see also Ellmann (1969, 1970), Beckson (1970), Tydeman (1982), and Raby (1997).

The passion of youth has a dangerous edge—whatever led the youthful Mrs Erlynne to leave her husband, it is clear that she feels that it was a terrible mistake. She lost her child and her marriage; her lover has disappeared or died, and she is thus left with nothing. The cruelty of social convention is one thing, its double standards another. The men, it is clear, can and do carry on as they please—sexual indiscretion is only held to be a fault in the women in the society pilloried by Wilde. The hidden reference to the unacceptability of homosexuality is obvious. This, too, is un-forgivable in late nineteenth-century Britain and indeed harshly punished by the law as well as by ostracism. Wilde's conspicuous sympathy for his female characters no doubt has something to do with his own complicated identity and identifications. "Society" is represented as cruel, cynical, and heartless, but at the same time the only place to be. There is simply no imaginable life worth living without conspicuous beauty, fine clothes, and surroundings (Oscar's passion in real life) and social position. To be outside this charmed circle is to be nothing. Possessions and invitations confer identity.

This surely is a state of mind we could link with a child's experience of exclusion from the adult world. "Society", in Oscar Wilde's childhood vision, is the world of the drawing-room, the club, the ballroom, the parental bedroom, where there is knowl-edge and sexuality, a world conceived of as held together by its smug possession of huge quantities of all that is desirable—leisure (these upper-class characters never work), people to do whatever one requires (servants), "love" (seen as mutual idealization), li-censed nastiness (malicious gossip), money (for clothes, carriages, flowers, or whatever else may enter one's mind), fun, and opportu-nities to show off (parties, etc.). One needs to bear in mind that the children of the privileged classes for the most part experienced in reality considerable emotional deprivation—brought up by serv-ants, sent off to boarding schools if they were boys, often having very little contact with their parents' world but for the tantalizing glimpses of adult excitements that are particularly difficult for children to digest when not tempered by more everyday concep-tions of the adult world. But the power of glittering society to seduce needs to be thought about primarily as a state of mind

Wilde wanted to explore—he shows us its emptiness and makes us aware of its lack of value while titillating us with the glamour of clothes and setting and the dazzling conversation attributed to the leisured class. Who could resist such splendour?

We are invited to savour the compulsive desirability of this world of glittering surface and to sense both its heartlessness and its irresistibility. Many of the most enjoyable speeches are those uttered by the most corrupt characters—the Duchess of Berwick, Mr Cecil Graham, and, in a more complex way, Lord Darlington. It is through their combination of realism and complete cynicism that Wilde's insights are expressed. When Lady Windermere objects to the compliments he pays her, Lord Darlington remarks:

> LORD DARLINGTON: Ah, nowadays we are all of us so hard up, that the only things to pay *are* compliments. They're the only things we *can* pay.
>
> [Act I, lines 36–38]

and later, after discussion of Lady Windermere's views on sexual morality:

> LORD DARLINGTON: I think life too complex a thing to be settled by these hard and fast rules.
> LADY WINDERMERE: If we had "these hard and fast rules" we should find life much more simple.
> LORD DARLINGTON: You allow of no exception?
> LADY WINDERMERE: None!
> LORD DARLINGTON: Ah, what a fascinating Puritan you are, Lady Windermere!
> LADY WINDERMERE: The adjective was unnecessary, Lord Darlington.
> LORD DARLINGTON: I couldn't help it. I can resist everything except temptation.
>
> [Act I, lines 140–148]

The irony at the heart of Lord Darlington's point of view is repeatedly noted:

> LORD DARLINGTON: Do you know I am afraid that good people do a great deal of harm in the world. Certainly the greatest harm they do is that they make badness of such extraordinary importance.
>
> [Act, I, lines 115–117]

Lord Darlington's undercutting of moral distinctions is matched by the Duchess's untroubled pursuit of money. Speaking of her husband's infidelities, she remarks:

> DUCHESS OF BERWICK: He was so extremely susceptible. Though I am bound to say he never gave away any large sums of money to anybody. He is far too high-principled for that.
>
> [Act I, lines 291–294]

Once the offer of marriage for her daughter Agatha has been secured:

> DUCHESS OF BERWICK: . . . I'm afraid it's the old old story, dear. Love —well, not love at first sight, but love at the end of the season, which is so much more satisfactory.
>
> [Act II, lines 378–380]

Fine words work within the play to seduce the unwary—Lord Darlington's pursuit of Lady Windermere, Mrs Erlynne's of Lord Augustus—and the audience. Wilde invites us both to ignore what is really going on and at another level to think about what we are lulled into neglecting. The contradictions and absurdities make us see the limitations of Lady Windermere's initial state of mind, where everything is black or white and one moves quickly from one certainty to another. Wilde teases us about the conventional expectation of certitude in this world, showing it to be continually undermined in reality. Dumby replies in contradictory ways to the same question, depending on what he thinks his conversational partner wishes to hear (the season is described as "delightful" and "dull" in successive speeches), and Lady Berwick's "dear little flying kangaroos" become "horrid creatures crawling about", and Australia a place from which one must be saved by settling in Grosvenor Square, "a more healthy place to reside in" with only some "vulgar people" to trouble one.[4]

---

[4] One can note the imperial presumptions of Lady Berwick's remarks about Australia. Grosvenor Square later figures in *The Importance of Being Earnest* as, in Lady Bracknell's mind, the putative site of a revolutionary outbreak.

Love and its Origins

But Wilde is certainly writing about serious matters too. Passion and confusion are there from the beginning in both Lord and Lady Windermere's states of mind, and intense emotion is also at the heart of Mrs Erlynne's other self—other that is than the society adventuress—as we see how she responds to the crisis in the Windermere household. All three of them are living with a perilously partial picture of themselves. At the opening, we see Lady Windermere struggling to convince herself that the flirtation Lord Darlington offers her has no appeal for her: as a "good" woman, it cannot. So the seductive compliments flow, but all is kept correct because she does not take his hand, busying herself with her flower arranging, reproaches him for paying court to her, and avoids him sitting too close to her. But her vulnerability is great, since her identity is founded on being "loved" by a man. Once she feels she has lost her husband's love because she cannot contemplate the idea that he might love her but also be interested in Mrs Erlynne (love for her must be exclusive or nothing), she has to attach herself to someone else and is thus drawn to accept Lord Darlington's counter-offer.

The background of all this is that she was a child who lost a mother. While her conscious belief is that her mother suffered a tragic early death, leaving her father broken-hearted, the unconscious thoughts and feelings stirred up by the events of her birthday tell a different story. Of course, it is important that it *is* her birthday—the day on which we all tend to be drawn towards thoughts about our own origins. As we later learn, this particular birthday produces a threat of repetition of the events that took place 20 years earlier, when she was the baby and her mother was the young woman leaving home. Wilde, like Freud, understood very well the power of the "repetition compulsion". The baby whose mother vanishes cannot but feel betrayed and abandoned, and it is the feeling of being abandoned by which Lady Windermere so quickly feels overwhelmed in the present. No other explanation of her husband's conduct can be imagined, despite all the evidence she has of his continuing affection for her. Her absolute condemnation of the "bad" Mrs Erlynne, even though she does not learn her true identity during the action of the play, gains its power

from these same unconscious roots: the bad betraying mother, the
sexual mother who has chosen her gratification at the expense of
the care of her baby, are the dominant images. An ordinary infant
may phantasize thus about an absent mother: how much more so
the baby whose mother disappears altogether. Lady Windermere
speaks of her upbringing by stern Aunt Julia, a lady no doubt
determined to instil a strong moral sense into a child who had the
misfortune to be abandoned by a profligate mother. The "Puritan"
identification Lady Windermere has adopted is one that links her
to Aunt Julia and to the condemnation of her mother. This leaves
out of account any other feelings she might have, such as her
intense desire to be loved. This, however, is also an important
aspect of her nature and as the play unfolds becomes linked to her
longing for the lost mother of her infancy.

Though she tries to leave her husband in a confusion of moral
outrage, humiliation, and jealousy, Lady Windermere in fact develops in a remarkable way in the course of the play—she has an
unexpected "coming of age" in which infantile simplicities are set
aside and values reassessed. She is given the final lines of the play
when she pronounces on Lord Augustus's intended marriage to
Mrs Erlynne. Between them (they are speaking to Lord Augustus),
the Windermeres highlight Mrs Erlynne's two essential qualities,
each from their own point of view:

> LORD WINDERMERE: Well, you are certainly marrying a very clever
> woman!
> LADY WINDERMERE [*taking her husband's hand*]:   Ah, you're marrying a
> very good woman!
>
> [Act IV, lines 427–430]

Earlier in the scene, Lady Windermere has referred to the red and
white roses in the garden of their country house at Selby—one is
reminded that these are the colours of the wars of the roses, united
ultimately in the Tudor rose of the pacified kingdom. The marriage, too, has reached a settlement. However, Lady Windermere
has had her eyes opened, and is planning to keep them open—
blindness is now seen not as protecting moral rectitude, but as a
source of danger. She needs to see clearly to escape the "land of pit
and precipice" (Act IV, line 401). She is Wilde's spokeswoman,
bringing into focus the play's subtitle in her final words.

And yet, of course, she only knows part of the truth. It seems that it will stay that way, since Lord Windermere has been frightened and to protect himself has retreated to condemning Mrs Erlynne's behaviour. The problem for him is that the exciting mixture of motives in his response to her arrival has unravelled in alarming ways. Consciously, he was protecting his innocent young wife from the potential shame of learning that her mother is alive and has a past that excludes her from good society. At the same time, the picture we get of the relationship between Lord Windermere and Mrs Erlynne, however magnified by malicious gossip, is of an affair conducted without sex—secret assignations, much time spent closeted together, enormous sums of money given to her, with blackmail clearly in the air. Lord Windermere is having some excitement on the side—very possibly stimulated to play the part of the loving protector by his wife's maternal preoccupation with their baby, in unconscious rivalry. When this little-boy-playing-big-Daddy meets up with evidence of Mrs Erlynne's sexuality, he is disturbed—that is why the encounter with her in Lord Darlington's rooms is so unbearable to him. He has felt powerful and in control of both women, wife and mother-in-law, while he is trying to engineer her re-acceptance by society. For him, the two women are not independent creatures, but characters in a script that he is writing.

The "Puritan" not-yet-grown-up state of mind shared by the Windermeres has its roots in a shared phantasy about an unreliable sexual mother who has to be denounced, controlled, or reformed—though, as Lord Darlington has warned, reform is a slippery matter. Because Wilde is writing a comedy, there can be a quasi-magical ending, and Mrs Erlynne can get her rich husband, but it is a near thing. The possibility that she may lose everything is recognized by each of the three main characters.

What of the significance of the fan and its central role in the action? The fan is an image that serves Wilde's purposes well—it can conceal in coquettish mode, but also reveals as its owner flutters it around; it draws our attention to sexuality, and the question of whether modesty or seduction is to the fore, and no doubt also to the ambiguity of sexual orientation so important to Wilde. A fan can create a refreshing breeze for its owner, or it may be used to heat up the atmosphere of sexual intrigue. It is a gift from a husband, but, like Desdemona's handkerchief, it can then become a potent symbol of betrayal. The shared first name of Lady Windermere and Mrs Erlynne inscribed on the fan underlines their primary link. When Mrs Erlynne departs, she takes as gifts both the fan, which had nearly brought about Lady Windermere's exposure, and a photograph of mother and baby together, recalling for the audience the earlier reference to Lady Windermere's fond attachment to the photograph of her mother as a young woman. The two gifts bring together a sense of woman both as sexually active and as idealized mother, the very combination so difficult for the Windermeres to imagine. Perhaps we are intended to hope that a new picture of woman is Mrs Erlynne's gift to them.

Surfaces and depths

Nonetheless the outcome leaves important secrets untold. Total recognition of what has taken place is denied us: Lady Windermere does not know consciously that Mrs Erlynne is her mother, and Lord Windermere does not know that his wife was indeed planning to run off with Lord Darlington and was in his rooms. The undisclosed secrets allow the play to remain a comedy, just as in *A Midsummer Night's Dream* the mortal lovers know little when they wake of what has taken place in the wood—the twists and turns of their allegiances are lost like forgotten dreams. Secrets, of course, feature large in Wilde's comedies, and the mysteriously abandoned baby reappears as the theme of *The Importance of Being Earnest*. Ellmann suggests that the attraction of the secret must be linked to his homosexual life, also hidden in part from public view. No doubt this is an element of the story, but it should be noted that the secret in these two plays concerns the birth of babies and their parentage. The "innocence" born of evasion of reality that characterizes both Lord and Lady Windermere centres on their avoidance of oedipal realities—that, we suggest, is what the fan was meant to shield them from. Mrs Erlynne's arrival produces a sharp confrontation with parental sexuality, which even the sexually mature young couple find it very hard to manage. They seem as ill prepared as young children to absorb the realities of generation and procreation.

Mrs Erlynne's intervention in the lives of the Windermeres depends on her being in touch with "society" at its most ruthless and cynical, and on her openness to real emotion. She is an astute schemer.

> MRS ERLYNNE: Well really, Windermere, if I am to be the Duchess'
> sister-in-law . . .
> LORD WINDERMERE: But are you?

("*Lady Windermere is watching them 'with a look of scorn and pain' but 'they are unconscious of her presence'*", Wilde writes in the stage directions.)

> MRS ERLYNNE: Oh yes. He's to call tomorrow at 12 o'clock! He
> wanted to propose tonight. In fact he did. He kept on propos-
> ing. Poor Augustus, you know how he repeats himself. Such a
> bad habit! But I told him I wouldn't give him an answer till
> tomorrow. Of course I am going to take him. And I daresay I'll
> make him an admirable wife, as wives go. And there is a great
> deal of good in Lord Augustus. Fortunately it is all on the sur-
> face. Just where good qualities should be. Of course you must
> help me in this matter.
> LORD WINDERMERE: I am not called on to encourage Lord Augustus,
> I suppose.
> MRS ERLYNNE: Oh no! I'll do the encouraging. But you will make me
> a handsome settlement, Windermere, won't you.
> LORD WINDERMERE [*frowning*]:   Is that what you want to talk to me
> about tonight?
> MRS ERLYNNE: Yes.
> LORD WINDERMERE [*with a gesture of impatience*]:   I will not talk of it here.
> MRS ERLYNNE: Then we will talk of it on the terrace. Even business
> should have a picturesque background. Should it not, Winder-
> mere? With a proper background a woman can do anything.
> LORD WINDERMERE: Won't tomorrow do as well?
> MRS ERLYNNE: No; you see, tomorrow I am going to accept him. And
> I think it would be a good thing if I was able to tell him that I
> had—well, what shall I say?—£2000 a year left me by a third
> cousin—or a second husband—or some distant relative of that
> kind. It would be an additional attraction, wouldn't it?
>
> [Act II, lines 410–438]

These speeches capture Wilde's knowledge of the languid but sharply egoistic talk of the society world. Marriages are made for convenience, and a worldly woman needs to make a good assessment of what is on offer. Lord Augustus may be old, but he's got money, he's foolish, and he's extremely well connected. Mrs Erlynne conveys how she can manage the whole business admirably, and at the same time startles her listeners with the absurdity of the idea that goodness is a surface matter. She is just about to discover quite the opposite in herself, as we shall see, but meanwhile is arguing the virtues of amorality. The commanding intimacy with which Mrs Erlynne proposes the idea of a settle-ment—calling him "Windermere", much as his bachelor friends might, instead of the more formal "Lord Windermere" of polite intercourse—establishes the illicit atmosphere of their relationship. Is she the mistress demanding her pay-off as she settles for a re-spectable old husband as a cover for what really interests her? But who, one might ask, usually provides settlements? Although she is in reality Lord Windermere's mother-in-law and a member of a generation senior to his, he is surely being invited to play the father to her girlish flirtatious self. Mrs Erlynne is aware of his weakness for patronizing and "taking care" of women perceived as depend-ent on his masculine strength, wealth, and worldly wisdom, and she is exploiting this. With the threat of the damage to Lady Wind-ermere's presumed innocence and delicacy which exposure of the facts would bring about, Mrs Erlynne is well set up as blackmailer. The mocking taunts about the "proper background" both draw attention to the splendour of the surroundings and touch on her threat to reveal an impropriety that would, at the least, disturb the social perfection of the Windermere household. It is, of course, hard not to recall Wilde's own terrible vulnerability to blackmail *vis-à-vis* his homosexual activities and marvel at the way he could draw on his own deep terrors in his writing.

In real life, Wilde was anything but ruthless in protecting his interests. His kindness (convincingly emphasized by Ellmann) and a self-destructive streak repeatedly combined to expose him to enormous risk. In his writing he has imagined in Mrs Erlynne a character who is like him in some ways—following her passions, doing great damage to spouse and child, nearly destroying her-self—but who can also use her understanding of upper-class hypoc-risies to turn the tables. We could almost see "society" as another character in Wilde's play and the one that is revealed in the worst light, while continuing to exercise its potent grip on all who live within it.

Just as Wilde could never take control of his self-destructiveness, despite much effort at times (he experienced his passion for Bosie—Lord Alfred Douglas—as ineradicable), so Mrs Erlynne is to be surprised by something beneath the surface that she had never expected to be disturbed by. When she reads Lady Windermere's letter to her husband and grasps what is happening, she feels impelled in an entirely unexpected direction:

> MRS ERLYNNE: Gone out of her house! A letter addressed to her husband! No, no! It would be impossible. Life doesn't repeat its tragedies like that. Oh why does this horrible fancy come across me? Why do I remember now the one moment of my life I most wish to forget? Does life repeat its tragedies?
>
> [Act II, lines 465–469]

She quickly hatches a scheme to get Lord Windermere out of the house and commands Lord Augustus's connivance in this, and this is how she describes her state of mind:

> MRS ERLYNNE: . . . What can I do? I feel a passion awaking within me that I never felt before. What can it mean? The daughter must not be like the mother—that would be terrible. How can I save her? How can I save my child? A moment may ruin a life. Who knows that better than I?
>
> [Act II. lines 491–495]

The contrast between manipulative surface and authentic depth ("a passion awaking within") is powerfully drawn. Wilde has touched on this same theme earlier when one of the detestable society fops, aptly named Dumby, is talking to Lady Plymdale, with whom he is conducting an affair. This dialogue follows Mrs Erlynne revealing his repeated attempts to call on her and inviting him to lunch.

> LADY PLYMDALE: *That* woman. . . . How intensely interesting! I really must have a good stare at her. I have heard the most shocking things about her. They say she is ruining poor Windermere, and Lady Windermere, who goes in for being so proper, invites her! How extremely amusing. It takes a thoroughly good woman to do a thoroughly stupid thing. You are to lunch there on Friday!

DUMBY: Why?

LADY PLYMDALE: Because I want you to take my husband with you. He has been so attentive lately, that he has become a perfect nuisance. Now, this woman is just the thing for him. . . . I assure you, women of that kind are most useful. They form the basis of other people's marriages.

DUMBY: What a mystery you are!

LADY PLYMDALE: I wish *you* were.

DUMBY: I am—to myself. I am the only person in the world I should like to know thoroughly; but I don't see any chance of it just at present.

[Act II, lines 229–249]

Lady Plymdale here seeks to manage her husband's feelings by turning them away from herself, while Dumby appears a pliable fool. However, Wilde even turns Dumby's lack of intelligence to poignant use. He contrasts the socialites' belief that by embracing cynicism they can understand themselves fully, with the reality of their failing to understand anything of significance, and in consequence getting little out of life.

In the scene in Lord Darlington's rooms between Lady Windermere and her mother it is striking that it is the appeal to Lady Windermere's feelings for her child that breaks through Lady Windermere's suspicions. This is the denied feeling of mother for child that Mrs Erlynne finds in herself and is then able to evoke in Lady Windermere. It is clear that it is the unselfish love of mother for daughter aroused in Mrs Erlynne that make her the good woman who interests Wilde. Wilde's affection for his own children comes painfully to mind, mixed as it was with so much neglect and harm, but one can perhaps also sense his exploration in Mrs Erlynne of the complex relationship between surface glamour and the world of seduction—she is the wittiest, prettiest woman on stage at the party—and the inner depths of human attachments that cannot be obliterated.

Wilde's many years of adoration of famous actresses has been linked, understandably enough, with the portrayal of Mrs Erlynne, and one is also reminded of the extraordinarily theatrical carryings-on during his boyhood of his own mother in this connection—a lady given to "improving on reality", as Ellmann (1987) recounts.

Wilde's two heroines—Lady Windermere and Mrs Erlynne—thus become three-dimensional as events unfold, and their femininity becomes powerfully located in their identity as mothers. We will now see that the theme of parenthood also figures largely beneath the apparently absurd surfaces of Wilde's most famous play.

The Importance of Being Earnest

The Importance of Being Earnest differs from Lady Windermere's Fan and the intervening comic plays, A Woman of No Importance and An Ideal Husband, in the completeness of his presentation of life as farce. The title, as in all his plays, encapsulates his point: no character ever makes a serious remark, as they are all playing a game of some sort. Even the servants join in. The brilliance of Wilde's wit is overwhelming and makes the tragedy of his foreshortened life as man and writer seem all the more acute. How can we understand the impact on us of this sustained drama of comic nonsense?

Audiences, seduced by Wilde's wit and eloquence, may be swept away by the desire to be as free of serious obligation, moral restraint, or, indeed, basic logic as all Wilde's characters. If only we could all get what we want as easily as these would-be lovers get their chosen partners at the end of the play.

Needs denied

The complete absurdity of an idea of love in which there is no need whatever for any interest in the reality of the loved one is, however, splendidly dissected. This reaches its climax in Cecily's revelation to Algernon (masquerading as "Ernest", the imaginary brother of her guardian, Jack Worthing) that she has been conducting an entire relationship with this mythical figure in her diary and that his arrival simply concludes the matter. She has been pretending not only for herself, but for her imaginary lover too. This conversation takes place perhaps half an hour after Algernon's arrival and first encounter with Cecily:

ALGERNON: . . . I don't care for anybody in the whole world but you.
I love you, Cecily. You will marry me, won't you?

CECILY: You silly boy! Of course. Why, we have been engaged for
the last three months.

ALGERNON: For the last three months?

CECILY: Yes, it will be exactly three months on Thursday. . . .

ALGERNON: Darling! And when was the engagement actually settled?

CECILY: On the 14th of February last. Worn out by your entire
ignorance of my existence, I determined to end the matter one
way or the other, and after a long struggle with myself, I accepted you under this dear old tree here. . . . And this is the box
in which I keep all your dear letters.

ALGERNON: My letters! But my own sweet Cecily, I have never written you any letters.

CECILY: You need hardly remind me of that, Ernest. I remember
only too well that I was forced to write your letters for you. I
wrote always three times a week, and sometimes oftener.

[Act II, lines 408–468][5]

It is made quite clear later in Lady Bracknell's investigation of the
suitability of the match for her well-born but somewhat impoverished nephew, Algernon, that Cecily has a lot of money, so we are
not allowed for a moment to forget that this is what dictates the
desirability of the marriage for Algernon, who is shown in his
perpetual eating of whatever is at hand to be a compulsively
greedy fellow.

One is struck also by a poignancy in the notion of a girl of 18
having to write love-letters to herself and invent an imaginary
relationship to fill the emotional void of her days sequestered in
the country with a dreary governess. The near-starvation of emotionally relevant and lively contact is turned on its head at surface
level when Wilde makes her so sophisticated a schemer, but the
reality of his characters being trapped in lonely and pointless relationships is inescapable. (One might doubt that Algernon will offer
Cecily any more emotional sustenance in the future.) The play's
absurd core, of the baby (Ernest) being left in a large handbag by

---

[5] Extracts from *The Importance of Being Earnest* are taken from *Oscar Wilde, The
Importance of Being Earnest and Other Plays* (Oxford: Oxford University Press,
1995).

Miss Prism at Victoria station, similarly places before us a wholly ridiculous image, at which everyone laughs, which nonetheless, if thought about for even a moment, is disturbing. We are hearing about a baby, already orphaned, entrusted to the care of a nanny whose capacity to know how to look after a baby is nil. However grotesque these images, we can certainly be in no doubt about the dire incapacity of this adult world to care for its children. Lady Bracknell may denounce Miss Prism in thundering tones in the present, but at the time she seems to have felt little compunction in abandoning her parentless nephew to his fate. A baby is not a creature of import in this world of glittering and ruthless self-advancement. Relationships are viewed as steps on the social ladder, and the natural dependence of a child has no place in the scheme of things.

Wilde's own fatherly interest in children and young people is shown in the stories created for his own children (one thinks particularly of "The Selfish Giant" as important evidence of his painful awareness of his own cruelty to them) and in the benevolent aspects of his relationships with his young men—lovers and pupils, but always people who, he felt, could expect much more from him than he from them, and for whom he felt responsibility, in however confused a way. The sense of guilt that may well have been a part of his refusal to take the opportunity to flee London and prosecution and instead to court harsh punishment might be linked to this. In *The Importance of Being Ernest*, the subtitle of which is "A Trivial Comedy for Serious People", we are told the story of a neglected and abandoned baby whose name nonetheless turns out to be his salvation in love, because of Gwendolen's capricious devotion to this as the name she wishes her husband to carry. As the child of dead parents, his name is one of the few things bequeathed to him: he regains it and—miraculously—his beloved with it. All the witty dialogue cannot completely obliterate the losses that lie behind the sustained mania of the play.

Avoiding reality

The misrepresentation of reality is brilliantly stated in the opening lines as one of Wilde's themes:

ALGERNON: Did you hear what I was playing, Lane?

LANE: I didn't think it polite to listen, sir.

ALGERNON: I'm sorry for that, for your sake. I don't play accurately—anyone can play accurately—but I play with wonderful expression. As far as the piano is concerned, sentiment is my forte. I keep science for life.

LANE: Yes, sir.

ALGERNON: And, speaking of the science of life, have you got the cucumber sandwiches cut for Lady Bracknell?

[Act I, lines 1–9]

"Accuracy" interferes far too much with narcissistic display and untrammelled licence. Lane's comment allows us to imagine the cacophonous outcome of Algernon's approach to music. His knowledge of his employer's weaknesses is the background to the servants' exploitation of their foolish master, for whom flattery and the turning of a blind eye is life-blood.

ALGERNON: Why is it that at a bachelor's establishment the servants invariably drink the champagne? I ask merely for information.

LANE: I attribute it to the superior quality of the wine, sir. I have often observed that in married households, the champagne is rarely of a first-rate brand.

[Act I, lines 17–21]

Algernon's greed, about to be expressed in his devouring of the cucumber sandwiches, leaves him unable to question his servants' behaviour. "Information" will not lead to any action, we can be confident, for the "science of life" means for him applying his mind only for the purpose of securing maximal personal comfort. Anything beyond that would be too much trouble.

Varieties of misrepresentation appear throughout the play, ranging from the overt lies of "Bunburying" (Bunbury is an imaginary friend whose supposed illness and need for visits serve as a cover story for whatever activities require concealment), to the fantasying of Cecily, the novel-writing and subterfuges of Miss Prism, the "chastity" of Canon Chasuble, and—by far the most fun—the extraordinary florid pronouncements of Lady Bracknell on every topic to which she turns her attention. There is no need at all, in her book, for any evidence to complicate her views or life, as long as "society" and money as its arbiter is maintained.

LADY BRACKNELL: I need hardly tell you that in families of high position strange coincidences are not supposed to happen. They are hardly considered the thing.

[Act III, lines 368–370]

She intervenes to forbid the proposed "christenings" of Jack (Ernest) and Algernon. This is another example of the plasticity of reality for Wilde's characters, but also of Lady Bracknell's insistence on controlling such primary matters as the naming and identity of the young, as well as taking her stand against unduly enthusiastic religious practices:

Enter DR CHASUBLE

CHASUBLE: Everything is quite ready for the christenings.

LADY BRACKNELL: The christenings, sir! Is not that somewhat premature?

CHASUBLE [*looking rather puzzled and pointing to Jack and Algernon*]:   Both these gentlemen have expressed a desire for immediate baptism.

LADY BRACKNELL: At their age? The idea is grotesque and irreligious. Algernon, I forbid you to be baptized. I will not hear of such excesses. Lord Bracknell would be highly displeased if he learned that this was the way you wasted your time and money.

[Act III, lines 289–298]

Lady Bracknell repeatedly points to the rules that have to be respected to ensure that the social order is preserved and reproduced.

LADY BRACKNELL: I do not know if there is anything peculiarly exciting in the air in this particular part of Hertfordshire, but the number of engagements that go on seem to me considerably above the proper average that statistics have laid down for our guidance. I think some preliminary enquiring on my part would not be out of place.

[Act III, lines 121–125]

Engagements, that is to say, should occur to order, and not at random. The enquiries she proceeds to make are, of course, all related to matters of birth and income, and she thus reveals what really matters in the making of marriages.

If people's lives are governed by such rules, there is unlikely to be much happiness around. The extravagance of words and character Wilde deploys conceals the misery implied by his characters' actual circumstances. The unrelatedness of surface and depth can go no further.[6]

Investigating Mr Worthing's eligibility, she is delighted with his claim to "know nothing":

> LADY BRACKNELL: I am glad to hear it. I do not approve of anything that tampers with natural ignorance. Ignorance is like a delicate exotic fruit; touch it, and the bloom is gone. The whole theory of modern education is radically unsound. Fortunately, in England at any rate, education produces no effects whatsoever. If it did, it would prove a serious danger to the upper classes, and probably lead to acts of violence in Grosvenor Square.[7] What is your income?
>
> [Act I, lines 479–485]

Wilde jokes thus about the absurdity of making a virtue of, by implication, sexual ignorance and of forms of education based on ignoring the realities of human nature, yet these social forces are about to destroy him. With a profound comic realism he plays at the dangerous edge of social convention, both as a member of the glittering classes of his day and simultaneously undercutting all they depend on. This could be the attractive double-edged thrill for his audience too. They are being carried along in illusory membership of so sophisticated and luxurious a life and yet able to enjoy the thrill of the most amusing and cutting criticism of society's mores. It is a position of oscillation between insider and outsider and offers the sense of winning either way. The exploitation of popular adulation of aristocratic consumption has, of course, its modern counterpart in the pervasiveness of film and television costume drama, but it seldom has either Wilde's edge or his verbal brilliance. What he offers, uniquely, is the combination of a knowledge of the seductive power of all that and a sense of underlying despair held elegantly at bay.

---

[6] Freud's hysterical patients presented him with another version of the quandary posed when the gap between emotional reality and social convention is quite extreme.

[7] Eventually, it did.

Wilde, in his lucid and powerful writings on aesthetic matters[8] and in his dramatic practice, was hostile to social realism and to the idea that the business of art or literature was to communicate moral or political ideas. In *Lady Windermere's Fan* and *A Woman of No Importance*, it is nevertheless not difficult to see his serious engagement with the situation and experience of women in society, as we have shown. But Wilde's most famous and popular play, *The Importance of Being Earnest*, often described as having the form of a farce, is more difficult to see as having a "serious" content. Is it possible to think of this play as making use of the public symbolic space of the theatre for any social purpose?

We contend that this is indeed how this play can be read, and that it is its particular engagement with its social context that has helped it to achieve its standing and popularity. *The Importance of Being Earnest* is as much a representation of the *ancien régime* of late Victorian England as Chekhov's great plays are of the last days of the gentry of imperial Russia. Lady Bracknell, its peerless principal character, is, in Mary McCarthy's phrase (McCarthy, 1963), a "dreadnought" of this world, but she reveals herself in almost all her speeches to have a mind that is filled by the social tensions that had begun by the 1890s to beset it. She evokes a crucial moment in the social history of her class:

> LADY BRACKNELL: To be born, or at any rate bred, in a hand-bag whether it had handles or not, seems to me to betray a contempt for the ordinary decencies of family life that reminds one of the worst excesses of the French Revolution. And I presume you know what that unfortunate movement led to?
>
> [Act I, lines 552–557]

When hearing that Algernon's friend Bunbury "quite exploded", she responds:

> LADY BRACKNELL: Exploded! Was he the victim of a revolutionary outrage? I was not aware that Mr Bunbury was interested in social legislation. If so, he is well punished for his morbidity.
>
> [Act III, lines 100–103]

---

[8] His four essays on art and literature, published under the title of *Intentions* (Wilde, 1891) are wonderfully articulate on the superiority—as Wilde saw it—of art, literature, and contemplation to the unprocessed experience of "real life" or action.

As we have seen, she regards education as dangerous and recommends ignorance, while herself making reference to statistics and keeping up to date in her own idiosyncratic fashion. She is very attentive to the changing climate of thought around her. While making hostile comments on social science, she herself adopts a scientific turn of phrase.

Here is Lady Bracknell on health and illness:

> LADY BRACKNELL: Well I must say, Algernon, that I think it is high time that Mr Bunbury made up his mind whether he was going to live or die. This shilly-shallying with the question is absurd. Nor do I in any way approve of the modern sympathy with invalids. I consider it morbid. Illness of any kind is hardly a thing to be encouraged in others. Health is a primary duty of life.
>
> [Act I, lines 331–336]

She is well aware of the declining profitability of land and the ensuing threat to the position of the landed classes. She enquires in her direct way about Jack's source of income:

> LADY BRACKNELL [*makes a note in her book*]:   In land, or in investments?
> JACK: In investments, chiefly.
> LADY BRACKNELL: That is satisfactory. What between the duties expected of one during one's lifetime, and the duties extracted from one after one's death, land has ceased to be either a profit or a pleasure. It gives one position, and prevents one from keeping it up. That is all that can be said about land.
>
> [Act I, lines 486–494]

Her characterization of Miss Prism shows her keen awareness of social differences, and also of how variously they are perceived:

> LADY BRACKNELL: Is this Miss Prism a female of repellent aspect, remotely connected with education?
> CHASUBLE [*somewhat indignantly*]:   She is the most cultivated of ladies, and the very picture of respectability.
> LADY BRACKNELL: It is obviously the same person.
>
> [Act III, lines 315–319]

She expresses firm views not only on fashionable social science, but also on literature:

> LADY BRACKNELL: ... A few weeks later, through the elaborate investigations of the Metropolitan police, the perambulator was dis-

covered at midnight, standing by itself in a remote corner of
Bayswater. It contained the manuscript of a three-volume novel
of more than usually revolting sentimentality.
[*Miss Prism starts in involuntary indignation.*]

[Act III, lines 336–340]

Wilde has, however, turned this aristocratic *fin de siècle* world upside down by having as its most articulate spokespersons powerful
women (Lady Berwick in *Lady Windermere's Fan* is another such[9]),
not men. Lord Bracknell is invisible, spoken of as the nominal
authority over his daughter's life but in practice kept in total ignorance of everything:

> LADY BRACKNELL: Her unhappy father is, I am glad to say, under the
> impression she is attending a more than usually lengthy lecture
> by the University Extension Scheme on the influence of a per-
> manent income on Thought. I do not propose to undeceive him.
> Indeed, I never undeceived him on any question. I would con-
> sider it wrong. . . .

[Act III, lines 78–83]

In *Lady Windermere's Fan* and *A Woman of No Importance*, Wilde
demonstrates a deep identification with women in this patriarchal
world. But perhaps a more effective assault on it is achieved by the
comic reversal by which, in *The Importance of Being Earnest*, he
places them in full if eccentric and surreal[10] control of their world.

The form of utterance that Wilde gives to Lady Bracknell, his
most memorable creation, is of course crucial to her extraordinary

---

[9] Lady Berwick expresses her conservative views in a more condescending
and less engaged way than Lady Bracknell. For example:

> LADY BERWICK: My dear nieces—you know, the Saville girls, don't you?—such
> nice domestic creatures—plain, dreadfully plain, but so good—well, they
> are always at the window doing fancy work, and making ugly things for
> the poor which I think is so useful of them in these dreadfully socialistic
> days, and this dreadful woman has taken a house in Curzon Street, right
> opposite them, such a respectable street too!
>
> [*Lady Windermere's Fan*, Act 1, lines 267–273]

[10] This play preceded the surrealist movement, and the later "theatre of the
absurd" (Esslin 1968) by many decades. Whereas dramatists like Beckett evoke
a world almost bereft of meaning, Wilde constructs a world which seems to be
extravagantly well-ordered. But its order is a brilliantly crafted illusion—it is
from this contrast between surface composure and underlying chaos and deprivation that its profound comedy derives.

effect. She speaks in orotund and unusually complete sentences, whose elaborate form conveys both her social authority and her commitment to decorum. She reproves Jack, finding him on his knees before Gwendolen:

> LADY BRACKNELL: Mr Worthing! Rise, sir, from this semi-recumbent posture. It is most indecorous.
>
> [Act I, line 402]

before delivering a brief lecture on the proper determination of a girl's engagements and then proceeding to interrogate Jack on his financial means and pedigree.

But while the form of Lady Bracknell's speech is authoritative declamation, its content reveals an extraordinary mental energy. Lady Bracknell is intensely engaged with the details of the modern social world as she encounters them. She offers a continuing commentary on their significance from her own point of view. Her character is constructed out of the tension between her restless flow of thoughts—almost a stream of consciousness and free association—and the necessity for her to encode all these thoughts in the stylized and mannered form attributed by Wilde to the aristocracy in these plays. It is this tension between her acute awareness of changing realities and a deep commitment to convention that leads to the wonderful paradoxes and epigrams that pepper Lady Bracknell's speech:

> LADY BRACKNELL: I'm sorry if we are a little late, Algernon, but I was obliged to call on dear Lady Harbury. I hadn't been there since her poor husband's death. I never saw a woman so altered; she looks quite twenty years younger.
>
> [Act I, lines 292–294]

The modern world figures much in the many references in this play to the railway. Lady Bracknell has come down to Hertfordshire by luggage train. She decides that she and Gwendolen must return in order to keep up appearances in face of this new public mode of travel:

> LADY BRACKNELL: Come, dear [Gwendolen rises], we have already missed five, if not six, trains. To miss any more might expose us to comment on the platform.
>
> [Act III, lines 285–287]

But the railway also enables Wilde to construct one of his most extraordinary comic feats, in the discovery, as a result of Lady Bracknell's pressing enquiries into his genealogy and upbringing, of Jack's having been found in a handbag in the left luggage office of Victoria Station. The hilarity of this episode depends on Lady Bracknell and Jack both attaching such overwhelming importance to birth and breeding that they will follow their investigation even down to the finest details of the particular railway line, the bag, and the station. This of course turns out to have an underlying emotional resonance for all of them, including Miss Prism, the nurse who originally mislaid the baby, since this is, after all, the story of an abandonment and a loss. Jack's excitement when he searches for the bag upstairs makes this clear. This episode allows Lady Bracknell to express a customary aristocratic dislike of displays of emotion:

> *Noises are heard overhead as if someone were throwing trunks about. Everyone looks up.*
> CECILY: Jack seems strangely agitated.
> CHASUBLE: Your guardian has a very emotional nature.
> LADY BRACKNELL: This noise is extremely unpleasant. It sounds as if he was having an argument. I dislike arguments of any kind. They are always vulgar, and often convincing.
>
> [Act III, lines 371–375]

Lady Bracknell's surreal literalism of mind allows her to engage with full seriousness in the investigation of a genealogy that derives from a railway line, rather than the more conventional line of blood. Unfazed by what she has just learned about Jack's origins, she goes on to enquire about the social background of Cecily, Jack's ward, whom Algernon, her nephew, now wants to marry:

> LADY BRACKNELL: Mr Worthing, is Miss Cardew at all connected with any of the large railway stations in London? I merely desire information. Until yesterday, I had no idea that there were any families or persons whose origin was a Terminus.
>
> [Act III, lines 126–129]

The effect of all this is, of course, to make the intense preoccupations of the real "society" of Wilde's day with birth and breeding seem entirely ludicrous. But because the objects of social condescension and indeed contempt are in this case not actual persons of a different social standing but handbags and railway stations, the wounding and rancorous qualities inherent in these social attitudes are miraculously removed from view. Wilde is able wonderfully to send up snobbery while circumventing its actual brutality. This becomes a satire on the pretensions of birth that avoids the resentment that would be evoked by a more realist representation of it. In bringing this off, Wilde can invest Lady Bracknell with some of his own qualities of mind—for example, the capacity to combine a formal perfection of utterance with a perception of the hollowness and harshness of this world.

Algernon, Lady Bracknell's nephew, is a somewhat unlikeable and spiteful figure. These qualities have not been not fully assimilated into the comic pattern of the play, so we find ourselves being made uncomfortable rather than amused by him. Eating the cucumber sandwiches intended for his aunt is one thing, but the reenactment of his greed later on, this time with Jack's muffins, is tedious. His spying on his friend and taking note of his country address, so that he can visit unannounced and investigate Jack's other life, is invasive and selfish. Algernon seems to have no real feeling for anyone except himself. It may be that in this picture of the two friends together there is an echo of Wilde's experience of Bosie, Lord Alfred Douglas, who was demanding, spoiling, and greedy of Wilde's time.

A kind of imaginative coherence to this story is restored in the eventual discovery that Algernon and Jack (Ernest) are indeed brothers. We come to recognize, perhaps, that they have each missed and lost something that they eventually find. Algernon is a younger brother whose elder brother has disappeared or, to all intents and purposes, died. His taking up all the available family space, and more, can be seen as an enactment of this situation. Somewhere, he unconsciously feels, there is someone who has or who at least deserves more than he, and he will spoil this more favoured life if he can. Jack has always wanted a brother. Both these brothers have made doubles for themselves. Jack is Ernest in the town, Jack in the country; Algernon has his imaginary friend, an excuse for getting away from his aunt when he wants, whom he calls Bunbury. Various meanings have, of course, been assigned to "Bunburying"—the double life of the homosexual in Wilde's society in particular. But an implicit explanation is offered within the play of these divided and double identities, and of the mutually bored and squabbling relationship of these two friends. Jack has been literally lost, as a baby, and no great effort ever seems to have been made to find him. There is thus, beneath the farcical action, an underlying atmosphere of emotional deprivation. What is magically remedied at the close of the play by the discovery of Jack's true origins is not only his lack of "breeding" in the sense of social respectability, a familiar ending of Victorian melodramas, but also of his emotional need to belong, to know his true parents. In Gwendolen's independence of her mother and the signs that both girls have minds of their own there is a suggestion that this bleak emotional history might not need entirely to repeat itself in the next generation.

Humour and reparation

In *Jokes and Their Relation to the Unconscious*, Freud (1905c) explained that through jokes and humour, feelings and desires can be expressed that are otherwise repressed from consciousness and communication. The double or metaphorical meaning of a joke licenses the forbidden desire, since its illicit significance can be overtly denied even while it is enjoyed in its "disguised" surface meaning. The joke conveys its charge of feeling while making us look the other way, and this is its source of delight to us. Freud mostly wrote in that essay about the inhibition and repression of sexual desires and their expression through jokes, but he also makes reference to emotions of hostility and hatred, in respect of which his argument can be further developed. Ted Cohen, in his *Philosophical Thoughts on Joking Matters* (1999), adds to this long-established psychoanalytic insight a more social understanding of humour. He describes the functions of jokes in creating shared communities of understanding and feeling between tellers and listeners. While Freud thought of the relief obtained from a joke as the effect of a discharge of repressed desire or emotion, both for its teller and its hearers, Cohen recognized that just as important as the discharge is the social recognition and acceptance of what has hitherto been unsaid or unsayable. Jokes do not only tear the social fabric, but they simultaneously sew it up again. Tellers and listeners share a new understanding and relatedness to one another as a consequence of their laughter. A more psychoanalytic way of putting Cohen's argument is to say that he explains how the anxieties evoked by the "forbidden" material of jokes are "contained" by the exchange between teller and listener. One could add that the laughter achieved by a successful joke, at some risk, ensures that love eventually predominates over hate in the humorous exchange, for those who share the laughter at least. (This may still be at the expense of the joke's "victim".)

These insights may help to understand something of the relationship to society that Wilde enacted through his comedies. By reproducing in his plays the style and glitter of what aristocratic society thought it aspired to, Wilde may have hoped to seduce this world into a kind of dialogue with him, in which serious realities could be explored.

The Importance of Being Earnest is more radical in its implicit social critique than the earlier plays, even though it might appear to be more superficial. Some audiences might fail to notice in their laughter that it is making any serious social point at all. By constructing such an extreme and wonderful version of an aristocratic—but also, it appears, originally *arriviste*—woman, sailing in full state through her world, and by investing her with a version of his own brilliance of mind, Wilde conveys that this social world is a completely ridiculous and untenable one. Surely, the implication is, even its inhabitants will now see this?

Well, they did and they did not. Wilde's plays made their contribution to the "de-centring" of the aristocratic world and the puncturing of its presumptions to authority. The choice of surreal humour as a preferred weapon of attack was itself a statement about social relations in England, and about a preference, shared even by Irishmen such as Wilde and Shaw, for avoiding the most bitter and violent means of conducting social conflicts. Wilde told André Gide that he had put his talent into his work, but his genius into his life (Gide, 1901, p. 34). There is genius enough in the work, while the life is now remote, despite the efforts of fine biographers such as Richard Ellmann. What one can, however, say is that Wilde wrote his plays as comedies but lived his life as a tragedy. In the comedies, the oppressiveness and brutality of society towards those who challenge or transgress its norms is overcome by humour and good fortune. But in life, Wilde's society did not forgive his challenge to it.

CHAPTER NINE

Arthur Miller:
fragile masculinity
in American society

The three plays that we are going to discuss in this chapter—
three of Arthur Miller's four most-performed and cele-
brated works, *All My Sons* (1947), *Death of a Salesman* (1949),
and *A View from the Bridge* (1955)—are plainly, in important respects, "social plays".[1] The stresses to which their principal characters are exposed, which lead in each case to their deaths, can be
traced through the action of the plays to deficits in their societies.
These plays are set in the United States in the time in which they
were written—thus they are manifestly critiques of Miller's own
society. This social critique is most explicit, as we shall see, in *All
My Sons*, where characters openly debate different moralities: in
Death of a Salesman and *A View from the Bridge*, Miller seeks to
embed social criticism only through the audience's response to the
imagined life and fate of his characters. Here, to a greater extent
than in the case of *All My Sons*, audiences learn to understand what

---

[1] *The Crucible*, the fourth play, is widely recognized as arising from Miller's
response to the McCarthy-led persecution of left-wing intellectuals in the post-
war period.

will destroy the central figures of these plays in ways that are not fully articulated by any of the figures themselves. Indeed, it is essential to the tragedy of the major characters in the later plays that they cannot understand what is happening to them. Miller represents this situation in different ways in these two dramas. *Death of a Salesman* enacts the psychological disintegration of its main character, with a force that it is extremely painful to watch or read, even at this distance from its writing. Miller pushes the form of "social drama" to a new interior intensity in the dialogue of this play. *A View from the Bridge*, by contrast, unfolds in a mode that deliberately recalls Greek tragedy, in that its main character, walled up in his identity, and defended against knowledge of his deprivation and pain, is pushed into his disastrous actions, which the audience is enabled to contemplate with understanding and compassion.

Ibsen was an important exemplar for Miller in his development of this kind of drama. Indeed, he published an adapted version of Ibsen's *An Enemy of the People* in 1950, in the middle of this formative period of his own writing. Miller, as he described in his many lucid essays on theatre (Miller, 1978), and in his autobiography, *Timebends* (Miller, 1987) was just as deeply estranged from contemporary American society as was Ibsen from the Norway of his time. Intellectual and artistic life in the United States of the 1940s and 1950s was subjected to intense anti-Communist persecution, to which Miller himself responded with integrity and courage. Miller saw many similarities between the oppressiveness and conformity of his society and that which Ibsen depicted in many of his plays, including *An Enemy of the People*. He also shared with Ibsen a commitment to a theatre that was serious, capable of exploring and illuminating the real issues of contemporary life for its audiences, in contexts in which most actual theatre was commercial and trivial. Clearly there was a connection in both Miller's and Ibsen's times between a climate of political and social conformity and an oppressive insistence that theatre should not rock any boats. This situation in Norway led Ibsen into a quarter-century of voluntary exile, until his international fame, and perhaps some opening-up in Norwegian society, led to his triumphant return there for the last years of his life. Miller did not leave the United States, and he has been able to continue to work there, even though he recognizes that he is in some respects better appreciated and loved as a dramatist in countries other than his own.[2]

For Miller, as indeed for Ibsen, "social drama", understood as the didactic representation of social issues and the conflicts of value that underlie them, was never sufficient as a conception of theatre. Partisanship was for him a limitation, not a strength, in a dramatist. Drama, he said, became "whole and capable of the highest reach" only when "social matters become inseparable from subjective psychological matters" ("On Social Plays", p. 54, in Miller, 1978). It is the enactment of what happens to imagined individuals, in relationship to one another and in a particular societal setting, not the dramatization of a pre-conceived social argument, that enables the crises of human lives to be most fully explored. In his later work Ibsen moved away from the more overt social criticism of his earlier plays, in which individual virtue is set against explicit social oppressiveness and hypocrisy. In plays such as *Hedda Gabler*, *John Gabriel Borkman*, and *Little Eyolf*, his main characters have been damaged in their lives in deeper and more interior ways, at the centre of their being. These plays dramatize their unsuccessful efforts to achieve self-knowledge and escape from their isolation from one another. Miller takes from Ibsen not only a contemporary equivalent of his social critique, but also his capacity to represent this through the conflicted inner experience of his characters.

A crucial influence on Miller in this respect was Greek tragedy, which, in the early 1940s, he said of himself: "I was coming to love as a man at the bottom of a pit loves a ladder" (1987, p. 94). He has written

> that his mind was taken over by the basic Greek structural concept of a past stretching so far back that its origins were lost in myth, surfacing in the present and donating a dilemma to the persons on the stage, who were astounded and awestruck by the wonderful train of seeming accidents that unveiled their connections to that past. [1987, p. 233]

---

[2]On Miller's writings and their context, see also chapter 4 in Christopher Bigsby, *Modern American Drama 1945–1990* (1992), and Christopher Bigsby (Ed.), *The Cambridge Companion to Arthur Miller* (1994).

Miller sought to give a contemporary form to this vision in several of his plays. In *A View from the Bridge*, these classical parallels are made explicit. The lawyer Alfieri tries to help Eddie Carbone recognize a potentially tragic pattern in what is going on and insists on the power of the "natural law", which Eddie is being drawn to transgress by forces he does not understand. Alfieri is given the role of a Greek Chorus. In *All My Sons*, the crucial myth has been constructed within the family—this family myth is the wilful denial of a son's death, and of a crime committed by the father, which together threaten to destroy the family if the denials are called into question, as they are during the action of the play.

Miller seeks to give a contemporary form to the idea of tragedy. In an early essay, "Tragedy and the Common Man", he argues:

> the tragic feeling is evoked in us when we are in the presence of a character who is ready to lay down his life, if need be, to secure one thing—his sense of personal dignity. From Orestes to Hamlet, Medea to Macbeth, the underlying struggle is that of the individual attempting to gain his "rightful" position in his society. Sometimes he is one who has been displaced from it, sometimes one who seeks to attain it for the first time, but the fateful wound from which the inevitable events spiral is the wound of indignity, and its dominant force is indignation. Tragedy, then, is the result of a man's total compulsion to evaluate himself justly. [Miller, 1978]

In addition, of course, Miller asserts his belief "that the common man is as apt a subject for tragedy in its highest sense as kings were". This is another link with Ibsen, although the threshold of "ordinary humanity" which Ibsen managed in his work to push out to include middle-class people—architects, doctors, journalists, and the like—Miller in the twentieth century extended famously to the figure of a salesman and a longshoreman, representing a common and indeed working-class humanity. He rhetorically insisted on this democratic purpose of his work when he demanded, through the mouth of Linda, Willy Loman's wife:

> LINDA: Attention, attention must finally be paid to such a person.
> BIFF: I didn't mean—
> LINDA: No, a lot of people think he's lost his—balance. But you don't have to be very smart to know what his trouble is. The man is exhausted.

HAPPY: Sure!

LINDA: A small man can be just as exhausted as a great man. He works for a company thirty-six years this March, opens up un- heard-of territories to their trademark, and now in his old age they take his salary away.

[*Death of a Salesman*, Act I, pp. 162–163][3]

Miller's plays show that the tragic sense for him both includes and goes beyond a commitment to personal dignity. Dignity is pos- sessed or lost with respect to values that extend beyond the indi- vidual and whose meaning depends on the possibility of their shared social recognition. In *All My Sons* it becomes evident, ulti- mately even to Joe Keller himself, that a commitment to fundamen- tal social bonds and obligations has been betrayed. It is because Joe's sense of self-value is tied, in however a vestigial family-cen- tred way, to this sense of social obligation that he can no longer bear to go on living. For Eddie Carbone, a feeling of public shame and indignity is crucial in driving him to his death, but this too depends for its power over him on values that he shares with his community, and which have made him what he is.

The psychological and the social

It is the fact that Miller succeeds in creating dramas in which "social matters become inseparable from subjective psychological matters" that makes it possible to write about the psychological subtleties of these three plays, integrally with their social mean- ings. The idea he draws from Greek tragedies of "a past . . . surfac- ing in the present and donating a dilemma to the persons on the stage, who were astounded and awestruck by the wonderful train of seeming accidents that unveiled their connections to that past", is a natural source of inspiration for the exploration of psychologi- cal depth in his plays. It provides an implicit connection with a psychoanalytic way of thinking about states of mind and behav-

---

[3] Extracts from *Death of a Salesman* are taken from *Arthur Miller: Collected Plays* (London: Cresset Press, 1958). Reprinted by permission of International Creative Management, Inc. Copyright © 1949 Arthur Miller.

iour in the present as the consequence of patterns laid down un-consciously in earlier experience.

The plays explore and reveal specific psychic structures and a configuration of generational and sexual dynamics within the family, which can be shown to be consequences of distinctive kinds of social organization, or disorganization. Audiences respond to the conflicts portrayed—internal and external—and it is through these that they are led to contemplate what it is in the society around them that leaves individuals so exposed to pain. The unfolding of the lives of members of whole families, and their impacts on each other, are the means by which Miller gives audiences access also to a larger social dynamic. Miller's drama thus achieves what C. Wright Mills asked that sociology should do—namely, demonstrate "the public meanings of private problems".

All My Sons

The title of *All My Sons* encapsulates the central act of moral recognition that takes place within the play. As it proceeds, both characters and audience come to understand the untenable nature of Joe Keller's identification with his family as the sole source of emotional and moral claims in his life. Keller, a successful manufacturer, has throughout his life put himself and his family first. His wife Kate, and his sons Larry, now dead, and Chris, who works with him in his business, are felt to exist as an extension of himself—they are allowed little space to be different from or independent of him. As we shall see, this claustrophobic quality of the American family is also an important theme in *Death of a Salesman* and *A View from the Bridge*.[4] Much of Miller's work can be seen as a critique of the individualism and familism of American culture and of its inability to extend human sympathies and identifications beyond the claims of family.

---

[4] It is possible that the intensity of family feeling and the ambivalence shown by the Kellers towards their non-family neighbours transposes the experience of Jewish families in particular. Even though Miller was Jewish, this is not an explicit point of reference in his plays.

We learn early in the play that Larry was reported missing, three years ago, at the end of the Second World War, in which he served as a pilot in the air force. Kate, Joe's wife, will not accept that he now must be presumed dead. Joe goes along with this, but his younger son, Chris, wants to marry Ann, formerly Chris's fiancée, and has invited her to visit them. She was brought up in the next-door house, and Chris's parents were important in her life, since Joe was her father's business partner. She has long ago accepted the fact of Larry's death and now wants to marry Chris. This situation, when she comes to stay with them, leads to a fierce battle with Kate, into which Joe cannot avoid being drawn. It emerges that Joe has allowed his weak partner Steve, Ann's father, to take the blame and consequent prison sentence for a cover-up of what happened in his factory: faulty aircraft parts were shipped out, leading to the crash of several planes and the deaths of their pilots. Ann's brother George has discovered that Joe was in fact responsible for this. He comes to challenge Joe and his son with this new information. and to prevent the marriage of his sister to Chris. He feels deeply guilty for having believed in Joe instead of his own father. Joe, through his power and self-confidence, had come to seem more like a real father to Ann and George than their own actual, vulnerable father. Ann finally tells Joe that she had received a letter from Larry before his death, which revealed that he knew about the court case. He had felt so disillusioned with the consequences for his comrades that he had crashed his own plane in despair. Kate begged Ann not to read this letter to Joe, knowing what it would mean to him. The realization that his actions have led to the death of his own son breaks Joe, who kills himself. His sons have taught him, at the end, that all the young men—not just his own—who fought in the recent war must be regarded as sons.

This play about small-town America in the post-war years shows a traditional division of labour, both practical and emotional, between husband and wife. Joe is succeeding in making a good living for his family and a substantial inheritance for his sons. He is a figure of local power who can afford to disregard his neighbours' actual suspicions, even knowledge, of his shameful crime. He lives by insistent denial and is able to hold the truth at bay without evident qualms or discomfort. Complacent and self-satisfied, he believes that he has the success he wanted. He relies on external signs of respect and recognition—the deference of employees, the acceptance of his hospitality and good-fellowship by his neighbours—to maintain his self-esteem. It does not matter to him that this respect may be given insincerely, so long as it is given:

> KELLER: Listen, you do like I did and you'd be all right. The day I come home, I got out of my car—but not in front of the house . . . on the corner. You should've been here, Ann, and you too, Chris; you'd-a-seen something. Everyone knew I was getting out that day; the porches were loaded. Picture it now; none of them believed I was innocent. The story was, I pulled a fast one getting myself exonerated. So I get out of my car, and I walk down the street. But very slow. And with a smile. The beast! I was a beast; the guy who sold cracked cylinder heads to the Army Air Force; the guy who made twenty-one P–40s crash in Australia. Kid, walkin' down the street that day I was guilty as hell. Except I wasn't, and there was a court paper in my pocket to prove I wasn't and I walked . . . past . . . the porches. Result? Fourteen months later I had one of the best shops in the state again, a respected man again, bigger than ever.
>
> [Act I, p. 80][5]

Joe depends for emotional sustenance exclusively on his close family. Identification with members of his family is thus the limit of his real connectedness to other people. He does not even care if the respect shown to him is genuine, so long as it is there. It is only disagreements with his wife and son that he finds uncomfortable and intolerable. He seeks to avoid conflict within the family by appeasing his wife's obsessional denial of Larry's death three years earlier, and by means of a collusive and mutually idealizing intimacy with his surviving son, Chris. His underlying sense of guilt is signalled to the audience in a rather literal symbolism, by a game he has made up with the local children, in which he sends them off as pretend policemen to look out for crimes, whose perpetrators could then be brought to the supposed "gaol" beneath his house.

---

[5] Extracts from *All My Sons* are taken from *Arthur Miller: Collected Plays* (London: Cresset Press, 1958). Reprinted by permission of International Creative Management, Inc. Copyright © 1947 Arthur Miller.

Kate, his wife, is disturbed by this game, which, she feels, merely draws neighbourly attention to the crime of which Joe was ostensibly acquitted three years before.

Most of the immediate costs of this psychological arrangement are borne by Kate, who is virtually hysterical (she is calling in astrologers to find out what happened to Larry) in her denial of the death that everyone else takes for granted is a fact. She lives in a state of repressed psychological desperation. She cannot tolerate the idea that her son Chris will marry Larry's former fiancée, since this would mean acknowledging that Larry is indeed dead. We learn as the play proceeds that she in reality understands more than at first appears. She recognizes that if Larry *is* dead, then her husband becomes for her morally guilty of the deaths of all the pilots who died as a result of the faulty parts. The fantasy that sustains her is that Larry is not dead. To deny the death of Larry is to deny the deaths of his fellow airmen.

> MOTHER [*to Chris*]: Your brother's alive, darling, because if he's dead your father killed him. Do you understand me now? As long as you live that boy is alive. God does not let a son be killed by his father. Now you see, don't you? Now you see.
> *Beyond control, she hurries up and into the house.*
> KELLER *Chris has not moved. He speaks insinuatingly, questioningly*: She's out of her mind.
> CHRIS *in a broken whisper*: Then . . . you did it?
> KELLER, *with the beginning of plea in his voice*: He never flew a P–40—
> CHRIS, *struck; deadly*: But the others.
>
> [Act II, p. 114]

Whereas for Joe the deaths of strangers do not count against his need to protect his business and his family, for Kate this is not so. She knows that other mothers feel as she does about their lost sons:

> CHRIS: Mother, I'll bet you money that you're the only woman in the country who after three years is still—
> MOTHER: You're sure?
> CHRIS: Yes, I am.
> MOTHER: Well, if you're sure then you're sure. [*She turns her head away an instant.*] They don't say it on the radio but I'm sure that in the dark at night they're still waiting for their sons.
>
> [Act I, p. 78]

When the crime her husband has committed is openly acknowledged by both of them, she says to him:

> MOTHER: Joe, Joe. . . . it don't excuse it that you did it for the family.
>
> [Act III, p. 120]

Her denial of Larry's death protects Joe from guilt for the deaths he
has caused, which is why he goes along with what he knows is a
delusion. Kate's state of denial is her defence of her husband and
family, but she is continually pulled between the claims made on
her by Joe, and by her surviving son. She finally enables Chris to
learn what has happened, refusing in the end to sacrifice his integrity to sustain her husband's position. Her character shows how a
mother in such a closed family can be torn to pieces by the oedipal
struggles between sons and husband. The hysterical, excessive
quality of her insistence that Larry is still alive arises from the fact
that she is repressing not the fact of his death, but her own knowledge of this, and her terror of what will happen if his death is
acknowledged. Mourning will then have to take place, but mourning for whom? And if one starts to mourn the deaths of all the
airmen killed by the lies practised in her husband's factory, where
will this lead, and who will have to take responsibility for what has
happened? This knowledge is unbearable to Kate, because it will
be unbearable to those she loves, so she struggles with all her being
to deny it. Kate Keller, like the wives in the other two plays we
discuss, has to bear a large emotional burden for others.

By her denial that Larry is dead, Kate also maintains the fiction
that Ann remains Larry's girl. Since Chris, long since returned
from wartime service in the army, is still living at home and working in the family business—now called "Keller and Son"—we may
conjecture that she would find the appearance of *any* potential wife
for her son deeply threatening, and that her rejection of Ann as a
wife for him is multiply determined. We get a sense of how much
she has lost, through her family's exposure to the half-disguised
contempt and hatred of her neighbours, but also in what we see of
her past happiness, when she recalls the days when the neighbourhood children were growing up. Her joy in seeing George again
brings back the years when she was the warm motherly figure for
a whole cluster of local children, happy in dispensing food, drink,

and comfort to all of them. Miller's stage directions describe her as someone "with an overwhelming capacity for love".[5]

The next-door family who have moved into the house of the disgraced and imprisoned Steve Deever show a different division of roles within a marriage. Here a greedy and forceful wife, Sue, has enslaved her doctor husband Jim Bayliss to the need to make as much money as possible, forcing him to sacrifice his real vocation as a medical researcher. Jim has been made by his wife to take the role that Joe took by choice. The idea of living by conviction or ideals is set in contrast to their actual absence in the lives of Jim, who has had to give up his ideals, and of Joe, who had none except that he and his family should be successful.

Miller thus explores the destructive relationships set up between the generations as well as between the sexes in this social order. In a world in which family ties are everything and non-family relationships have little depth, children face intense pressure to identify wholly with their parents and find little space to differentiate themselves as individuals. Chris idealizes his father—and we may suppose that Larry did too when he was alive. This has led him to accept his father's version of the shipment of the defective cylinder heads. Ann and George, on the other hand, have completely rejected their father and refused to visit him in prison or even send him a Christmas card. A father, in this universe, is either all good, or all bad. Ann says to Chris: "You're the only one I know who loves his parents." Joe surprises them by showing no resentment of their father and indeed offering him a place back in his firm, and to use his business connections to get George a job as a lawyer. This enacts Joe's belief that it is to be expected that an inferior will "take the rap" but will be given some later compensation for this. These ethics are not far removed from those of a Mafia family.

When Chris finally realizes that his father was guilty of the crime and cover-up, he becomes wild with rage. He now rejects his

---

[5] Compare the tenderness towards her husband shown by Linda in *Death of a Salesman*, as she pleads with her son: "And be sweet to him tonight, dear. Be loving to him. Because he's only a little boat looking for a harbor" (Act II, p. 176).

father as totally as Ann and George have earlier rejected theirs. It is
Joe's recognition of his rejection first by Larry and now by Chris
that leads to his suicide.

Miller is perceptive here about a perverse and destructive kind
of idealism that arises from intense splitting between good and
bad, represented as the opposites of total idealization or rejection
of fathers by their children. Chris becomes as single-minded and
self-righteous in his rejection of his father as he was in his previous
idealization of him. The extremist and paranoid-schizoid nature of
this idealism (unable to tolerate in depressive mode the unavoidable good and bad qualities of its objects) is as much of a problem
as the presence or absence of idealism itself.

Miller shows how well he understands the effects of this kind of
idealism through his description of its effects on Jim, the doctor
neighbour. His wife describes him as having an unhealthy admiration for Chris, seeing in him the idealism that he used to have but
has now given up. Although she has her selfish reasons for wanting her husband to be left to make money from his patients without
worrying about deeper values, her suspicion of his idealization of
Chris has its point. Miller shows that the "idealism" that emerges
in this corrupted world can be as problematic as the indifference
and worldliness against which it defines itself.

It is the characters in the play who are able to bear suffering,
and who struggle to live with the recognition of imperfection, who
are its most sympathetic figures. These are the doctor, who is
mourning his idealistic youth but sees no way back to its hopefulness; Ann, who clings to Chris as the only safety she can imagine;
George, who has been virtually broken by his guilt at his rejection
of his father; and Kate, who has been driven nearly mad by the
need both to share and to deny her husband's guilt. But none of
these figures, nor Joe's final suicide, which brings a kind of retribu-
tive justice, offer much hope of redemption in the world Miller
presents to his audiences.

It would be easy to miss another quality in Miller's plays,
which underlies their capacity to bring about such inspiring experiences in the theatre. Miller continued to love the society he depicted and criticized it from close to its heart. Unlike Ibsen's
relationship to Norway, Miller never exiled himself from the

United States—indeed, he married its most famous actress. We see this deep affection in the sheer intensity of feeling of his characters for each other, which is more often love turned in on itself than hatred or indifference. In *All My Sons* there is nostalgia for a genuine warmth of neighbourliness—for a society everyone wanted to belong to. Miller's heroes live by what he thinks of as inadequate aspirations—to make money, to live for family alone—but they live, nevertheless, with intense passion. It is in this intensity of feeling and aspiration, whatever its particular objects may be, that Miller seems to locate his continuing hopes of betterment. We will see these paradoxical and very American qualities just as clearly in *Death of a Salesman*.

Death of a Salesman

The weight of the tragedy in this play is hard to bear. The story has a haunting quality, disturbing us through the sense of inevitable doom, reminiscent, like the subsequent *A View from the Bridge*, of the atmosphere and impact of classical Greek tragedy. Miller's technique combines realistic elements—the setting in the family home of Willy Loman, the salesman, his wife Linda, and their two grown-up sons, Biff and Happy, and the scenes of edgy, anxious dialogue in the family and at Willy's workplace—with a representation of Willy's inner state of mind using snatches of memory, almost dream-like monologues, and reconstructed events from an earlier period of his life. The staging of this interweaving of real-time events with what is evoked in the characters' minds is a powerful rendering of Miller's interpretation of the ongoing interplay of external and internal reality and is, we argue, one source of the play's power to move us.

The death we are to witness is not only Willy's despairing suicide but the process of a dying identity and a mind disintegrating. Miller's social theme is the terrible vulnerability of individual identity when family and community confirmation, solidarity, and support are lost—the disappearing neighbourhood, with the old suburban houses replaced by high-rise blocks, the growing irrelevance of the travelling salesman's role and consequent loss of employment, Willy's role as father of young sons lost as they reach adulthood. How is he to live? How is growing old to be faced? The psychological core of Miller's study is the representation of Willy's crumbling grasp on reality and the investigation of his loneliness and weakness. Miller's choice of name for Willy draws our attention to the way in which his lack of potency and of masculinity is closely linked to a sexual identity rooted not in interdependence but in a quasi-adolescent demand to rule the world through the sheer impressiveness of his phallic self-assertion, an over-identification of man and phallus.

Miller has created a character whose capacity for evading reality is immense. He is working in the same territory as in his earlier creation of Joe Keller, but the subtlety and many-layered depiction of Willy's bad faith is more textured, carrying a deeper punch. Linda and the two boys, whose growing-up is as crippled as Willy's growing old, contribute to the perpetuation of unreality through placation and a repeated failure to confront the truth. They edge towards it, but the "blind" love to which Linda adheres and which she defends, and the sons' dread of facing Willy's damaged state and their own difficulties and despair, serve to bring about repeated retreat. Finally comes Biff's realization that he can survive only if he stands out against his father's dream and makes his own way, however humdrum that may be. So great is the entanglement of father and sons that Willy cannot survive their defection: Biff's blistering uncovering of the family myths leaves Willy with nothing to hold on to and is the precursor to his suicide. Willy's mind is no longer able to feed on truth but is confused to a deadly degree by the years of falsity—the audience may long for Willy to feel relief at Biff's courageous struggle, but Willy's resources are too enfeebled by the long years of self-deception, and we watch him lose himself again in the past and his tormenting envious memories of his more adventurous and successful brother. It is his failed competitiveness with brother Ben that fuels the frantic longing for Biff to succeed.

The world of untruths in which the family is trapped includes the consequence of many lies told—by Willy to himself and others, by his sons in a similarly indiscriminate way, and by Linda through her collusion, turning away from what she knows to be true to a fiction that will help to sustain Willy's fiction of himself. Cheating is endemic—Willy cheats at cards, he cheats on his wife (and discovering this was a devastating blow to the younger Biff's idealized picture of his father), he cheats on insurance, and he encourages Biff to cheat at school. Stealing becomes a partial way of life for Biff to solve the problem of the gap between reality and his desires: he steals the answers to the maths problems from Bernard (father agrees and indeed urges it); the balls from the school locker-room; and later on emblems of potency (balls/pen) from employer/boss figures. Here too Miller is interested in the failure of role identity—there is no solid properly rooted masculinity available to a boy growing up in the shadow of a figure like Willy. Biff's identification with the short-cut to success, the belief that he has a right to succeed without effort just because of who he is—Willy Loman's son—undermines all sense of reality. If anything gives the lie to his fantasy, there is a paranoid response—he feels picked on, unfairly treated. Only when he moves out of the family sphere can he see straight—recognize his limitations, tell his story, and imagine a future:

> BIFF: I'm one dollar an hour, Willy! I tried seven states and couldn't raise it. A buck an hour! Do you follow my meaning? I'm not bringing home any prizes anyhow, and you're going to stop waiting for me to bring them home!
>
> [Act II, p. 217][5]

Biff, the school-boy sporting champion, has ended up a casual labourer and a thief, served a prison sentence, but stopped himself as he ran off with Bill Oliver's pen:

> BIFF: I saw the sky. I saw the things I love in this world. The work and the food and the time to sit and smoke.
>
> [Act II, p. 217]

So he tries to break out of Willy's "phoney dream", to set a boundary around himself—the opposite of the earlier strategies of stealing to swell the self in a delusional fashion—and to attempt to separate from his father. The tragic outcome of this for Willy is due to his identity being so confused with his sons—an agglomeration, echoed by Happy and Biff when they fantasize about being "the

Loman Brothers". Without Biff as an extension of himself, about to make it, Willy shrinks and collapses. He has said of him earlier:

WILLY: That boy is going to be magnificent. Can you imagine that magnificence with twenty thousand dollars in his pocket?

[Act II, p. 219]

These vast hopes invested for so long in Biff no longer hold him together when he realizes Biff is really going to leave and he thus feels exposed to his catastrophic internal state.

The intolerance of reality is linked in Miller's political voice to the insubstantiality of the American dream—the free-standing man who can conquer the world single-handed and who needs no more than himself to do this. In *All My Sons*, Miller gives Chris political speeches to make this point, but in *Death of a Salesman* he goes deeper into the nature of character in his tragic hero. Willy is shown as a man profoundly dependent on wife and children for the support of his fragile unreal identity, but also on his neighbour Charley, who helps him out financially. He cannot bear to recognize his dependence, since it conflicts with his image of the self-made man. He attacks both Linda and Charley when their actions threaten to penetrate his carapace of illusory grandeur. As Miller gradually provides us with a richer understanding of Willy, we grasp that this thick-skinned defensive armour is protecting him from a quite unmanageable sense of deprivation and loss—too early a loss of his own father and abandonment by his bolder elder brother have led him to a grandiose assertion of independence which he cannot sustain. This is how he describes to his boys the life of a travelling salesman:

WILLY: Well, I got on the road, and I went north to Providence. Met the Mayor.
BIFF: The Mayor of Providence!
WILLY: He was sitting in the hotel lobby.
BIFF: What'd he say?
WILLY: He said "morning!" And I said "You got a fine city here, Mayor." And then he had coffee with me. And then I went to Waterbury. Waterbury is a fine city. Big clock city, the famous Waterbury clock. Sold a nice bit there. And then Boston—Boston is the cradle of the Revolution . . .

BIFF: Gee, I'd love to go with you sometime, Dad.

WILLY: Soon as summer comes.

HAPPY: Promise?

WILLY: You and Hap and I, and I'll show you all the towns. America is full of beautiful towns and fine, upstanding people. And they know me, boys, they know me up and down New England. The finest people. And when I bring you fellas up, there'll be open sesame for all of us, 'cause one thing, boys: I have friends. I can park my car in any street in New England and the cops protect it like their own.

[Act I, pp. 144–145]

Willy feels part of this glorious New England America as if it were a family in which he has a recognizable individual place looked after by the authority figures. He has the same expectation of his employer—a ruthless younger man who has no sense of obligation to an old retainer. Attaching himself to these powerful idealized paternal figures in the outside world has been Willy's solution to the absence of inner strength based on the experience of feeling cared for.

Willy says to Ben, his brother:

WILLY: Can't you stay a few days? You're just what I need, Ben, because I—I have a fine position here but I—well Dad left when I was such a baby and I never had a chance to talk to him and I still feel—kind of temporary about myself.

[Act II, p. 159]

Miller's portrayal of how this deep insecurity is also at the core of Biff's distress is vivid. Biff has just this same temporary perpetually on-the-move way of living, he can't settle, he can't "find" himself:

BIFF: I can't take hold . . . I'm looking around . . . travelling.

[Act II, p. 161]

His identification with his father's restless searching seems constructed from a conjunction of his boyhood emulation of a still-admired father and of his unconscious response to his father's powerful and destructive intrusion into his personality—a process by which Biff is taken over by aspects of his father's inner world, becoming a receptacle for parental projections.

The need for care and protection is located in Linda—there is no place for it in the version of male character Willy aspires to. Feelings of dependence are attributed instead to the women who are felt both to exploit the men and to be incapable of taking adult responsibility. While the audience can see that Linda is keeping the household finances in some limited order, Willy clings to his authority, just as he has forgotten that he must have been brought up by his abandoned mother. Women are doubly demeaned in Willy's world-view—either childishly full of complaint or sexual and greedily exploitative. Men are to be above all this, and to espouse strength and independence. Willy's house-rebuilding projects are the essence of this, but the dishonest basis of Willy's identity is again rammed home with the evidence that the construction work is all with materials stolen from a building-site and that the boys have been dragged into this theft.

In the painful remembered sequences of Biff's discovery of his father with a prostitute in a Boston hotel we can sense the problem for Willy of being away from home. Without Linda to contain for him his hated neediness and sense of deprivation, he cannot bear his loneliness and is driven to seek relief for himself in an enactment of his phantasies of female exploitativeness. The instability of his identity is starkly realized in his desperate and volatile behaviour to the woman in his room—at one moment giving her silk stockings to secure company and the next driving her out half-dressed, telling mad cover-stories to Biff to explain away the sordid reality.

His enormous difficulties in logical thinking evident on this occasion are a profound part of his tragedy—he has not been able to understand that the collapse of Biff's belief in his father that these events precipitated is at the heart of Biff's own failure to complete the maths course that would have given him entry to college and his subsequent descent into aimless wanderings. He has "forgotten" what happened in Boston because the pain and guilt that reflection would entail is quite beyond him. Willy cannot make use of his own observations and pursue their contradictory logic. Within a short space of time he can remark confidently that he is a "well-liked man" and puzzle momentarily that "people don't seem to take to me", or boast in an all-American bubble of pride that the Chevrolet is "the greatest car ever built" and complain when it breaks down that "they ought to prohibit manufacture" of this unreliable vehicle. His grandiose self-assessment as friend of everyone can shift to an unhappy description of himself as "fat" and "foolish to look at". There seems no possibility of modulation or linkage. Each thought is isolated from the wider context, and integration cannot take place. When there is talk of fearlessness, Ben says it's needed but Charlie that it can land you in jail. Willy flounders, unable to find any grounding in his own mind and to exercise judgement. His manic flow of talk protects him from the impact of his disturbing inner state and functions as a frantic effort to reshape reality in a more pleasing shape. He exhausts himself in this form of flight, and one could perhaps see his final flight as he drives off bent on suicide as his exhausted refusal to struggle any longer. The insurance money he expects Linda to receive soothes his guilt.

The emotional abuse of Biff and Happy to which Willy is driven by his inner situation is the motor of the family catastrophe. Biff's failure to establish himself in the world makes him the tormenting representation of Willy's lack of success. Willy's oscillation between denunciation and unrealistic and mindless encouragement and flattery bemuses Biff, combined as it is with his burdensome awareness of his father's desperation. To be the "Adonises" Willy demands his sons to be, they would have to solve the problems that have defeated their father, and each is crippled by unconscious identifications with his weaknesses. Happy is no better off than Biff—he carries for Willy the cynical "I can get away with anything" conviction that delinquency has no cost and that seduction will always carry the day. His physical attractiveness becomes a weapon to inflict humiliation and destroy people. The terrible scene in which the sons abandon their father at a supposed birthday celebration to go off with girls they have picked up at the restaurant is a grim reversal of the Boston hotel debacle. Everything is recycled across the generations, unmodified by understanding, as minds caught in this maelstrom cannot function. Action continually replaces any possible pause for thought.

The twin poles of father's weakness and strength are present in the sons' relationship to Willy and in his relationship to the other male figures. As children, the boys respond to Willy in a bizarre jumping-to-it puppet-like obedience, and this is linked to their realization of his dependence on their support. They are like a fan club. Ben (his absent brother) and Charlie (his old friend next-door) represent the split nature of Willy's internal father image—Ben is the idealized, successful, rich, super-independent one, Charlie the denigrated ordinary dependable father able to stand by a family. Thoughts of Ben's triumphs come to haunt Willy and continually undermine any realistic assessment of things. Hence he has to turn down Charlie's offer of a modest job, closing his eyes to the cold-heartedness of these adventurers and to his fury about being left behind. This leaves him exposed to dangerous rage turned against himself and expressed in suicidal impulses.

The oedipal aspects of this constellation are manifest. Happy is addicted to oedipal triumph and gets his kicks from seducing the women of his superiors at work. His childhood jealousy of his father's rights is thus endlessly acted out in philandering. He takes thoughtlessly what he does not really want and then tosses it aside as used goods, spoilt and valueless. Willy's failure to retain a sense of a mother from his childhood and his deadly focus on the attractions of the undependable father has been lived out in the next generation—he has not been able to give his sons a picture of parents functioning as a couple. Instead, they are invited to believe that they look after their mother by joining up with father's orders. Mother disappears as a real figure and force within the family, and the "boys" together run things. The delusional aspects of Willy's assertion invite us to sense the little boy playing at manliness, which is a plausible back-cloth to his flawed adulthood. He, too, like his father before him, abandons the family, despite a life-long feverish effort to make real a family experience quite the opposite of this.

The profound links explored by Freud between the compulsion to repeat in human life and the destructive forces within us are exemplified in this drama of failed mourning, manic denial, false selves, and failure of development. The intensity of the text does not fade with renewed study—indeed, if anything, the agony of it seems increased as one gets close to the intolerable world the family all inhabit. The knitting-together of a psychologically credible intergenerational family nightmare and a picture of an atomized and harshly individualistic social fabric, which renders people even more vulnerable to the destructive forces within them, is

Miller's achievement. It is little surprise that this play also became a powerful film, achieving Miller's aim to use drama to present modern society's tragedies to its people as the Athenians did in their amphitheatres.

A View from the Bridge

In *All My Sons* and *Death of a Salesman*, the entire burden of social connectedness in a competitive society is shown to rest on the family, and, as we have shown, the effects of this situation are to break and destroy its members. *A View from the Bridge* is set in a different social milieu—a neighbourhood of Italian–American longshoremen in New York. In this world, social bondedness does stretch further than the immediate family: to the extended family of origin in Sicily and to the working community, joined together to some degree in resistance to harsh employers and to the immigration authorities. Miller achieved a further extension of the scope of theatre by making a dockworker the central figure of a tragedy. But while the play demonstrates a different kind of connectedness between Eddie Carbone's family and his social world from that of Joe Keller or Willy Loman, his ultimate exposure and isolation is shown to be similar to that of Miller's earlier heroes. The dynamics of generation and gender that are shown to have been so troubled in the middle-class environments of the two earlier plays are equally fraught with difficulties, and ultimately as catastrophic, in the world of the longshoremen.

In *All My Sons* and *Death of a Salesman*, the oedipal relationships between parents and children are worked out principally with sons. Both Willy Loman and Joe Keller have two sons and no daughters. While the possibility of a grown-up son's marriage and independence is a point of crisis for Kate Keller and there is some flirtation between Joe and his son's girl, Ann, which implicitly threatens to confuse the differences of generation, there is little scope in these plays for the exploration of a father's difficulties with the oedipal transition in relation to daughters.

A View from the Bridge focuses, however, on this particular aspect of the inevitable oedipal transitions that occur in any family. It is in this respect, as well as in its social location, that this play differs from the two that preceded it. From the beginning of the play, we see that Eddie is unable to tolerate his separation from his niece Catherine, and her emergence as a separate sexual being. His anxiety about the attention being paid to her on the street and his disparaging comments on the men of the neighbourhood who look at her are a projection of his own desires—these men who, he asserts, are not good enough for her and who wish her no good, are men like himself. He imagines that it might be different if she worked in a "better class" of office, but in fact he is more disturbed by the attentions of Rodolpho, who feels at home in the emerging consumer city, with his aptitudes for fashion, food, and music, as by that of his fellow dockers. This is because Rodolpho competes with Eddie, not only in terms of his physical youth, but also in terms of his modern identity, in ways that the longshoremen do not. Beatrice, Eddie's wife, has lost her sexual interest for him, as she reminds him; her main hope seems to be to live through this painful period of abandonment by Eddie and to help Catherine to escape into a life of her own, in the hope that Eddie might then return to her. Although Beatrice is struggling honourably to look after her niece and the newly arrived illegal immigrants, we see that she has already had to tolerate being pushed aside for some period. She has to put up with an intensity of feeling between Eddie and Catherine that is both humiliating to her and dangerous to them.

Why are Eddie and Beatrice not able to allow Catherine to grow up into sexual adulthood? The capacity of one generation to tolerate the emergence of the independence of the next depends on the sense that the older generation's life has had its own value and meaning, and on this generation's capacity to identify with what is to follow. The hardships of Eddie and Beatrice's lives, which have been lived for others, not for themselves, have left them with an unresolved and unrecognized bitterness about what they have missed in their own lives, and thus towards the next generation, who can hope for something better. Beatrice manages these painful feelings through self-abnegation. Having no children of her own, she has brought up Catherine for her dead sister, and she is ready to give up part of their house and livelihood to help her newly arrived cousins from Sicily. Eddie is living his emotional life through his niece. He has held on to the intimacy of her childhood well into her adolescence, and in the course of the play tries to prevent her involvement with Rodolpho, as he would with any man of her own generation. There seems to be an absent centre from the lives of Eddie and Beatrice, which have, instead, to be lived through the lives of others.

Miller represents this family as having to fight to survive in a harsh and competitive world. Eddie angrily describes his periods of lay-off, when he has had to seek work all over the city:

> EDDIE, *with a helpless but ironic gesture*:   What can I do? I'm a patsy, what can a patsy do? I worked like a dog so a punk could have her, so that's what I done. I mean, in the worst times, in the worst, when there wasn't a ship comin' in the harbour, I hustled. When there was empty piers in Brooklyn I went to Hoboken, Staten Island, the West Side, Jersey, all over—because I made a promise. I took out of my own mouth to give to her. I walked hungry plenty days in this city. . . .
>
> [Act I, p. 409][6]

The community of longshoremen and Italian–Americans imposes obligations on him—for example, to give support to newcomers—but provides little for him in return. In this dockworking environment, unions and the employers are in league with one another. Immigrant workers are brought in illegally, are allowed to work until they pay off their debts, and must then hustle in competition with all the other casualized and often-unemployed dockworkers. This is the world of "racket-ridden longshoremen" described at around the same time in Elia Kazan and Marlon Brando's film *On the Waterfront*, and in a classic sociological article by Daniel Bell (1961). There is neither a structure of class solidarity nor a culture of familial and neighbourly support to make Eddie's and Beatrice's sacrifice feel fully bearable and worthwhile. Their self-abnegation is given little social recognition. There is to be no big party to celebrate Catherine and Rodolpho's wedding, and this does not seem to be only because the marriage had to take place in a hurry,

---

[6] Extracts from *A View from the Bridge* are taken from *Arthur Miller: Collected Plays* (London: Cresset Press, 1958). Reprinted by permission of International Creative Management, Inc. Copyright © 1955 Arthur Miller.

to give Rodolpho rights of citizenship, or because Eddie so hates it. Miller represents this family as having few kin or friends who could celebrate such a marriage with them. Eddie poignantly expresses the fear that when Catherine leaves home, she will move far away, and Beatrice and he will seldom see her. The parents' sacrifices will thus have been for nothing, and will leave them in their own later years feeling depleted and empty.

The picture of intergenerational mobility that is set out in this play is a depressing one. The older generation has invested everything in the lives of their children's generation, but for this reason impose exceptional and oppressive demands on them. Hopes and expectations that have not been fulfilled in the parents' lives must be fulfilled in the children's, but this must be on terms and in ways that the parents control. The children must live for their parents, give the parents the satisfactions that they have had to sacrifice for themselves. This gives them little scope to live their own lives in their own way and also places on them intense spoken or unspoken demands for gratitude. Although Catherine gives Eddie no good reason for his fear that he will be abandoned when she marries, her violent disillusionment with him at the end of the play does reveal the latent potential for complete breakdown in the relationship between the generations within a family when so much pressure has been placed on it by the family's isolation. The play suggests that the immense opportunities that have been created for individuals in America have been obtained at the price of a loss of supportive solidarity both within and between the generations.

By contrast, Rodolpho's hopefulness, as a newly arrived Sicilian in New York, already attuned to the American way of life, is not presented in the context of the play as necessarily ill-founded, and the play suggests that he may well eventually achieve his desires. Rodolpho is accused by Eddie—though not to his face—of wanting to marry Catherine to gain the right to stay in America and become a U.S. citizen. Eddie has his own jealous reasons for this suspicion, but it is true that the marriage is desirable to Rodolpho and his elder brother for more than one reason. In a world in which most people are out for themselves, Eddie's unworthy suggestion that this might be true, or might come to be true, of Rodolpho too is not to be entirely discounted. What is clear is that the precarious and isolated situation in which they all find themselves allows no one any space to reflect on these different possible motives for action and to ensure that they each have their understood and acknowledged place.

Although the longshoremen do give some reluctant help to their immigrant kinsfolk, it seems to be given more from a sense of obligation and shame than from affection. The union's role in the admission of these illegal immigrants, and by implication the role of the dockworking employers, is in no way altruistic. For the employers, as Eddie perceives, these illegitimate workers enable them to undercut the wages of existing workers and to keep the latter in a state of insecurity and dependency. For the corrupt unions, there are kickbacks and bribes to be taken. Eddie is contemptuous of the desperate poverty of his kinsmen back in Sicily and feels that he has left their world far behind. The impulse to close the door on the newcomers, to lessen the competition among those who have previously arrived, is not far from the surface. Miller seems to have some nostalgia for an older world in his depiction of the respect for familial authority shown by the Sicilians, but this only throws Eddie's transgression of all of their moral boundaries into sharper contrast.

Rather than take pride in the hope that the children can do better than their parents and live a fuller and more open life than they have been able to, Eddie feels threatened by the changes he perceives taking place around him. This play long anticipated and prefigured the crisis that would decades later strike the "rustbelt" economy in the United States and in other countries, such as Britain, and would devalue the skills and identities of its male workers. This is one reason why it can still have such intense social resonances when it is performed.[7] Catherine and Rodolpho's success would in his own eyes make his life seem a failure. Eddie is shocked when he learns that Catherine, in her first job, will make more money than the normal wage of an adult longshoreman.

---

[7] A particular resonance of this kind was achieved in a recent (1995) production at the Bristol Old Vic, in which the actor who played Eddie Carbone (Bernard Hill) was already memorable for an earlier performance in a television film classic, *Boys from the Blackstuff*, in which he had played Yosser, a working-class man at the end of his tether, notably in "Yosser's Story". The crisis of male working-class identity that Eddie represents has been the subject of many recent imaginative works—for example, the films *The Full Monty* and *Brassed Off*.

Rodolpho's expressiveness and his feeling for the opportunities of America make Eddie feel resentful and inadequate. He persecutes in Rodolpho those aspects of himself that have had to be repressed in his lifetime of physical endurance.

Most fundamental is the fact that the deprivations and absences in Eddie and Beatrice's lives are not able to be recognized or mourned. They never refer to their own childlessness in their conversations together. Catherine's mother is referred to only once, and her father never. When Eddie reminds Catherine of his promise to her mother on her deathbed, this is to insist that he now has full responsibility and ownership of her. He denies all recognition that Catherine has different natural parents and that this might give her an additional right to make her own life in her own way. A large part of the tragedy that unfolds on the stage is that Eddie has no language for what is happening to him and refuses the understanding that others (Beatrice, Alfieri) offer, in which lies the only hope of change.

The deprivation of Eddie and Beatrice and the possibilities of an incestuous relationship between Eddie and Catherine are, of course, made more convincing by the fact that Eddie and Beatrice are without children and that Catherine is not their own natural daughter. The additional strain that this situation places on the oedipal dynamic of parent-child relationships makes it easier to expose its risks and dangers without causing excessive public outrage. This displacement of a universal situation onto this more vulnerable family constellation gives audiences more space to absorb and reflect on its meaning. By this device Miller offered his "interpretation" of a common experience of American family life in a way that his audiences would be able to respond to. Nevertheless, it seems clear that the crisis portrayed in this play—of a parental generation unable to mourn its own losses past and future and unable to identify with their children's autonomous lives as a fulfilment of the meaning of their own—was intended by Miller as a representation of a wider contemporary American experience.

Miller's plays demonstrate a deep moral and indeed political engagement with his own country and its development, though he believed that drama should be devoted to the exploration of reality, not the propagation of ideology. In Athol Fugard's later terms, drama should be an act of witness, not of advocacy. Miller's great achievement, following in the footsteps of Ibsen, Chekhov, and his other great realist predecessors, was to insist that the modern theatre should explore the lives of ordinary citizens, and that modern tragedies could be located in everyday contexts—hence the importance of Miller choosing as his heroes a salesman and a longshoreman. Each modern generation of dramatists, from Ibsen onwards, has given a further expression to this democratic commitment.

Miller may nevertheless have encountered some difficulties of technique or confidence in representing a working-class world in the 1950s to his largely middle-class audience. The role in the play of Alfieri as the educated lawyer, both advising Eddie and interpreting the evolving situation to the audience, may have been a product of this dramatic problem. Alfieri functions as a mediator and is a means by which someone like the author could himself be present in this social milieu, making it seem less alien to the audience.

The role of Jim Bayliss, the doctor, in *All My Sons* is similar to this, in permitting an articulate elaboration of issues at stake in the action which would not fall within the compass of the more representative characters. Charley, Willy's next-door neighbour and friend, is given a comparable last word in *Death of a Salesman*, in the scene called "Requiem", finding meaning in Willy's tragedy:

> CHARLEY [*stopping Happy's movement and reply*]:   You don't understand: Willy was a salesman. And for a salesman, there is no rock bottom to the life, He don't put a bolt to a nut, he don't tell you the law or give you medicine. He's a man way out there in the blue, riding on a smile and a shoeshine. And when they start not smiling back—that's an earthquake. And then you get yourself a couple of spots on your hat, and you're finished. Nobody dast blame this man. A salesman is got to dream, boy. It comes with the territory.
>
> ["Requiem", pp. 221–222]

Athol Fugard, in *Valley Song*, found another solution to this need to find a place for understanding within the action itself by including "The Author" as a major character, thus giving himself a direct presence in his play.

In *A View from the Bridge* Miller frames this mediating role in the idiom of classical tragedy, making use of the link of the action with

Sicily as a justification for making these overt parallels between ancient and modern ways of representing social tragedy. This device imparts an additional dignity to the play, establishing its deep seriousness and perhaps keeping at a useful distance two more immediate frames of reference that could have impinged on it in a harmful and didactic way. One of these is the contemporary political context that must have been in Miller's mind (this was soon after the period of McCarthyism, and its repression of political radicalism in the USA). The other is the world of more abstract ideas—for example, those of psychoanalysis itself, which it would have been of no help at all to this play, or indeed most others, to make explicit. Perhaps the device of Alfieri's comments on the unfolding inevitability of the action may also signify Miller's sense that as a socialist intellectual, writing at a time of political gloom and defeat, he could chart the tragedy of an American working class helplessly divided against itself in many ways but could see no resolution of it. This sense of a world whose contradictions, confusions, and potentials for catastrophe can be witnessed and charted, but within which there seem to be few genuinely reparative or redeeming forces available, is a powerful theme common to all of the three plays we have discussed. The seriousness of Miller's social vision matches his profound sense of the tragedy of the individuals who people his plays.

CHAPTER TEN

Beckett:
dramas of psychic catastrophe

W hat are Beckett's plays about? Even 45 years after the first production of *Waiting for Godot*, this remains a challenging question, though many people, including Beckett himself, have thought this was not necessarily a productive place to start from, since it threatens to lead one away from the plays themselves. We might see this as analogous to Bion's distinction (Bion, 1962a) between knowing about and getting to know— that is, the idea that there is a form of knowledge that evades the essence of the thing studied, and which should be clearly distinguished from an engagement with experience. This latter is necessarily an ongoing process and does not claim to take possession of the object of enquiry. The "known" will always retain some element of mystery.[1] The question arises nevertheless because of Beckett's break with previous expectations of what a modern play

---

[1] Arguments for the particular quality of understanding achieved through imaginative literature, whether by Coleridge or F. R. Leavis, have often made parallel distinctions between "abstract" knowledge and knowledge that emerges from "realized" or embodied instances. This is a relevant parallel to draw in a book that tries to explore dramatic writing through a psychoanalytic perspective.

was supposed to be—that is, a representation of a more-or-less familiar patch of social life (usually taking place in a house or a room) with characters who are at least in part identifiable versions of social types. This apparent correspondence between the staged play and recognizable social and domestic reality had become especially the case for modern drama, in the work of its great masters, such as Ibsen, Chekhov,[2] and Miller, as we have explored. Indeed, part of the achievement of modern dramatic writing had been to invest with tragic dimensions the experiences of characters whose social identities were not so different from those of the majority of their audiences.

But in *Waiting for Godot*, Beckett put on to the stage two nondescript characters, Estragon and Vladimir, who had little in common with those conventionally represented in the theatre. They are in some respects like vagrants (with ill-fitting boots, sleeping in ditches, eating raw turnips, radishes, half-eaten chicken legs), yet some of their routines are like those of circus clowns. The play has no plot or action to speak of, except that of "waiting" for Godot, whose identity is a mystery and who in any case does not come. The absence of action or plot—the extreme difficulty of Vladimir and Estragon in doing anything, even moving from the spot—is what distinguishes the action of this, and of Beckett's other full-length plays, *Endgame* and *Happy Days*, from most previous drama.

This is a more extreme dramatic strategy than that of Chekhov, Beckett's outstanding forerunner in his attention to the "real time" or "here-and-now" of his characters' interaction with one another. In Chekhov's work what happens, or does not happen (the failure to sell the cherry orchard until it is too late, for example), is mostly moved by the states of mind of his characters and their relations with one another. Beckett is more radical than Chekhov in that Vladimir and Estragon, Winnie and Willie, Hamm and Clov are in a world in which virtually nothing can happen at all, since they have lost the capacity for agency. Another way of putting this is to say that Beckett is representing characters who are trapped in their own mental states.

---

[2] Chekhov, however, as Richard Gilman (1995) has pointed out, is one of Beckett's major forerunners, in the ways his plays give preference to the depiction of often paralysed states of mind over conventional action.

There are three questions one might ask about this dramatic method. The first is, why does Beckett choose to depict, in all of his plays, characters with such vestigial social identities? A second question is, what is the nature of the mental states in which these characters are in their different ways imprisoned? And a third is, why should these distinctive *mises-en-scène*, and the mental states that are explored in them, have such continuing resonance? Clearly we have to understand the mental states in order to enquire why Beckett chose to represent them as he did and why it is that audiences should feel, over nearly 50 years, nourished and enriched by their representation.[3]

We will begin with some reflections on *Waiting for Godot* (1952), then offer some thoughts about *Endgame* (1957) and finally turn to *Happy Days* (1961).

Waiting for Godot

Estragon and Vladimir appear to have virtually nothing except the clothes they wear. They have no project, except, at Vladimir's insistence, to wait for Mr Godot, who has promised to see them and who seems to offer some kind of indeterminate hope. They are vulnerable to attack—Estragon says he has slept the night in a ditch and has been beaten up by ten men. They have nothing to eat except the odd raw vegetable, which they carry in their pockets. Estragon's boots hurt him. Vladimir finds urination acutely painful. They repel each other through their smell. These are images of infantile helplessness and persecution. Clowns likewise represent for the audiences extreme physical vulnerability and liability to attack, failure and humiliation of all kinds, reminding us of our own memories of vulnerability, though encoding this in the relatively safe external form of the clown, whose underlying sadness

---

[3] Much valuable information about Beckett's life and work is provided in two recent biographies, by Anthony Cronin (1996) and James Knowlson (1996). Guidance to contemporary work on Beckett can be gained from John Pilling (Ed.) *The Cambridge Companion to Beckett* (1993).

is, however, often made evident. Beckett was in fact an admirer of Buster Keaton and cast him in his only film.[4]

However, these figures have other imaginative referents. One could hardly forget that this play was written in the years just after the Second World War, when Europe was full of displaced persons and the victims of war. There are fragmentary evocations of death and disaster throughout the play, references to "billions of others", "dead voices" that make a noise like wings, leaves, sand, or ash, voices for whom "to have lived is not enough".[5]

Estragon and Vladimir express a shared memory of more deaths than any mind can bear to think of, which makes it impossible for them to think of anything else. They share the burden of these thoughts, as if what could not be thought at all by one may perhaps be just bearable if the two of them share the task. Suicide is no good to them, they recognize, unless both of them can die, since unless there is someone with whom to share their terrible thoughts, to live on would be unbearable.

Theirs is a strategy of bare psychic survival, and their dialogue is its main resource. The rhythms, repetitions, flow of ideas, irony, playfulness, and rejection in their talk gives some containment to the anxieties and terrors that beset the characters. The audience, brought into the dialogue as spectators of these bizarre events, is also caught up in subtly shifting identifications. The point of Beckett's choice of Chaplinesque or Keatonesque figures as his two central characters must have been that audiences could identify with them as stylized representations of ordinary vulnerable citizens in a senseless world. The play's frequent silences, abruptness, and apparent inconsequence creates unease and anxiety as it disrupts the normal theatrical expectation of a seamless and naturalistic flow of dialogue and action. It is the release of this unconscious anxiety in the audience that underlies much of the humour of the play. (As Freud understood, humour and anxiety are closely connected.) It is important in staging it that the despair and desola-

---

[4] The story of this episode is told in Cronin (1996).
[5] From *Waiting for Godot*. In: *Samuel Beckett: Complete Dramatic Works* (London: Faber & Faber).

tion—the dead and dying objects—that underlie the comedy remain real presences. Laughter must only be a partial escape from unbearable mental pain.

There is, we think, some gradual movement towards greater hopefulness and perhaps recovery as the play proceeds. Pozzo's blindness and consequent vulnerability is less terrifying than his earlier arrogant bullying—Vladimir and Estragon no longer have to worry about violence from that quarter. The concluding comic exchange of the play is around the macabre subject of their project to hang themselves—they don't have a rope, they need each other's help to hang, their rope breaks, and Estragon's trousers fall down when he takes out his belt. All this has the effect of containing their despair and, of course, the audience's. What the audience is perhaps left with is that these two traumatized victims of terror and disaster have just about survived. And they occupy our minds insistently.

Our belief is that this play has to be seen in part as a response to the catastrophes surrounding the Second World War. While there are references to philosophical and religious themes, the sufferings evoked on the stage seem altogether more tangible than these, although the echoes of these more abstract discourses provide some fractured language in which the near-destruction of life and hope can be represented.[6] There has perhaps been some reluctance to acknowledge the actual all-too-recent horrors hinted at in the play in some critics' insistence on more metaphysical interpretations, though Beckett's own text provides grounds for these.

Vladimir, Estragon, Lucky, and Pozzo are a collection of names that evoke the turbulence of post-war occupied Europe. They appear to be beset by guilt as well as by fear and hopelessness, though it may be the guilt of survivors, and a sense of general complicity, as much as of perpetrators. Vladimir's interest in one of the two thieves on the cross with Christ who was spared, according

---

[6] The tree which has put forth leaves in the second act calls to mind the last chapters of *Revelations*, which describe "a new heaven and a new earth":

In the midst of the street of it, and on either side of the river, was there the tree of life, which bare twelve manner of fruits, and yielded her fruit every month: and the leaves of the tree were for the healing of the nations. [*Revelations*, 22.1]

to the account given in one Gospel, expresses his sense of identification with this guilty victim. Will one of them be spared, he is
asking, but also, what crimes have they committed? Athol Fugard
told his actors, when he was directing *Waiting for Godot* in South
Africa, that

> Estragon and Vladimir must have read the accounts of the
> Nuremberg Trials, or else they were at Sharpeville, or were the
> first in at Auschwitz. Choose your horror—they know all about
> it. [Fugard, quoted in Graver, 1989, p. 103]

Of course, they seem hardly capable at this point of doing anything, but we learn more of what this state of mind might mean
when Pozzo and Lucky come onto the stage.

Pozzo holds Lucky as his slave on a leash. He controls him by
the threat of the whip. Lucky has been turned into a wholly abject
instrument of his master's will, picking things up, putting them
down, fetching and carrying them, in a way that makes clear that
his continuing total obedience is his master's purpose for him. This
demonstration of a broken will, of the turning of a person into a
sub-human being, is surely an evocation of the fate of the victims of
the ghettos and concentration camps.[7] At one point, Lucky is in-
structed to keep a few paces away from Pozzo, as the SS required
their concentration-camp victims to do.

Estragon and Vladimir witness this treatment of a victim even
worse off than they themselves and display different reactions to it.
This includes some sympathy for Lucky, and protest to Pozzo. But
they discover that Pozzo has something—food—that they want,
and his self-confidence and bluster is in any case intimidating.
Estragon's gesture of trying to help Lucky leads to his being kicked
in the shins. That is the end of any sympathy for him. Pozzo explains as a matter of obvious fact that pain has to be lodged somewhere, and that Lucky has just got rid of a bit of it into Estragon.

These events are made to seem an ordinary enough part of
Vladimir's and Estragon's lives. They are thus represented as
ordinary, powerless, witnesses to and accomplices in abuse and

---

[7] Beckett had a friend and Resistance comrade, Alfred Peron, who died soon
after his release from Mauthausen.

atrocity. No wonder they experience guilt, impotence, and hopelessness. Lucky's fate could easily be theirs, and even observing
Lucky's fate is destructive enough.

As one of Pozzo's two exhibitions of his damaged capabilities,
Lucky is made to dance. For the other, he is made to "think"—that
is, to make a speech in which thinking is supposed to take place.
The speech draws incoherently on a variety of cited references. Its
underlying theme, however, in so far as one emerges, is that man,
in spite of apparent consolations and activities and academic
knowledge, "wastes and pines, wastes and pines". The speech culminates with repeated references to "the skulls", and "labours left
unfinished". The emerging image is of total desolation, and of a
mind destroyed.

The end of this speech produces a brief moment of triumph
for the others, as Lucky's hat, symbol of his thought, is crushed.
Vladimir and Estragon then co-operate with Pozzo in trying to
restore Lucky—by propping him up—to some measure of servile
functioning. Not only has Lucky's mind been destroyed by his
experiences, whatever they were, and its devastation publicly ex-
hibited, but the sense is that these established kinds of thinking
(philosophy, scholarship, citations) and activities ("the strides of
physical culture the practice of sports such as tennis football running cycling . . .") have lost all meaning and worth.

There is another kind of thinking that does go on in this play
and provides the basis for its residual hopefulness. This is the
thinking embodied in the conversations between the two friends,
Vladimir and Estragon. Even the worst that can befall, Beckett
seems to suggest, is made more bearable by its being shared.

The two friends have moments in which they can help each
other, offering to share the meagre food available (turnips or car-
rots) and achieving some understanding of each others' states of
mind. They are often verbally in tune with one another, even if they
appear to start off with a difference of opinion. In fact, their dialogues are plainly what enable both of them to think.

Their anxieties and uncertainties, about what day of the week
it is, about whether and how to kill themselves, about being beat-
en up, are all alleviated by the fact that they can put them into
words and know that they are understood by the other. Their
double act is the disguise, the outward form of the joke that con-

ceals the desolate truths that it is the main work of the play to share with its audience. The "charming evening", which is "worse than being at the theatre", wrenches our guts as we laugh. The exchange of words is likened to a game ("Come on Gogo, return the ball, can't you, once in a while?"), but the underlying matter is deadly serious.

The problem, to which Beckett's method in this play was a solution, is what has been described as the impossibility of representing in art the terrible sufferings of catastrophes such as the two world wars and the Holocaust. Beckett lived through the war in Occupied France.

It seems crucial to Beckett's method not to allow his audiences the mental comfort of references to circumscribed, recognizable events. Definition, narrative, description, would all be defences, ways of pushing away anxiety onto some named "other", in a place, a nationality, a recognizable "type" of some kind. A symbolic containment of the horror need *not* to be available for its true meaning to be conveyed. The strangeness of these Beckett characters, the surreal quality of the scene and the dialogue, evoke the impossibility of reaching an understanding of catastrophic events such as those of war, persecution, and torture. We could say, using Bion's terms, that a loss of contact with good objects and the experience of the environment as wholly unreliable and persecuting engenders a sense of "nameless dread".

Al Alvarez, in *Beyond All This Fiddle* (1968), was one of the first to write about the emergence of a post-war literature that sought to do justice to the extremes of emotion and experience of our time.[8] Beckett, with his exceptional sensitivity to mental pain and his gift for representing the essence of this, was the pioneer in theatre of this exploration, as Alvarez discussed in his *Beckett* (1973). After Beckett, with Pinter[9] and others, it became possible to recognize that bizarre and extreme states of mind were common features of our social world. It is, however, noteworthy that with Pinter, too, the exploration in his writing of psychotic states of mind has been

---

[8] See also on the difficulties of such writing George Steiner's near-contemporary *Language and Silence* (1967).

[9] Anthony Cronin's (1996) biography of Beckett describes Pinter's admiration for and friendship with Beckett.

accompanied by his increasing sensitivity to political atrocity. Dramatists, who need a theatre, are perhaps particularly aware of the importance of external containment.

Although there remains some vestigial structure of night and day in *Waiting for Godot,* its characters exist in a disordered relation to time. Estragon, Vladimir, and Pozzo torment each other with the uncertainty of whether they can remember what took place yesterday or recognize each other when they meet again, and they are tormented by the unending unchanging quality of their states of mind. The play investigates the response to a small change in this environment: at the beginning of the second act, the tree has sprouted a few leaves. Spring—hope?—has perhaps surfaced in this dead landscape. Vladimir's response is to sing a song about a dog stealing a bone and being beaten to death by the cook and the other dogs. It is clear that it is dangerous to allow hope to emerge: a dog who sniffs out a bone and believes he can get nourishment is in for trouble. Not only does the cook fail to respond to the dog's hunger, but all the other dogs unite in murderous rage because of their own deprivation. No one can therefore feel safe. It seems that it is better not to notice the leaves or to smell spring in the air: one will only provoke the envy of the others and end up worse off than ever.

This bleak situation underlies the problem Vladimir summarizes thus: "What is terrible is to have thoughts." There are repeated attacks on the possibility of thinking, both within and between characters. For instance, Lucky's monologue, with its crucial remnants of thought that could provide meaningful clues to the catastrophe they are living, is the cue for the others to steal and crush his hat, representing the head from which the mangled thoughts have come. The intolerance of the reality that his words have made real for his hearers is thus enacted. The routine that follows, with Vladimir and Estragon passing the hats back and forth as they try them on for fit, registers their confusion as black comedy.[10]

The place to which the characters have retreated is of course rife with infantile anxieties, though they struggle to hold these at bay

---

[10] Beckett once began rehearsals of the play with Lucky's speech, saying that this was the key to it (Graver, 1989, p. 49).

through their immobility. Beckett shows us the fundamental fear of the void, of falling out of contact with a supporting internal or external object. There are many episodes of actual falling, responded to at times with concern and an attempt to pick up the one who has fallen, and at others with cruel delay in responding. "When we wait with folded arms", says Vladimir, evoking the image of the stony parent who fails to respond to a distressed child. The panic the characters experience provides a theatrical representation of the infantile terror described so well by Bick (1968). Her account draws attention to the infant's helplessness and need to be held together by material care and by being held in mind. And, on the other hand, of the infant's dread of annihilation through melting or falling to bits, which underlies the need for such containment. Vladimir asks Pozzo: "What do you do when you fall far from help?" Of course the answer can only be that he waits. Meltzer's later work (Meltzer, 1992), on the defensive use of intrusive identification to evade the terror of the dependence on an object (this is one way of avoiding the anxiety of awareness of separateness), is visibly exemplified in the relationship between Vladimir and Estragon. "There you are again at last," says Vladimir, as Estragon reappears and falls into his arms. They are "playing" at Pozzo and Lucky, but it is deadly serious for each of them if they cannot maintain contact with the other. "Where were you? I thought you were gone for ever," Vladimir continues, and when they are separated again a few lines later, Estragon says, "I'm in hell."

The version of mutual dependence that their relationship exemplifies is a parody of a benign tie between parent and child. For their hell is as much in being together as in being apart. "Get up till I embrace you" well expresses their contradictory feelings, as they both love and repel each other, moving swiftly from a comforting embrace to hostile rejection: "You stink of garlic." They have brought this relationship of ambivalence to a fine art, playing much of it out as a game and managing their dependence on and aggression towards each other in this way. *Waiting for Godot* gives the image of a couple joined together in hopeless and hostile mutual dependence one of its most resonant expressions.

Even though there is some development in an otherwise repetitive and static state of affairs, the characters remain trapped by their unbearable pain. In Act II, Vladimir tenderly helps Estragon to go to sleep and comforts him when he wakes up in panic. But Vladimir, though kinder to Estragon than in the parallel scene in Act I, still cannot bear to hear about Estragon's nightmare and proposes walking off instead. Estragon's anxious complaints finally drive Vladimir to furious rejection, of the "bellyful of lamentations".

Their suffering is engendered by the act of waiting, which the play sets out to investigate. They are waiting for someone else to intervene and make a new direction possible. When the infant has to wait for too long, the problem of trusting in Godot/God or mother and father can be extreme. Vladimir and Estragon do not hang themselves, and their knowledge that they are waiting is evidence that they are not wholly trapped in the claustrum-type of mental world described by Meltzer (1992). (Estragon speaks of being in "another compartment".) They still wish to meet up with someone outside this hellish place.

The image of birth offered by Pozzo is relevant in this respect: "They give birth astride of a grave, the light gleams an instant, then it's night once more." The brief gleam has not been extinguished, so death has not completely won, despite the dreadful confusion of creation with the grave. The baby is being born momentarily into a world of light (a mother looking at her baby with love is the image suggested), and this possibility has not been entirely destroyed by fear and hatred.

Endgame

Endgame is the bleakest of Beckett's plays. The sense of imprisonment of the characters in their relations with each other and in the physical space they inhabit is almost total. The absolute greyness of the room's interior, added to by the colourless world Clov briefly describes when he peers through the small high window, takes us into a bleached-out world lacking much potential for elements of discrimination and depleted of vitality and the means to sustain life. Dry dog biscuits may be all that remains in the larder, there is no blade of grass in the landscape, a real dog is replaced by an

incomplete toy replica. The appearance of a flea provokes panic
and a determination to exterminate this disturbing sign of life as
speedily as possible. What has happened to humanity?

The setting stirs echoes in our minds of the prison cell, of a
house whose inhabitants have moved away or died—the rags cov-
ering Hamm's face and the dustbin-lids remind one of dust-sheets
over abandoned furniture. In terms of literary associations, Sartre's
Huis Clos and Koestler's *Darkness at Noon* come to mind. If we
attempt to locate this place somewhere in time, might we consider
a place of exile in Stalinist Russia as offering an external analogy to
the internal landscape depicted in the play? There are references to
the barren land, to the steppes, in stark contrast to the Ardennes or
Lake Como—beautiful places known in the past when Nagg and
Nell were alive in the world and had not yet been consigned to
their dustbin-prisons. Now, though so close, they cannot see each
other and can only communicate through speech . . . one might
think of prisoners in their cells tapping or calling through the cell-
walls to establish a link with another live being.

Beckett's awareness of the horrors of Stalinism must have been
growing in the early 1950s in common with intellectuals throughout the West. The Algerian colonial impasse may be another background preoccupation—the master/slave relationship described
by Hegel was powerfully exemplified in the French settlers' relationship to their Arab subjects, and the future of Algeria troubled
all France through this period.

Hamm, in his wheelchair, blind behind his dark spectacles
and unable to walk, is as incapacitated as Nagg and Nell, in a state
of identification with the dead internal objects that these figures
embody. The dustbins are called ashbins, perhaps expressing
Beckett's sense of the deadness they contain: the ashes of a crema-
torium, the ash left after the fire has burnt up all that is combust-
ible.

The relationship between Hamm and Clov is a present-day
version of Hamm's picture of the relationship he has had with his
parents, as we gradually learn. Its circular sado-masochistic structure is at the heart of the state of impasse depicted in the play.
Victim and tormentor fit together in a horribly perfect unchanging
system. Each day is as every other. There is no movement through
time, no change, just repetition. Pleasure has become attached to

the infliction of pain. For example, we can hear the delight in Clov's voice at the idea of inserting the catheter into Hamm. There is awareness of this perversity: "No one that ever lived ever thought so crooked as we."[11] Triumphant glee and sadness vie for expression in this sentence.

Hamm is desperate to assert his omnipotent control—via the whistle, via his position as the master, via his knowledge of the combination that can unlock the larder. He gets into a terrible panic if anything seems to suggest that his control is not absolute: he must be right in the centre of the room in his chair, and obsessional anxiety torments him as he demands adjustments this way and that. He has to occupy the central position, linked in the infantile mind to the nipple that crowns the breast, and he gives access to the breast's contents, like the key to Hamm's larder, because only thus can he inflict the pains of hunger and helplessness on the others. Nell must be told there is no more pap (baby-food). The dread being held at bay is that if Hamm were not himself the controlling tyrant, he would be subject to such tyranny himself. Later in the poignant conversation with Nagg we learn of Hamm's sufferings as a baby: left to cry, ignored by his parents. At first it seems as if at least father was going to respond to baby Hamm's night-time distress, even if mother has shut him out of her mind, but this too then turns out to be a pipe-dream. Hamm's revenge on the parental objects in his mind is what we observe in the play: they are shut away, no food, warmth, comfort, human touch, no possibility of moving (like babies who cannot yet go and find the longed-for person), an endless recreation of the infant's loneliness and the terror of abandonment and death.

This picture only emerges in fragments: Beckett's language brilliantly captures the nature and consequences of the minute splitting of experience that has been used to destroy what has been unbearably painful. The minute fragments defy reconstruction into meaningful shape or narrative. Instead, we have ash, "smithereens", "a bit of all right". Only bits, not wholes. Linked to these processes of destruction via minute splitting are the jokes—a des-

---

[11] Fom *Endgame. In: Samuel Beckett: Complete Dramatic Works* (London: Faber & Faber).

perate effort to create something lively out of the quasi-faecal indeterminate world of fragmented objects. For example, the story of
the tailor and the making of the pair of trousers is an elaborate anal
joke that follows the narrating of the marriage at Lake Como, with
its potential for generative sex, which has been attacked in rage
and envy. If we can laugh enough at the tailor story, we may not
notice the catastrophe that is taking place: instead of a couple
together who might produce a baby, we have a brilliant display of
verbal masturbation. The competitive infantile self can produce
enough shit to drown the oedipal pains that might otherwise have
to be suffered.

The relentless attacks on couples are perhaps the hardest parts
of the text to bear: Nagg and Nell are not allowed to reach to kiss;
they "crashed in their tandem" instead of going somewhere, having a real adventure in the world; nor are they being allowed to
link up in any kind of creative intercourse. Parents and children
suffer a similar fate: Hamm and his mother are not brought together in the night; the destitute father and his young son are not
allowed to be together. The horrible cruelty of the sequence when
this needy child is abandoned at Hamm's command (a brutal instance of identification with the aggressor) is at the root of the
vicious point-scoring between Hamm and Clov: Clov threatens to
leave, in which case Hamm would become the abandoned helpless
starving child, as happens at the end when he is left to die. Most of
the time Hamm and Clov are hand-in-glove in destroying meaning: the panic engendered by the discovery of the flea is the
epitome of this. It must be destroyed, as otherwise "Humanity
might start from there! Oh God." Couples are held in a state of
suspended animation (like Nagg and Nell in their bins), with all
creative contact broken off. The children, represented by Hamm,
are then identified with the deadened depressed objects and cannot move, see, or feel. The sight, hearing, and memory of Nagg and
Nell are failing. Nell dies, and Hamm is also gradually dying. In
psychoanalytic terms, we are observing the consequences of projective identification with destroyed internal objects whose state of
near-death is consequent on their imprisonment in the child's
phantasy. Meltzer's book The Claustrum (Meltzer, 1992) describes
this state of affairs, and the type of claustrum relevant to this text is
very obviously the rubbish-filled mind equated with a bottom.

All this killing of creativity, of links and of awareness of pain has reached a climax in the play because the pain-killers have run out. Awareness of Hamm's psychic state is not bearable for him. There is a poignant reference to the fontanelle, the tender vulnerable spot on the baby's head when the protective skull is not yet fully in place and where even a tiny touch could do great damage. The images of horror in the play, like the child never fetched by its father and left to starve, expose us as watchers to feeling our nerve ends exposed to traumatic shock as we quiver like a baby's still-exposed fontanelle. Beckett's delicacy of mind seems to us important in protecting his audience from being exploited when they are opened up to the levels of psychic pain he is describing.

It is worth noting some of the important features of the reduced world of which Hamm is the tragic ruler. First, it is a deeply boring place: "I love them, the old questions, the old answers." We are in a timeless world of repetition, where deadly familiarity is the most that can be hoped for. There will be no New Year. It is also immobile: there is a conversation about setting off on a journey—"Let's go from here . . . South"—but quickly the idea of going to the sea becomes impossible: the travellers would encounter sharks. The sadism that rules within the prison-room is feared outside it: if Hamm and Clov were to make a dash for freedom, they have no doubt they would become victims in their turn. It is a world overtaken by dirt: filthy handkerchiefs, sex reduced to anality. As Hamm puts it, "we're down in a hole." It is dominated by distorted perception, as in the story of the madman who can only see ashes. It is heartless: helplessness is systemically projected and then mocked. A dog implores for a bone, baby Hamm cries for mother, Clov begs for food. It is deeply uneasy: there is always a suspicion that procreation may creep back in somehow. The small boy, the fleas, are reminders that the upside-down world in which the perverse has triumphed might be challenged by evidence of another reality, however blind to this the protagonists have made themselves. So there is a terrible lack of security. In political parlance, that is why so-called security police are needed so badly. The grandiosity of Hamm's opening speech is perfectly paralleled by the devastation of his last lonely soliloquy.

Psychoanalysis ponders on the meaning of the death instinct and the fear of death in the infantile part of the personality. This play provides an extraordinary tableau of the death instinct triumphant in its characters but of course imagined by its author, whose capacities of mind and language thus represent the continuing struggle of the life instinct to assert its power. It also offers a very moving delineation of our primitive fears of physical deterioration and death. In the dialogue between Hamm and Clov after the shared fantasy about sailing off on a raft is disrupted by the fear of sharks, Hamm questions Clov about his·bodily powers—his eyes, his legs, which Clov says are "bad"—and Hamm's vicious rage builds to a chilling climax.

The dialogue continues with its cruel teasing interchanges replacing the unbearable desolation of helplessness Hamm has described, and a little later the terrible speech in which Hamm tells the story of the man who begged in vain for food. This reveals how the failure to pity, to feel for each other, to sustain life leaves Beckett's characters in an inner world dominated by despair and failed reparation.

Such grief would be felt if the bitter laughter stopped that it would drive men mad. *Endgame* is about an extreme state in which the terror of encountering the reproachful ghosts is defended against by a deadly game that only intensifies the persecution.

Just as Ibsen was probably exploring aspects of himself in *John Gabriel Borkman,* so *Endgame* may in part be seen as a harsh self-exploration of the mind and work of the writer. Hamm is trying to tell a story, and Clov is prompted to ask him about it, to keep it going. Clov is forced to be the feed-man in this bleakest of Beckett's comic routines, with Hamm's reference to "technique" as what keeps him going. Under this parody of narcissistic writer's talk is a deeper story of the malevolent control that the writer may feel he tries to exercise through his mind. We don't really know what has happened and what has been imagined or invented by Hamm. Did a man come pleading, was there a child left to die, how did Clov come to be there at all? All our revels now are ended, Hamm says, when Nell dies, but in fact the scene is more reminiscent of *The Tempest* than of *A Midsummer Night's Dream.* Instead of a beautiful island, Hamm and Clov inhabit a hell-hole in which all sign of procreation and love is hated. Your move, says Hamm, reminding us of the chess game in *The Tempest.* And among the props is a gaff (a pole used to spear fish) serving as a vestigial staff, though this

cannot even move his chair. This writer's mind is filled with omnipotence and hatred of life, killing parents and children alike,
creating characters only in order to control and humiliate them.
But just as the play of language brings some glimmer of hope in
these dramas, so also in *Endgame*, as in *Godot* and in *Happy Days*, a
vestige of life survives, as Clov manages to leave, pushed to escape
perhaps by Mother Pegg's death and his recognition that while he
and Nagg can mourn her, Hamm cannot.

Happy Days

Happy Days is unusual in Beckett's work in having a central female
character. The play is set in blazing light on scorched ground.
Centre-stage is Winnie, buried up to her waist in a mound. At the
back of the mound is her husband, Willie, who spends most of the
time invisible to the audience, hidden in his burrow. This powerful
image takes us straight to the theme of the play. Here is a marriage
in which communication has almost dried up, despite the wonderful haunting eloquence of Winnie. The two are so near, and yet so
far from each other, hopelessly trapped in heart-rending near-iso-
lation. Being characters in a Beckett play, they are committed to
surviving, though with ever-present thoughts of death, represented by the gun in Winnie's bag, and their survival is based on a
residual capacity for thought and feeling, including shafts of brilliant humour. What catastrophe has taken place?

We can consider this at a number of levels. We might see the
landscape as a world in which life has been almost extinguished—
a post-nuclear world. As Winnie remarks, "flesh melts at so many
degrees".[12] There are also powerful echoes of seaside narcissistic
loneliness. Winnie's parasol-umbrella evokes a beach scene, her
all-important bag is like a beach bag full of the necessary equip-
ment to maintain her glamour while she cooks in the sun. As the
bell rings to wake her for the day, we might think of an old people's
home, with the partially helpless inhabitants hanging on desper-

---

[12] From *Happy Days*. In: *Samuel Beckett: Complete Dramatic Works* (London:
Faber & Faber).

ately to the remnants of their old selves, waiting endlessly for something to happen that will provide them with a sense of being persons who mean something to someone else. Winnie remembers, perhaps enviously, that Willie has a marvellous gift in being able to sleep through the bell, not wake up to the anxieties about deterioration with which she struggles as she cleans her teeth, does her hair, reconstructs her face, and puts on her hat, ready to face the world. The intense light is holy but also hellish. There is something it is very important to see, but it is truly terrifying to do so. Winnie's pain is clearly in her mind, and the hellishly bright light makes her feel in need of medicine to deal with her loss of spirits. She empties the bottle, and the audience feels the anxiety of how she will be able to endure her position without such magic potions.

Winnie's attempt to order things for herself is in counterpoint with her flow of disordered recollections. The "happy day" she would like to have is undermined by thoughts of hogs—castrated male swine, as Beckett reminds us in due course. A sexual catastrophe has taken place. The play explores this in Winnie's memories and in the present relationship between Winnie and Willie.

The picture of the woman who is sinking further into the dried-up ground despite repeated appeals for help to an impotent husband brings to mind an infant's image of desolation—the mound–breast is not alive with the intercourse of mother and father but is, instead, a place where parental figures cannot reach each other and are increasingly weakened by this failure of restorative contact. The bell that wakens Winnie might then be linked to her maternal preoccupation with an infant who needs to be attended to—an external infant calling her to provide maternal care, or an infantile part of herself still holding on to life (in contrast to Willie's marvellous gift for ignoring the demands of living) and calling her to attend to the state of her mind and body, an infant who refuses to lie down and die, as she refuses to pull the trigger on herself. Winnie longs for help—to be seen, to be heard, to be acknowledged, as she tries to sustain life—but her partner is in a much more deteriorated state. Willie spends most of his life stuck up the backside of the mound. His predominantly anal preoccupation interferes massively with his capacity to communicate with Winnie. Pornographic postcards, his snot, titbits from the newspaper occupy his mind. He reads out advertisements—"Opening for a smart youth", "Wanted, bright boy", which refer both to homo-sexual invitation and to the child that Winnie, and perhaps he too, may have wanted but could not create. "Lift up your eyes and see me", she says. Such Biblical references are frequent in Beckett and underline the possibility of salvation that human relationship offers us, but which can also be refused. When an emmet (an ant) and eggs are noticed by Winnie, evidence that life remains in mother earth, Willie's brilliant joke about "formication" brings the couple together in laughter, and Winnie finds a moment of joy in Willie's mirth.

But this joke simultaneously reminds us that all sex is for him illicit, dirty, a subject for mocking laughter. The text suggests that Willie's impotence and retreat to masturbatory preoccupations may be rooted in the unbearable realization of his incapacity to make a difference to her. In the play, we are a long way down the line, faced with ageing and loss of faculties and hope, but the couple's history seems to turn, in part, on the significance of the little girl, Mildred, of whom Winnie speaks. One aspect of what we learn about Mildred suggests that she represents Winnie's terrified frigidity, the part of herself unable to engage in mutual sexual exploration, the woman Willie could not reach.

Beckett's imprisoned Winnie, who used to have the use of her legs and who, in the course of the play, loses the use of her arms and any vestige of bodily freedom, is an image of a mother cut off from father. The problem is "visible flesh", says Winnie, and we can thus suggest that the son/sun has been enraged by a vision of intercourse. Infantile vengeance is represented by the burning up of mother and father and the remorseless gazing at this vision. The exposure of their sexuality is ruthless and full of hate towards father. The claim made from this hostile child-view is that father is a dirty bugger when he enters mother. Mother is presented as narcissistically preoccupied but is shown in a more tender light because her attention to herself is clearly seen as replacing the love she craves. Winnie is still wonderfully beautiful in the play, and the infantile disaster confronting us is perhaps related to that described by Meltzer as a potential response to the baby's encounter with mother's beauty. The too-bright light that is so hard to bear (or to forget once one has seen the play) is the infant's experience of being completely overwhelmed by too brilliant a vision. The audience has to struggle with this intense brightness and its overtones of exposure, helplessness, and absence of protection (not even shade is available). There is shock in the realization that such theatre depends on the writer's and actors' capacity to modulate the impact of intimate exposure.

In the second act, the childhood background of Winnie's distress is probed further. As her need for contact with another person to sustain her conviction in her own existence is heightened (a neat reversal of Descartes's axiom) a troubling figure reappears in her thoughts. Charlie, the Reverend Dr Carlos Hunter, has emerged from Willie's newspaper, "found dead in a tub". Charlie the priest is remembered as a seductive figure. Winnie's anxiety increases, and she speaks of the earth losing its atmosphere—a phrase encompassing post-nuclear devastation, a sense of the loss of liveliness and hope, and a horrible glimpse of a world disconnected from the universal order of things. Beckett's talent for sketching endless nightmares in a phrase is extraordinary. Her thoughts wander to the Browning gun, turned into her pet, the Brownie. "Happy days" are those when there are sounds to interrupt her monologue.

Winnie begins to tell the story of Mildred, a little girl who explored forbidden territories in the middle of the night, undressing her beautiful doll beneath the table and then terrified by a mouse running up her leg. Mildred, perhaps primarily a little-girl aspect of Winnie, is curious about the mysteries of mother's body and horrified to discover that it is not all hers to possess. Is the mouse perhaps a perception of father's penis, which moves between mother's thighs, or of the baby they might make in intercourse? The awareness of parental sexuality bursts into Mildred's mind in an unbearable way; she screams and screams, and perhaps we can sense that the infantile disaster of the too-bright maternal breast is re-evoked and intensified by the later oedipal encounter. Winnie goes on to speak of the bitter pain of her marriage. Willie had seemed a source of hope—his love might pull her out of the fragile retreat in which she was perhaps already stuck, but Winnie is herself deeply imprisoned inside objects pictured in ways that make development, movement, and growth almost impossible. Winnie's Willie is a denigrated penis that cannot rescue her. For Willie, the failure of the marriage involves a despairing retreat; for

238 MIRROR TO NATURE

Winnie, the repetition of a degraded version of sexuality consequent on the shocked withdrawal from encountering the overwhelming unknown. At the play's close, there is an acutely painful
restatement of the impasse: Willie emerges from his hole, all
dressed up for a dance, and murmurs "Win" as he scrabbles unsuc-
cessfully across the mound towards her, only to slip back. Winnie
sings a dance-hall lyric about love, and they look at each other and
smile. Their humanity remains poignantly alive as they each acknowledge that this moment of contact sustains their existence.
Their infantile anxieties have not been surmounted and their sense
of damage is huge, but the characters share with their audience the
emotional power of the truth of their lives. They do not believe in
the romantic dream, but they understand why they cling to it.

In this play Beckett's despair about the human condition is
modified not only by the extraordinary wit and intelligence of the
text but also by the pity and understanding of the characters for
each other.

Beckett's deep sympathy is evident in his creation of a woman
who is holding together the remnants of her existence. She has, we
infer, lived by a code that required her to take most of the responsibility for her and her husband's life, with little love or comfort
from him. Her sense of herself depends on her sense of attractiveness, which she has to sustain in the absence of anyone who will,
for most of the time, acknowledge it. What courage and fortitude is
required for someone to survive in so isolated a situation!

The resonance of the play arises from the fact that its dramatized excess of deprivation and loss, which seems to be fast approaching a state of living death, evokes more recognizable and
ordinary human pain. As we have mentioned, among these are the
catastrophes of war, the vulnerability of age and sickness, a callous
public world in which others are regarded as if they were despised
objects in a freak-show. The intensity of the play comes from its
juxtaposition of Winnie's love of life, which she evokes intensely in
her audience, and of the psychic pain that she bravely suffers, with
the extremity and enormity of her plight. The play has the quality
of a homage towards a maternal object—everyone's maternal object—who has suffered so much unrecognized and uncomplaining
pain.

CHAPTER ELEVEN

Psychic spaces
in Harold Pinter's work

Our chapter on Beckett drew attention to the implicit back-ground of violence and social devastation in his work. We made reference to critics who have suggested that a major challenge to writers of the post-war period has been to explore the meaning of the extreme historical events of the twentieth century and their dire implications for human lives.

Harold Pinter's work occupies a contiguous space. His friendship with Beckett, and his admiration for his work, suggests that he clearly recognized this. In post-war Britain, the dominant middle-class culture had to absorb not only the magnitude of these ter-rorizing facts, but also the entry into its cultural space of many new social experiences and voices. Writers, film-makers, actors, and critics from the working class began to obtain a hearing for their work, sometimes in the context of an explicitly political chal-lenge to the "establishment", as it came to be called. Plays, films, and novels came to feature working-class heroes and milieux in a new way.

Pinter's work belongs within this broader trend, but in a highly individual and in some ways dissident way. He brought together in his early plays, we might say, both the extremity of experience of this post-war, cold-war era and the marginal social subjects hitherto little represented in the theatre. Many writers articulated their antagonism to the established cultural elites in explicit passages in their novels and plays, or indeed organized their whole action as its expression—John Osborne and Kingsley Amis are examples. Others, like Lindsay Anderson, wrote manifestos to explain the subject matter and form of their work (usually a version of stylistic realism) in political terms.

Pinter would have none of this. He declined to provide explanatory commentary or interpretation of his plays in any terms that belonged outside the work itself. "I start off with people, who come into a particular situation. I certainly don't write from any kind of abstract idea. And I wouldn't know a symbol if I saw one" (Pinter, 1991). Pinter set out to create an experience for his audiences in the theatre, and he did not wish to dilute or contain this experience within any frame of rational explanation. This would only have the effect, he thought, of keeping the audience at a distance from what the play had to offer them. This is the exact opposite of the strategy of George Bernard Shaw, whose Prefaces usually set out to explain and amplify the ideas that his plays sought to animate. In this refusal of commentary on his work Pinter is, of course, close to Beckett.[1]

The social world that Pinter sought to represent bore little or no relation to that articulated by more politically committed dramatists. Conventionally left-wing writers tended to represent working-class people as heroes or victims, thus giving class struggles a cultural voice. The principal character of Pinter's first successful play, *The Caretaker*, is, however, a vagrant who has more or less fallen out of society. The play displays his extreme vulnerability, but also his own chronic difficulties in sustaining any viable hu-

---

[1] Whatever Pinter may have thought about the value of commentary, there has been a great deal of writing about his work. Among valuable contributions are Martin Esslin, *Pinter the Playwright* (6th edition, 2000); Michael Billington, *Life and Work of Harold Pinter* (1996); Peter Raby (Ed.), *The Cambridge Companion to Harold Pinter* (2001); and earlier collections of critical essays edited by Lois Gordon (1990), Michael Scott (1986), and Arthur Ganz (1972). Pinter's *Various Voices: Prose, Poetry, Politics 1948–1998* (1998) describes his own approach to play writing.

man relationships. He is shown to be in a sense responsible for, as well as undoubtedly the victim of, his fate.

Many of Pinter's radical contemporaries were at pains to elaborate their identification with their "roots" (*Roots* was, of course, the title of one of Arnold Wesker's plays) and to represent themselves as the articulate voices of a hitherto unrecognized way of life and its values. Richard Hoggart and Raymond Williams are examples of this chosen "representative" function from the field of cultural and social criticism. It is crucial to Pinter's work that he did not see himself as representing any shared collective experience. Indeed, it seems to have been his own experience of dissociation from his location of origin and of having found a highly personal way of engaging with the realities of class that informs his work.

Pinter has described, though at no great length, his upbringing in Hackney as the child of a Jewish family—his father was a tailor. During the war he was evacuated from home twice—an experience he referred to as painful and disorienting. He describes his neighbourhood as having been full of threats, both immediately to himself—for example, the risk of being beaten up by young men if they identified him as Jewish—and more generally in the context of the anti-Semitic street campaigning of the Fascist Mosley in the East End, and in the wider recent context of the war and the mass murder of the Jews. One can see signs of Pinteresque exaggeration in these descriptions, but there is nevertheless no reason to doubt their essential truthfulness. One can see his work, as Stuart Hall (1965) pointed out early on, as a disturbing footnote to Young and Willmott's *Family and Kinship in East London* (1957).[2] Where Young and Willmott wrote of the cosy matriarchal *Gemeinschaft* of Bethnal Green (the district of east London adjacent to Pinter's Hackney), Pinter populates his work with unstable, violent, and vulnerable individuals some of whom who are identifiable as gangsters, pimps, and prostitutes.

While a radical political tradition liked to attribute to the working class the reassuring virtues of collective solidarity, another and more widely shared attitude was to regard the lower orders with a mixture of fear and fascination. Here was the dangerous "other" of

---

[2] Hall, writing in *Encore* in 1965, is quoted by John Stokes in Raby (2001, p. 32).

the world of middle-class respectability—it was perceived as more violent, more frightening, more sexual, and also more exciting than "conventional" society. Popular culture drew much of its vitality from representation of this "other" world, for example in such genres as gangster and crime movies and novels. In the 1950s and early 1960s prostitution was highly visible on the London streets, gangsters like the Kray twins became celebrities, and association by both a government minister and a Russian spy with Christine Keeler—like Mandy Rice-Davies an object of nation-wide sexual fascination—destroyed the career of the minister and even put in doubt the survival of the government of the day. While "sleaze" in the latter years of the Conservative government of the 1990s was largely a matter of money, its equivalent in the 1960s was a much more sexual affair. Appropriately, the minister concerned in that scandal sought redemption by undertaking good works in the East End. Films like Nicholas Roeg's *Performance,* in which Mick Jagger starred, powerfully evoked this underworld, which later figured in *The Long Good Friday* and *Mona Lisa.* Such films were more direct and powerful than most of their British predecessors in evoking an atmosphere of violent excitement, cruelty, and terror.

Pinter's plays, in particular *The Birthday Party* and *The Home-coming,* brought the fascination with criminality and violence that gave popular culture some of its vitality into the English theatre, from which hitherto it had been mainly absent. Pinter succeeded in wholly subverting the conventions of "drawing-room comedies", noted for their absence of intense feeling or disturbance, and bringing new dimensions to domestic ceremonies like tea parties or to the everyday event of the arrival of an unexpected visitor. In the early part of his career, Pinter had acted in much of the standard repertory in provincial repertory theatre. He was thus able to work as a playwright to transform genres that he already knew from within as a performer. While radical cultural critics wrote polemics that denounced the complacency of middle-class dramatic conventions, Pinter wrote plays that turned these inside out.

Pinter's relationship as outsider to the established cultural world was most crucially expressed through the distinctive speech-patterns of his plays and the idiosyncratic use of language of nearly all of his characters. What is distinctive about this is not so much what it includes—although his language is intermittently violent and extreme, as befits the states of mind of the characters who speak it—as what it excludes. What is invariably lacking is a consistent capacity on the part of any of his characters to keep powerful and unsettling feelings out of their conversation. Whatever they are saying, however apparently factually based their narratives or articulate their points of view, sooner or later the audience becomes aware that what is being said is more than the character himself or herself fully understands or intends to give away. Characters unsettle each other, by *non sequiturs* and apparently random digressions. Speeches seem sometimes to proceed by free association, reflecting the speaker's stream of consciousness but oddly related to what seemed the initial point. Yet characters seem to be themselves unaware of any oddity in what they are saying: with each speech, they encounter their own thoughts and feelings as if for the first time. Although they seem frequently to be speaking under the pressure of an "internal script", which forces all kinds of unexpected thoughts and associations to the surface, they have no awareness or memory that such an internal script exists. Indeed, clear and consistent memory, and a habit of self-reflection, are just what Pinter's characters markedly lack. This is why their identities appear to be so unstable. It is the fact that his characters are always liable to be surprised by their own thoughts as these are evoked by their contact with each other that make his plays such distinctively "live" and authentic experiences for actors and audiences.

Pinter has pointed out that he never went to university. He dropped out of RADA, having found it socially remote from his own experience, although he later trained at the Central School of Speech and Drama. His attachment to the theatre, and also to cinema, seems to be rooted in his fascination with and knowledge of their constituent crafts. Abstract discussion of these matters interests him scarcely at all. His relationship to other writers is intense but highly individual. There are memorable stories of his walking around Hackney in his youth with his English teacher, reciting passages from Webster to passing trolleybuses, and of his meetings with Beckett in Paris. He seems characteristically to relate to other writers from the inside of a writerly community, and never as a commentator or critic. He has had for example an intense and craftsmanlike relationship to a number of writers through his work on adaptations and screenplays, including one for Proust's *À la*

Recherche du Temps Perdu. It will not do to underestimate in any way the depth of Pinter's understanding of those writers who are most important to him, who include Kafka and Beckett.

What Pinter has chosen to avoid is to be assimilated into the conventional routines of discursive writing with its disciplines of logic, respect for fact, and impartiality of tone. These "academic" codes require above all that writers and speakers learn to keep their own feelings out of their subject matter, until such time as they can introduce them as a particular additional dimension, as evaluation or grounded expression of opinion. Pinter never seems to have wanted to engage with such impersonal codes. It is possible that he feared that if he started down that road, he would lose contact with his own voice and his capacity to imagine voices and states of mind for his characters. This lifelong insistence on working in "creative" and not "critical" or discursive modes has been a distinguishing feature of his writing. It has given him the capacity to recognize beneath the surfaces of formal language unconscious currents that are liable to disturb. Another of his telling devices has been the capacity he gives to socially lowly or marginal characters, like Mick in *The Caretaker*, to set off on astonishing flights of language, all the more unsettling because their content—such as a recital of the bus-routes of London—is so bizarre. Pinter sometimes infuses everyday forms of speech—for which, as critics have pointed out, he has a remarkable ear[3]—with his own virtuosity with language. He is able at the same time to both capture and transform these idioms with astonishing effects.

For the last two decades Pinter been a highly committed political figure, not only in public declarations about many issues, but also in the subject-matter of several of his plays, which are more or less directly about political violence and torture. This is in marked contrast to his earlier refusal to assign or discuss any exterior "meaning" to his work, political or otherwise. Retrospectively, it is perhaps possible to see the lines of linkage in his work in a different

---

[3] When one reads certain verbatim transcripts of life histories, which have been delivered with few interruptions or promptings from interviewers, one sees how close Pinter is to everyday rhythms of speech, especially in his capture of disjointedness and the pressure of emotion on thought.

way. McCann and Goldberg, the thugs who come to take Stanley away in *The Birthday Party*, might now be interpreted with hindsight as precursors of political terror, even if for reasons of dramatic form they were not identified as such. So short was the actual interval between the Nazis and the Latin American dictatorships of the 1970s, which aroused such strong feelings of moral outrage and human sympathy in Pinter, that it might seem odd that this connection was not spotted in the first place.

It is, however, possible that the fundamental thrust of Pinter's imagination was going in a different direction. It seems to us that Pinter became engaged early in his work in exploring and developing a particular "structure of feeling", in which sado-masochistic states of mind and their particular excitements and anxieties loomed large. His plays repeatedly explored this structure of feeling. The effects on audiences were exhilarating—something was certainly being done in British theatre for the first time, and what was being done was bringing into the theatre new areas of feeling, and by implication new kinds of awareness of social and personal realities.

Perhaps the realization that the scenes of emotional violence and abuse that his plays were representing had a contemporary political reference came later, as a kind of political awakening. Possibly it was at this point that Pinter himself came to recognize that his preoccupations also had a political context and origin in the memories of his early life, both conscious and unconscious.

The terror represented by McCann and Goldberg in *The Birthday Party* is not very distant from the more explicit kinds of political terror of later plays, such as *The New World Order*, *The Mountain People*, or *Ashes to Ashes*. This evident equivalence—the crystallization in his plays of what might be thought of as the essence of the relationship between the perpetrator of violence and his victim—has led Pinter to his forceful protests against political terror and collusion with it. It is a paradox that the writer who, in the 1950s and 1960s, seemed to be the least politically committed and outspoken has become one of the most politically engaged in recent decades.

Little has changed in the structure of the plays themselves, and this continuity derives from aspects of Pinter's underlying vision.

The emotional environment of plays such as *The Birthday Party* or *The Homecoming* is a closed one in which the characters are wholly trapped or by which they are destroyed. These plays are based on the creation of a paranoid-schizoid atmosphere, from which few if any characters can escape. Conscious and unconscious hatred and envy are pervasive, and undermine such attempts as are made to make different kinds of relationship. In *Betrayal*, a later play, it becomes clear, in similar vein, that the chief excitement of the betrayals of the marital relationships lies in the acts of betrayals themselves, in the victorious position in which they appear to place lovers over betrayed husbands and wives. The pleasure that the lovers take in being with each other seems to have been shallow and insignificant compared with the pleasures of shutting the third person out.

The location of paranoid-schizoid structures of feeling in a political context may have the effect of putting it at some distance, even though what is intended, and achieved, is to enable audiences to experience its horrors. Pinter clearly intends his audiences to learn from their unwilling identification with the torturers as well as their victims—it is this that gives these plays their disturbing force. In these dramas of terror there seems to be no point in seeking a way out, and change is not possible. Protest against the torturers, driving them from the face of the earth, seems the only adequate response to the reality represented, and this, of course, is what Pinter has come to demand in his public advocacy.

But, of course, Pinter's worlds were never merely representations of external reality. They are at the same time projections of an internal reality. What becomes lost in the politicized version of this structure of feeling is that it is in part internal in its origins and logic, so that if we become trapped within it, this becomes a fact about ourselves as much as about the world. Sartre's play *Huis Clos*, in which "hell is other people", was an earlier exemplar of this insight. (Existentialist writing was one of the early formative influences on Pinter, as on many writers formed in the early postwar period.)

To respond adequately to violence and torture at a political level, it is necessary to do more than denounce it. It is important to seek to understand the states of mind involved, to recognize the repressed and unbearable pain of the perpetrator as well as of the victim. The evenly given compassion and sympathy that character-izes the work of Chekhov and Beckett is essential if the theatre is to offer possibilities for emotional transformation. Pinter has done more than any dramatist to represent on the stage these extreme states of mind, in ways that engage and disturb audiences, and this has been a major contribution. There may be some question, however, about the addictive quality of these sado-masochistic relationships between master and victim. In the end, perhaps, these plays convey an underlying despair about the possibilities of escape.

The Birthday Party

When this play was first produced (in 1958), it was not a success, and it is small wonder that so disturbing a representation of the psychological disintegration of a human being should have deeply upset audiences. It is, however, a brilliant dramatic account of events we can understand as happening within or between peo-ple—that is, one can think of the characters both as aspects or fragments in personified form of one man's internal world and as an encounter between a group of damaged characters, each with their own pre-history. We argue that it is the fit Pinter achieves between the structure of the tormented inner world of Stanley and the cast of individuals assembled within the house for the birthday party that gives the play its compelling coherence.

The play opens with a glimpse of the childish marriage be-tween Meg and Petey, a couple in their sixties. Their relationship is made up of Meg's girlish dependency and Petey's childish link to her as a maternal figure who provides oral gratification. She speaks like a little girl trying to please Daddy, playing at being grown-up and begging for titbits of knowledge about the great world outside the kitchen. Petey is reading the paper, and she says: "Will you tell me when you come to something good?" He informs her, "Someone's just had a baby", and she responds: "My, oh, they haven't! Who?"

PETEY: Some girl.
MEG: Who, Petey, who?
PETEY: I don't think you'd know her.
MEG: What's her name?
PETEY: Lady Mary Splatt.

[Act I, p. 11][4]

This crude absurdity suggests the failure of this couple to achieve any adult sexual link: the name implies that a baby is pretty much equivalent to a bit of shit. In their conversation, each misses the adult potential of the other, and they thus remain stuck in an infantilized state. The comic and tragic nature of their impasse is conveyed with economy—after Petey has consumed the cornflakes Meg offers, she excitedly announces that she has got something else for his breakfast. This turns out to be fried bread, and the audience squirm with the awareness that this is not a proper dish: it should be the extra to the seaside boarding-house English cooked breakfast, not its sole feature. Of course Pinter is drawing on his experience of pinched digs during his repertory years as an actor, but he is also pointing out that this is not a solid meal, only a gesture towards one. Later Stan's derogatory abuse of her unappealing food amplifies this point.

Petey casually mentions that two men he met on the beach where he works as a deckchair attendant have asked for a room—they are going to call today. This intrusion into the Meg–Petey–Stanley household seems mysterious, but before they arrive we learn more of Meg's relationship to Stanley, their long-term lodger. He is a man in his late thirties, in retreat from the world outside, as she is. Together they are playing out an oedipal entanglement—she announces she will "wake that boy", and calls up flirtatiously, "I'm coming to get you", as a mother might to a small child who needs hurrying out of bed. Does Stan represent the son she and Petey failed to have? Over the living-room table they squabble excitedly, and the sexual edge is repeatedly visible. Stan threatens to go off to get a decent breakfast at a "smart hotel on the front", but when asked if the fried bread was nice, replies: "Succulent." Meg hears

---

[4] Extracts from *The Birthday Party* from H. Pinter, *The Birthday Party and Other Plays* (London: Methuen, 1960). Reproduced by permission of Faber & Faber Ltd.

this as a sexual reference (out of ignorance and simultaneous grasp of Stanley's underlying meaning) and their mutually provocative banter is only punctured by Stanley's distaste for the stewed tea and Meg's disorganized efforts to tidy up. She is playing mother to his tyrant son, but the mothering isn't up to much, his own sexual energy is depleted, and the confusion overwhelms and disgusts him.

> STAN: And it isn't your place to come into a man's bedroom and—
> wake him up. . . . I can't drink this muck.
>
> [Act I, p. 19]

Meg gets her own back by mentioning the two gentlemen expected, arousing Stan's fear and jealousy. He tries to puff himself up, boasting of the job as pianist in a nightclub in Berlin he is "considering at the moment", but this quickly collapses in memories of the concert he played at to which his father did not come. Stanley shrinks to his current status as weak man, in retreat from a world he could not manage or make sense of and then attempts a further reversal by threatening Meg that "they" are coming with a wheelbarrow. Who are "they", and who are they coming for? Meg and Stanley are both fearful of the disruption of their protected enclave, and we are filled as readers with visions of what they are fleeing from. Are they both in flight from a past within a mental hospital? What authorities are they so fearful of?

The arrival of Lulu, a girl in her twenties, reveals the extent of Stanley's retreat from the world. She proposes letting in some fresh air (a metaphorical necessity in the infantile and markedly anal atmosphere of the Meg–Stanley relationship) and suggests a walk and a picnic. Stan's despairing refusal of this offer of real life makes it clear how desperate things are. She is the girl he could love but won't stir for.

> STAN: How would you like to go away with me?
> LULU: Where.
> STAN: Nowhere. Still, we could go.
> LULU: But where could we go?
> STAN: Nowhere. There's nowhere to go. So we could just go. It
> wouldn't matter.
> LULU: We might as well stay here.
> STAN: No, it's no good here.
> LULU: Well, where else is there?

STAN: Nowhere.

. . . . . .

LULU: So you're not coming out for a walk?

STAN: I can't at the moment.

LULU: You're a bit of a washout, aren't you?

[Act I, pp. 17–18]

After their devastating exchange, the two visitors arrived—a sinister couple, Goldberg and McCann. They talk while Stanley is in the back garden. Goldberg is an assertive talker, and McCann supposedly his assistant. Who are they? What is their "mission", and who sent them? There is a Kafkaesque description of their task when McCann seeks information about the job.

> GOLDBERG: The main issue is a singular issue and quite distinct from your previous work. Certain elements, however, might well approximate in points of procedure to some of your other activities. All is dependent on the attitude of our subject. At all events, McCann, I can assure you that an assignment will be carried out and the mission accomplished with no excessive aggravation to you or myself. Satisfied?
>
> McCANN: Sure. Thank you, Nat.

[Act I, p. 32]

Thus we learn that their subject, whoever that may be, is to suffer while they are to be cocooned within a righteous bureaucratic rationalization of cruelty. The sense of threat is palpable.

Meg arrives and offers them the information that today is Stanley's birthday, and a "party" can be planned for him, however unwilling he proves to be. The two arrivals run rings around Meg, combining seductiveness with arrogant manipulation. She is the excited little girl, looking forward to the party for which they have a different agenda. When she tells Stanley about them, his anxiety is roused. The tension is intensified as Meg gives Stanley his birthday present—a toy drum, to replace the piano he no longer plays. As Stanley is constrained to play the part of the grateful child and put it around his neck, he flips and becomes openly panic-stricken. Meg's "dismay" (Pinter's stage directions) conveys her unreadiness and incapacity when faced with the loss of control the drum evokes. As Stanley beats it wildly at the close of Act I, what are we hearing? The drumbeat presaging war? Or execution? Terror stalks the stage.

Act II opens with Stanley attempting to join up with McCann in fake bonhomie, as if a pairing could be established that would protect him. There is suggestive talk of Maidenhead, which they are both supposed to be familiar with, and of the delights of Ireland (McCann is Irish), but the manic flow collapses gradually as Stanley's sense of persecution breaks out:

> STANLEY: Where the hell are they? Why don't they come in? What are they doing out there?
>
> [Act II, p. 44]

Goldberg and Petey are in the garden talking, and they represent for Stanley the threat to the inside-the-house takeover he has been engaged in—the possessive and demanding relationship with Meg, which he believes he will be accused of by Father (Petey) made hostile by alliance with the threatening Goldberg, who has arrived in a very authoritative mode. "Don't call me sir", he says desperately to McCann. He had been masquerading as "sir", the important chap around the house, and he now dreads being revealed as an impostor.

"You want to steady yourself", advises McCann, and Stanley goes on to reveal that the external-world counterpart of the current situation in the house is some prior betrayal he was engaged in for which he believes the visitors have come to arraign him. A gangland scene is suggested, with the revenging East End hoodlums, with their neo-Nazi style, in pursuit.

When Goldberg comes in, a scene of bullying unfolds in which Stanley is reduced to catatonic terror and confusion. He loses all grip, and his glasses are taken by McCann, who plays hard man and echo to Goldberg's mad-making eloquence. The accusations are of his driving people mad, betraying "the organization", his bride left waiting on the porch, his father and mother betrayed (by his changing his name). Goldberg summarizes the vicious verbal assault thus:

> GOLDBERG: You're dead. You can't live, you can't think, you can't love. You're dead. You're a plague gone bad. There's no juice in you. You're nothing but an odour!
>
> [Act II, p. 55]

We are in a nightmare world of impossible-to-answer accusations, confusion, and bombardment. Stanley's terrifying experience is of a persecutory self-accusatory voice that has been keeping a tally of all his failings from the beginning of time becoming externalized in the villainous pair. He is, as they announce, Judas, the betrayer incarnate, responsible for the destruction of the principles of loyalty and love. Crazed voices in the mind, the schizophrenic experience of one's mind being possessed, is before us on the stage. Stanley's glasses, removed in a threatening fashion (and later broken), represent his frail link to reality and the possibility of being able to have a mind of his own, a way of seeing that can withstand the psychic assault of this ruthless superego.

When Meg and Lulu arrive for the party, Stanley's grossly disturbed state is not immediately obvious to them, as Goldberg and McCann confuse things further by putting on a display of apparently "normal" social behaviour. Meg is invited to toast Stanley and reveals her love for him as surrogate child, to the accompaniment of Goldberg's loud laughter. The attack by the two intruders on the evidence of Stanley's capacity to inspire affection in Meg and Lulu is shocking in its intensity. In increasingly drunken games, Stanley is provoked to such a degree of jealous rage and confusion as the two women become excited by the seductive advances of the visitors that we see him first threaten to strangle Meg and later rape Lulu. He has become the beast that his persecutors accuse him of being.

This breakdown—the forcible breaking apart of his precarious grasp on himself—is shown also to permit Goldberg and McCann, whose own unstable relationship has more than once threatened their pseudo-unity—for example, in the many jibes about Goldberg's Jewishness—to sustain their position. With Stanley subdued by a combination of emotional assault and physical manhandling, they can stay on top and avoid being too troubled by their own conflict.

The final disaster for Stanley is that Petey's defence of him is impotent in the face of the omniscient intruders. Petey is aware of Stanley's breakdown, and he has the idea of a doctor being needed—but Goldberg has got there first with the plan to "take him to see Monty". We are left to wonder whether Monty is a nasty psychiatrist or the gang-boss, but in no doubt that no good will come of it. Petey as father, the one who has some connection with a real outside world of the town, a job, the beach, people who he plays chess with, is unable to challenge the ascendancy of the perverse pseudo-normality that the intruders represent. The link between inside and outside (inner and outer space and internal and external reality as a whole) has broken down, and this is the state of affairs the play depicts. There is no news in Petey's newspaper that can penetrate and enliven the timeless state of being that has taken over in the household. He has retreated to chess as a way of escaping from his lifeless relationship with Meg, and yet he has not quite given up. Just as Lulu wants to invite Stanley to go for a walk and is convinced that a walk and fresh air would do him some good, so Petey retains a dim sense of what is needed.

Michael Billington in his discussion of the play (Billington, 1996, p. 79), emphasizes Petey's final statement to Stanley ("Stan, don't let them tell you what to do.") as critical to Pinter's vision. He suggests that this rebellious and critical spirit is what has inspired much of Petey's anti-authoritarian beliefs. However, Petey's strength is limited, and he cannot take command within his own house, just as he has been unable to battle with Meg's wish to be "the belle of the ball" for Stanley or the visitors because of the depth of her unconscious disappointment and anger. So Stanley is kidnapped by his persecutory accusers, and there is no protective figure to intervene effectively. The passive collusion with the fascist torment and degradation is first seen in Stanley's collapse—the terror and shame are too much, and the evasion of the guilt he fears to encounter weakens his resistance fatally. Petey's feebleness is an echo of this.

Lulu is not rendered silent and does denounce Goldberg, with whom she has spent the night after Stanley's sexual attack on her. She still has her head and perceives the way in which their sexual activities were intended to make her feel used and dirtied, to be a receptacle for Goldberg's hatred of human feeling. She, too, is a victim, but one who can leave, saying:

LULU: I've seen everything that's happened. I know what's going on. I've got a pretty shrewd idea.

[Act II, p. 85]

Just as she arrived from the outside, inviting Stanley to join her out there, so she has somewhere to go to that is not dominated by the horrible events of the night. Although infantile modes of thought and feeling—and, in particular, acute persecutory dread—dominate the atmosphere, Lulu escapes. It is no doubt a troubling irony in Pinter's choice of name that Wedekind's play *Lulu* tells the story of a young woman who cannot escape her self-destructive sexual destiny. Pinter returns to this theme in a later play, *The Homecoming*.

The Caretaker

Caretakers are objects of ambivalence in the real world—often depended on, but mistrusted—and this social fact gives the play's title some of its ironic punch. None of the three characters in *The Caretaker* (1960) has much capacity to take care even of themselves, though they seek alliances with each other that might improve their deteriorated state. The dilapidated house for which a caretaker might be sought is the external representation of the littered, fragmented, and punctured inner space that they all uneasily inhabit. In this, his most continuously successful play, Pinter is framing the action in a space that has both internal and external meaning, and allowing his characters to define themselves with reference to the one room from which they come and go throughout the play. Who owns the space, who can enjoy the immensely limited but nonetheless valued protection from the frightening world outside that it provides, is the crux.

The powerful opening shows Mick sitting alone in the room and gazing around at its contents. A heavy silence is interrupted by the sound of a banging door and the sound of voices: Mick gets up and glides out silently. Aston and Davies, the elderly tramp, arrive. When Aston invites Davies to sit down, he has to pull a chair from a heaped-up pile of assorted debris in order for there to be anywhere to sit. The idea of there being no place to sit, no hope of getting a rest from a state of homeless wandering, is evoked. We are in a room intended to provide domestic comfort, which in fact threatens to deprive its inhabitants of any sense of finding a place for themselves. It soon becomes clear why this is so—Davies complains of not finding anywhere to sit in the place he was working in:

DAVIES: Ten minutes off for tea break in the middle of the night in that place and I couldn't find a seat, not one. All them Greeks had it, Poles, Greeks, Blacks, the lot of them, all them aliens had it. . . .

[Act I, p. 88][5]

Davies's world has been invaded by "aliens", the unfamiliar and hated immigrant arrivals, linked in his mind to a picture of hordes of invading greedy rivals, who take up the space and resources that he believes should be his—a grievance-laden image of a man still trapped in a world in which the new arrivals are equated with new babies stealing away mother's attention. The mother-country is felt to have been taken over by denigrated, hated, and feared rivals. When Aston explains where the lavatory is, Davies's panic resurfaces—

DAVIES: You don't share it, do you?
ASTON: What?
DAVIES: I mean you don't share the toilet with them Blacks, do you?
ASTON: They live next door.
DAVIES: They don't come in.

[Act I, p. 88]

Even though Davies has been invited in by Aston in a friendly spirit and is receiving a warm welcome (cigarettes, offers of a bed, cash, and time to "get himself fixed up"), his conviction is that that this haven of respite will be swiftly shattered by the necessity to share space with others. There is no proper boundary between internal space, a mind in which his fantasies of persecution continuously threaten to engulf him, and external space, the house whose separateness from other houses is not believed in. His awful fear of not being able to defend himself in his weakened old age from his attackers, as in the fracas from which Aston rescued him, intensifies his paranoia. What is dreaded is the dirt that he longs to

---

⁴ Extracts from *The Caretaker* from H. Pinter, *The Caretaker* (London: Methuen, 1960). Reproduced by permission of Faber & Faber Ltd.

locate outside himself. He recounts the story of the precious soap provided in the Shepherd's Bush convenience and boasts "I've had dinner with the best", "eaten off the best of plates", "I'm clean", and he excoriates the "pigs" who are hounding him. These pigs are variously the Blacks next door, the "Scotchman" he was fighting with, his wife whom he left after a fortnight because

> DAVIES: I took the lid off a saucepan, you know what was in it? A pile of her underclothing, unwashed. The pan for vegetables, it was. The vegetable pan. That's when I left her and I haven't seen her since.
>
> [Act I, p. 9]

Primitive terrors of contamination in which bodily dirt and food become entangled and contact with the unclean cannot be avoided seem at the heart of Davies's tramping life—settling in a place means that one cannot always get away from the feared dirt by moving on, which was his solution. The fight had been occasioned by his being expected to "take out the bucket"—an intolerable task for him because of the weak discrimination he makes between what is outside and what is inside. Would he be throwing out the rubbish, or is he himself the unwanted rubbish, as in the story he tells of his trip to the monastery at Luton to beg, where the monk said: "Piss off."

While Davies reveals his painful fugitive situation, Aston is trying to mend a toaster; the connection has gone. Not only are we becoming aware of the damaged, partially disconnected state of Aston's mind alongside his efforts to think and to relate to the tramp's worries, but we become disturbed by the idea that there is nothing for them to eat, not even a piece of toast. The gas cooker (another feared object for Davies, who suspects poisonous leaks) is not connected, the toaster is broken, the thin undernourished state of them both seems related to the image of the vegetable pan full of underclothes, and the woman associated with that who cannot be relied on to produce any food one could trust. Somewhere else, behind "them heavy big curtains" next door, there might be family life, a protected space in which children could have parents, but in the world Davies and Aston are inhabiting there is an overpowering sense of being excluded from any ordinary expectation of care or human attachment. The piled-up furniture and assorted objects convey Aston's longing and failure to construct a home; all that can be managed are things that could, if ordered and linked up, create domesticity, but whose unavailability for use mocks the desire of their owner. Neither mothers nor fathers provide what is needed—cafés, pubs, and monastery kitchens all disappoint. The shoes Davies wants are what might set him up in life—give him a solid feeling of connection with the ground of reality, and of proper support, but even the ones Aston acquires specially for him are not quite right. Aston's Buddha statue, with its combined male and female quality, seems to speak of the longing for something "well made"—an idea of human relationships that might create links rather than threaten to exclude—but its actual fragility (it is smashed later on) is obvious.

The sense of lost identities and lost histories becomes explicit when Davies talks about his "papers", down with a man in Sidcup for the last 15 years or so, and his two names—one that gives him "no rights", and the "real name", which might allow him to re-connect with the scattered aspects of his life. As Aston tries to establish the reality of the planned trip to Sidcup, Davies becomes more incoherent. The almost manic eloquence he can summon in his states of delusional paranoid conviction deserts him.

ASTON: Sure he's still got them?
DAVIES: He's got them.
ASTON: Might have moved.
DAVIES: I know the house he lives in, I tell you! Once I set foot in Sidcup I could go there blindfold. Can't remember the number though. I've got a good mind to . . . I've got a good mind to . . .
Pause.
ASTON: Well, you ought to try to get down there.
DAVIES: I can't go in these shoes. It's the weather, you see. If only the weather would break.

[Act I, p. 21]

The microclimate of Davies's internal world does not favour the possibility of regaining the lost strands of his identity lodged in the abandoned papers.

Later the men sleep. Aston is disturbed by Davies's dreaming, his groans and "jabbering". His own absent peace of mind and

psychological frailty is matched by Davies's frantic assertion that
he "never had a dream in my life".

DAVIES: Maybe it were them Blacks making noises, coming up
through the walls.

[Act I, p. 24]

The worrying noises, the evidence of inner disturbance, are pushed
away and disowned in an effort to re-establish a sense of control.
Aston, for his part, wants to take forward his project of regeneration of the house through acquiring more tools. He has seen a jig-
saw he wants to buy.

ASTON: Ther's a lot you can do with a jig saw, you see. Once you've
fixed it . . . to this portable drill. You can do a lot with it. It
speeds things up.

[Act I, p. 26]

As each man flees his inner terrors in characteristic ways, Davies by
massive emptying of himself and Aston by anxious and feeble
gestures towards potency and reconstruction, their shared fantasies
emerge. Aston describes being approached by a tart; an ordinary
conversation in a café was suddenly invaded by sexual provocation and suggestiveness. Each man is occupied with the thought
that he is desired by exploitative women who are best avoided.
Aston tries to pin Davies down: "Where were you born?" thus
approaching the territory of the relationship to mother. Davies's
mind cracks:

DAVIES: I was . . . uh . . . oh, it's a bit hard, like, to set your mind
back . . . see what I mean . . . going back . . . a good way . . . lose
a bit of track, like . . . you know . . .

[Act I, p. 27]

Aston busies himself in looking after Davies before going out. He
perhaps gains thus some relief from his own fractured sense of self.
The act ends with Mick's creeping in and attacking Davies, now
alone.

Who is Mick? His alarming assault comes from nowhere and
seems to have no reason save the pent-up aggression and desire for
power we sense in him. Having established his superior strength,
he starts a strange cross-examination, which leads on to a lengthy

speech composed of confusing free association. We listen to this aware that it is intended to terrify and befuddle Davies further, but perhaps also getting a first taste of Mick's own unstable pseudo-rationality. His sudden repetitions and lightning tour of parts of London through his train of thought are dictated by an invisible internal logic, which the listener cannot discern. What impresses is the force and violence of his personality. The long speeches are interspersed with question-and-answer dialogue, which makes Davies more and more anxious. The rhythm is totally unpredictable and creates tension. Mick accuses Davies of fibs, but the larger point is that the world Pinter is writing about is one with no shared points of reference. Things may be true—or not.

Mick tunes into the predominant terror in Davies unerringly— he accuses him of being a stinking intruder, and the theme of intrusion and violation is revisited, with Davies now equated with his own bad objects (the Blacks). We do not know whether Mick actually believes any of this to be true or is merely playing with Davies's fears in a sadistic way. He refers to the police, prison, and a threat of "daily check and double check" by a solicitor. Davies, the man without papers and properly stamped insurance card, is being tormented by a master of cruelty, a "joker" of devilish precision. The sado-masochistic pairing is chilling. Only Aston's return signals an end to the torment and provides us with an answer as to Mick's identity as Aston's younger brother. After the panic and speed of the Davies/Mick exchanges of words and violence, Aston and Davies continue their laboured mode of conversation as if nothing much has happened, and as if the project of renovation could move ahead. Aston says of his plans:

> ASTON: Once I get that shed up outside . . . I'll be able to give a bit more thought to the flat, you see. Perhaps I can knock up one or two things for it. I can work with my hands, you see. That's one thing I can do. I never knew I could. But I can do all sorts of things now, with my hands. You know, manual things.
>
> [Act II, p. 42]

He muses on the partition he plans to erect in one room. The world of total disorder and unpredictability that Mick had conjured up in his monologues is imagined potentially transformed into a space with differentiated areas and the possibility of separateness and discrimination. From this vision of a house put to rights comes the notion of the role of caretaker, which could provide Davies with a meaningful identity. Aston's offer serves briefly to link the two men in a benign pairing (old father and younger son?) with the shared task of taking care of the house. They discuss the necessary implements hesitantly and start to get involved in the hopeful fantasy, but mention of the doorbell stirs Davies's panic: if one settles inside the house, his conviction goes, the "queries" he will be supposed to answer at the door immediately become dangerous intruders. There is no peace, for those with the good fortune to be insiders must expect to be disturbed by the envious outsiders. Pinter's dramatic line leads straight on to Mick's second and more bizarre series of attacks on Davies's precarious sanity. This is indeed the psychological logic following its inevitable path: the room that could seem homelike is turned for Davies into a place full of incomprehensible dread, with lights turned off and the Electrolux suddenly roaring into life. Just as unpredictably Mick pretends it was all "spring cleaning", "upkeep of the premises", intended for his benefit.

> MICK: I'm sorry if I gave you a start. But I had you in mind too, you know. I mean, my brother's guest. We got to think of your comfort, en't we?
>
> [Act II, p. 48]

Mick then seduces Davies into an alliance with him based on encouraging Davies to patronize and denigrate Aston as the "slow worker", the "funny bloke". Davies is to be a caretaker/interior decorator appointed by Mick the landlord.

This new option naturally destabilizes the Aston/Davies relationship. Davies, now emboldened, begins to complain of the draughts, the absence of new shoes, the leak in the roof, and his mention of the café and cup of tea he cannot get stirs Aston's terrifying memories of his schizophrenic breakdown of years ago. He describes falling out of contact with people, hallucinations, and his traumatic incarceration and experience of enforced treatment by ECT. Betrayal is the essence of what he felt—a mother who permitted the treatment despite his pleas, and doctors who offered him "a chance", which he experienced as an assault on his mind from which he is still struggling to recover. This is a picture of parents joining together in cruelty to suppress a child's terrors either because of their unwillingness or incapacity to understand him or their hatred or intolerance of his neediness.

> Aston: They always used to listen. I thought . . . they understood what I said. I mean I used to talk to them. I talked too much. That was my mistake.
>
> [Act II, p. 57]

The fear of either being too much for people to bear or of being exposed to an unremittingly hostile world is thus Aston's deep dread, just as it is the underlying condition of Davies's world picture. Their damaged minds cannot cope with life.

> ASTON: I don't think my spine was damaged. That was perfectly all right. . . . The trouble was . . . my thoughts . . . had become very slow. . . . I couldn't think at all. . . . I couldn't . . . get . . . my thoughts . . . together . . .
>
> [Act II, p. 60]

The Mick/Davies axis breaks down because Davies tries to establish that they are to be the favoured couple and exclude Aston, now seen as the source of all that disappoints. The inherent instability of the trio created by Davies's arrival is resolved by his ejection, and his final broken-up sentences echo Aston's earlier description of his shattered mind. Aston's assertion of his rights to his room and demand that Davies leave arises from his refusal to betray his regenerative project. When Davies abuses his project for a garden shed, his belief in the "good wood" and his positive investment in himself as a man who can make things is under attack; he defends his potential space by forcing Davies to confront his nastiness—not just his "stinking the place out" literally, but more so the dirty trick he tried to play in attributing all the madness and "bad dreams" to Aston, at the same time forgetting his initial kindness. Aston holds firm, and Mick offers Davies no way out, because the two brothers have re-established an equilibrium that depends on being able to reject the disruptive impact of their visitor. Aston is back to mending the plug, and the *status quo ante* is being reconstructed. The noise, the hallucinations, all that might disturb are to be shut out of the house with Davies. Inside is to be a place protected from intercourse with the outside world, a place without a sense of time passing.

The Homecoming

The Homecoming (1965), like the two earlier plays, is set in a house. In this instance, it is the family house to which Teddy and his wife Ruth return on the homecoming visit that gives the play its title. Teddy finds, as he expects, that his father, Max, his two brothers, Lenny and Joey, and his uncle, Sam, are still living there together, as they were when he left for America six years before. Introducing his wife Ruth to his family is the purpose of their unannounced visit. His mother, Jessie, we learn, has died many years before.

The house is the space within which most of the life of this family seems to have taken place. This space has various zones— kitchen, bedrooms, the ancillary domestic space of Sam's car—in which different parts of the family's life are enacted. It becomes evident that Max, Sam, Lenny, and Joey have all been unable to move out of this "home" despite, or because of, the mother's death. We learn that they are also trapped in a pattern of relationships in which the past of their family is the continuing and unavoidable point of reference for all of them. The action of the play reveals this also to be true for Teddy and for Ruth, his wife, who tells them all that she was "born quite near here", and whose first action on arriving has been to go out alone in the dark for a walk, suggesting that she feels at least as much at home here as her husband, even though he was born and brought up in the house.

In *The Homecoming*, Pinter enables his audience to piece together from what happens and what is said a more complete family history than he usually offers. The dramatic situation makes it natural that its characters should explain themselves to each other, since they are meeting for the first time for many years. The "family reunion" that the play enacts lends itself to reminiscence, though this turns out to be a savage and grotesque parody of the exchanges that one might expect to take place in such a situation. The shocking effect of the play arises from the gross discrepancy between conventional expectations and representations of family relationships and what actually takes place on the stage.

What does take place is an ongoing attack on all those elements of family life and its memories that can be said normally to have a quasi-sacred quality in the minds of family members. (Max in one moment of reminiscence refers to his father's "last sacred words".) Nearly everything is inverted. At the beginning of the play Max says of his wife:

> MAX: Mind you, she wasn't such a bad woman. Even though it made me sick just to look at her rotten stinking face, she wasn't such a bad bitch. I gave her the best bleeding years of my life, anyway.
>
> [Act I, p. 9][6]

His opening remarks when he comes downstairs in the morning and unexpectedly encounters Teddy and Ruth are in a similar vein:

> MAX: Who's this?
> TEDDY: I was just going to introduce you.
> MAX: Who asked you to bring tarts in here?
> TEDDY: Tarts?
> MAX: Who asked you to bring dirty tarts into this house?
> TEDDY: Listen, don't be silly—
> MAX: You been here all night?
> TEDDY: Yes, we arrived from Venice—
> MAX: We've had a smelly scrubber in my house all night. We've had a stinking pox-ridden slut in my house all night.
> TEDDY: Stop it! What are you talking about?
> MAX: I haven't seen the bitch for six years, he comes home without a word, he brings a filthy scrubber off the street, he shacks up in my house!
> TEDDY: She's my wife! We're married!
>
> [Act I, p. 42]

We gather that Max's rage with his wife and his brutal attack on Ruth and Teddy may be connected. He goes on:

> MAX: I've never had a whore under this roof before. Ever since your mother died. My word of honour. [To Joey] Have you ever had a whore here? Has Lenny ever had a whore here? They come back from America, they bring the slop bucket with them.

---

[4] Extracts from *The Homecoming* from H. Pinter, *The Homecoming* (London: Methuen, 1965). Reproduced by permission of Faber & Faber Ltd.

They bring the bedpan with them. [*To Teddy*] Take that disease away from me. Get her away from me.

[Act I, p. 42]

The ambiguities yet to be explored include whether Max's wife or Ruth is the tart-bitch in his mind. There is no need for any introduction, since all women are known to be much the same. The whole family lives in a state of suppressed violent rage, directed in particular towards women. Lenny waits for Ruth to return from her walk outdoors (has she already been on the game, we wonder?) and tells her this story about a woman he knows:

> LENNY: This lady had been searching for me for days. She'd lost track of my whereabouts. However, the fact was she eventually caught up with me, and when she caught up with me she made me this certain proposal. Well, this proposal wasn't entirely out of order and normally I would have subscribed to it. I mean I would have subscribed to it in the normal course of events. The only trouble was she was falling apart with the pox. So I turned it down. Well, this lady was very insistent and started taking liberties with me down under this arch, liberties which by any criterion I couldn't be expected to tolerate, the facts being what they were, so I clumped her one. . . .

[Act I, p. 31]

He describes how he had thought of killing her, decided that it would be too much bother:

> So I just gave her another belt in the nose and a couple of turns of the boot, and sort of left it at that.

[Act I, p. 32]

Lenny tells two other brutal stories, one about how he became annoyed with an old lady who had asked him to help her move her iron mangle. He feels humiliated by not being able to lift it and infuriated by the fact that she is "not even lifting a little finger to give me a helping hand". So he tells her to "stuff this iron mangle up your arse", contemplates beating her up, but instead "I just gave her a short-arm jab to the belly and jumped on a bus outside." He later reminisces sadistically about a night when he and Joey forced two tarts in Paddington to have sex with them without contraceptive protection.

The hatred felt by Max and Lenny towards women is all-pervasive. Women are betraying whores. The trauma that seems to have brought about this state of mind focuses on Jessie, Max's dead wife. It emerges that it is her betrayal—but also the fact of her death, which has left them doubly deprived and been interpreted as a betrayal—that has led to this family's being sunk in misery and barely suppressed violence. Max refers to his "bedridden" mother and his own "crippled family", so it is perhaps suggested that this state of deprivation goes a further generation back.

The absence, and need, of a mother in the family is painfully apparent. The family of men who survived her has remained completely stuck, held together by mutual antagonism and unable either to care for one another adequately, to find partners for themselves, or to leave. A more light-hearted version of a grown-up father and son glued together by need, failure, helplessness, and paranoia was later explored in the television series *Steptoe and Son*.

The family has attempted to go on functioning, after a fashion. Max provides food, Sam washes up, they try to share the resources of the house but continually quarrel over details—where are the scissors, who has eaten my cheese roll, and the like. They are tormented by an idea of the warm-hearted sociable East End family they would like to have been but are not. Max, thinking of the grandchildren that his dead wife will never see, talks about her in a parody of what a proud East End father might be expected to say:

> MAX [*to Ruth*]: Mind you, she taught those boys everything they know. She taught them all the morality they know, I'm telling you. Every single bit of the moral code they live by—was taught to them by their mother. And she had a heart to go with it. What a heart. Eh, Sam? Listen, what's the use of beating around the bush? That woman was the backbone of this family. . . .

> [Act I, p. 46]

In fact, we already know what he thinks about his sons' "moral code". He oscillates continuously between this sentimental picture of the good old days of his family and foulmouthed abuse of women in general.

Teddy and Ruth's arrival provokes their feelings of rage and deprivation. Teddy has insulted his family, in Max's view, by getting married and leaving without even telling them: a double insult. The family, the male gang, wants to control its members and is enraged by the defiance of its rules by a member who thinks he can be an individual and join up with an outsider to become a couple. Max imagines the big family wedding they should have had, while Ruth tells them that when they married "there was no-one there". If Teddy and Ruth have chosen to treat the family like dirt, the family in return will show them how dirty they can be. Max imagines his three grandsons left in America—the possibility of a new start, just like his own fatherhood with three sons—but the reminiscences that emerge of what it was actually like bringing up his boys are often mocking and cruel. Max cannot bear being reminded of this past.

> MAX: Stop calling me Dad. Just stop all that calling me Dad, do you understand?
> LENNY: But I'm your son. You used to tuck me up in bed every night. He tucked you up too, didn't he, Joey?
> *Pause*
> He used to like tucking up his sons.
> LENNY *turns and goes towards the front door.*
> MAX: Lenny.
> LENNY [*turning*]: What?
> MAX: I'll give you a proper tuck up one of these nights, son. You mark my word.
>
> [Act I, p. 17]

Each of the normal rituals of parenting and family life—providing meals, bathtimes, bedtimes, and so on—whether remembered from the past or taking place in the present, is subjected to ritual desecration. Max, in his own view, has had for much of his life to try to be both mother and father to the boys, and indeed to his brother, and his efforts are continuously attacked and denigrated. While hatred of the sexual aspects of women is projected onto tarts, real and imaginary, onto Ruth, and, of course, onto the memory of Jessie herself, hatred of the more nurturing aspects of mother is directed at Max and Sam.

There are many hints of how physically and sexually abusive this family has always been, not least in its inability to maintain any boundary in its conversation between everyday decency and

the obscene. At one point Max is barely able to maintain his authority. He knocks Joey down with his stick and insults and humiliates
his younger brother, Sam. But Lenny makes it shockingly clear that
Max now remains head of the family only on sufferance, and that
he can no longer tell him what to do. His role as father is tolerated
because he alone provides food and some feeble semblance of care
for the others. Max tells Sam that he will be thrown out when he
can no longer bring in any money, and we realize that Max could
be talking about what is likely to happen to him as soon as he
ceases to be of any practical use to his sons. This is part of Max's
own terror and pathos.

Teddy and Ruth's visit raises the question for the family of
whether there could be any other way of life. They set about attacking the new arrivals in many different ways—abusing Ruth as a
tart, telling her intimidating stories about Lenny's violence towards women, mocking Teddy's academic career. Teddy can find
no words to resist his family's sado-masochistic view of the world
and cannot avoid being drawn back into it—indeed, we come to
realize that the attraction to him of his family's perversity has been
the reason for his homecoming. His escape into abstract intellectu-
ality and material affluence in distant America has done nothing at
all to clarify his relationship to his family in his mind. When he
does eventually suggest that Ruth and he should leave ("We might
as well . . . cut it short, I think"), Ruth tries to get him to talk about
his family. "Don't you like them?" she asks. He says, "It's so clean
in America," thinking of his sons by the pool. She insistently asks if
he finds it dirty here? (He has earlier said that the local swimming
pool is a "filthy urinal".) If he does, the implicit suggestion is, he
must find her dirty, since this is after all where she comes from too.
She is asking him to confront their shared past, from which they
had tried to escape together. But escape into a lifetime of denial
and silence will not do—only if he could acknowledge their shared
origin and begin to think about its meaning for them would there
be any chance of real escape from this world.

It is immediately after this conversation that Ruth tells Lenny,
who at least appears to be interested in what she says, about her
earlier career as a model, a "photographic model for the body",
and soon after this she is kissing Lenny and then Joey, with Max
looking on. She goes "upstairs" for two hours with Joey; Lenny

picks a quarrel with Teddy over a cheese sandwich and tells him what he thinks of his campus life, while Teddy attempts vacuously to assert his intellectual superiority over them. Lenny sings the praises of the family in superficially meaningful terms:

> LENNY: No, listen, Ted, there's no question that we live a less rich life here than you do over there. We live a closer life. We're busy, of course. Joey's busy with his boxing, I'm busy with my occupation, Dad still plays a good game of poker, and does the cooking as well, well up to his old standard, and Uncle Sam's the best chauffeur in the firm. But nevertheless we do make up a unit, Teddy, and you're an integral part of it. . . .
>
> [Act II, p. 66]

The family, buoyed up by this fake unity and feeling euphoric, return to describing Ruth openly as a whore and arrive at the idea of setting her up in Greek Street, to earn money for them, while she also looks after them at home. Their triumph is all the more intense because it involves the degradation and destruction of Teddy and Ruth's marriage, and of her role as a mother. Teddy is invited to join this enterprise or, in a perversely imaginative extension of it, to solicit clients for her in America. The extravagance of these fantasies is, of course, amusing as well as horrific.

> LENNY: No, what I mean Teddy, you must know lots of professors, heads of department, men like that. They pop over here for a week at the Savoy, they need somewhere where they can have a nice quiet poke. And of course, you'd be in a position to give them inside information.
>
> [Act II, p. 75]

Teddy passes on the family's invitation to his wife:

> TEDDY: Ruth . . . the family have invited you to stay, for a little while longer. As a . . . as a kind of guest. If you like the idea, I don't mind. We can manage very easily at home . . . until you come back.
> RUTH: How very nice of them.
>
> [Act II, p. 76]

Things have come full circle. The family seem to have in Ruth a reincarnation of Jessie, their alluring but abandoning mother, who will thus be recaptured and punished. It is at the moment when the family have succeeded in achieving this repeat version of their history, this time in apparently full triumph, that we finally learn in more definite terms what the family history has been. Sam, whose residual decency and sense of reality has been offended by the macabre spectacle being played out in front of him, blurts out:

SAM [*in one breath*]:   MacGregor had Jessie in the back of my cab as I drove them along.
He croaks and collapses...

[Act II, p. 79]

This is the last of many references to MacGregor and Jessie during the play, this one finally making clear what has only been repeatedly hinted at earlier. Max's first abusive tirade against Jessie took place in the first scene, immediately after he has talked about MacGregor, a six-foot man with whom he used to "knock about". After describing their past as a pair of gangsters ("We were two of the worst hated men in the West End of London, I tell you. I've still got the scars"), he continues:

MAX: He was very fond of your mother, Mac was. Very fond. He always had a good word for her.

[Act I, p. 9]

He goes on immediately to give a revolting picture of their marriage.

When Sam is mocked for his impotence by Max:

MAX: Above having a good bang in the back seat are you?

[Act I, p. 15]

Sam replies with an innuendo.

SAM: Yes, I leave that to others.
MAX: You leave it to others? What others? You paralysed prat!
SAM: I don't mess up my car! Or... my boss's car! Like other people.
MAX: Other people? What other people?
Pause
     What other people?
Pause
SAM: Other people.

[Act I, p. 15]

MacGregor and Jessie are recurrently talked about in the same breath, particularly by Sam, who seems unable to get them out of his mind, continually needling Max with references to them:

> SAM: I want to make something clear about Jessie, Max. I want to. I do. When I took her out in the cab, round the town, I was taking care of her, for you. I was looking after her for you, wasn't I, when you were busy, wasn't I? I was showing her the West End.
>
> [Act I, p. 19]

He feels guilty that he has actively colluded in the betrayal of his brother by driving Jessie and MacGregor around, Jessie perhaps a tart and MacGregor her pimp. This is the "family secret" that everyone has really known about all along—this is why Max is so venomous towards his dead wife, and why for his sons (including, in the end, Teddy) all women turn out to be tarts. Lenny's elaborately offensive question to his father about the moment when he was conceived invites Max to remember the horrible meaning that sex had in this family:

> LENNY: I'll tell you what, Dad, since you're in a mood for a bit of a . . . chat, I'll ask you a question. It's a question I've been meaning to ask you for some time. That night . . . you know . . . the night you got me . . . that night with Mum, what was it like? Eh? When I was just a glint in your eye. What was it like? What was the background to it. I mean, I want to know the real facts about my background. I mean, for instance, is it a fact that you had me in mind all the time, or is it a fact that I was the last thing you had in mind?
>
> [Act I, p. 37]

Max tells Lenny in reply that "You'll drown in your own blood" , and Lenny says, "I should have asked my dear mother. Why didn't I ask my dear mother? Now it's too late. She's passed over to the other side."

The profaning of a family can go no further, and Max spits at him. This conversation puts one in mind of the invasion of the minds of some sexually abused children by memories of the events they have witnessed and suffered and their difficulty in restoring normal psychic boundaries. Lenny's implication may also be that someone else—MacGregor perhaps—was his father, and not Max at all.

MacGregor has been the big boss, and Max, for all his vainglory, has had to do whatever he was told. The manic near-orgy at the end when Ruth seems to be making love to several of them at once while they discuss the comfort she is going to keep them in is the other side of the past that they have previously remembered with misery and hatred. This time, the young prostitute mother of three will keep them happy. In reality, the tormenting memory of their actual mother has left their lives in ruins and, for all their bravado, apparently sexually incapable too.

Whether all this has a real basis in the family's history or is a shared fantasy that has become dominant in the family group is left for the audience to struggle with.

Why does Ruth go along with the family's plan to install her in Greek Street? Is the audience being drawn perversely into identification with the family's pornographic fantasies? Her decision to stay with the family and to be prepared to discuss their offer of a career as a prostitute is perhaps to be interpreted as her decision to return to a self that at least has some reality for her, compared with her false life as an academic wife in America. It seems profoundly unlikely that Pinter regarded the life of a Soho tart with Lenny as her pimp as any kind of liberation, though some critics have argued along these lines. Since Ruth has already sexually triumphed over Teddy, Joey, Lenny (who was dismayed by her apparent sexual invitation to him at their first meeting), and Max, she may be imagined to be at this point in full control of the situation, whatever plans Lenny and the family might think they are able to make for her. But here Pinter seems to have found it easier to create a seductive and perverse mental universe than to identify any believable way out of it. Pinter's imagination may itself have been impoverished as a consequence of recycled visions of deprivation and depravity, which can be addictive and enslaving in their impact on the mind.

The play puts into stark relief the divided image of woman as both whore and saint, Max moving from one description to another within single torrents of words. Pinter has his characters express both a sentimental vision of a respected and revered Mum and her converse image as a diseased and hated tart. They seem to have lived their lives in a constant condition of bitter rivalry—sons competing with their father, and with each other, for access to their mother, and all of them pushed out by the dominant figure of MacGregor, the real boss in this violence-dominated world. They have adapted to this war of all against all in different ways, but what they all share is the despair that they can have anything at all outside the prison of their home in which they are doomed to humiliating repetition of their failure to confront the doubled images of the abusive, greedy father(s) (Max and Mac) and betraying mothers (Jessie and Ruth). Internal reality is projected outside themselves and remains unmodified.

The audience of this play is confronted with the task of bearing a penetrating assault—peace of mind is shattered by the immediacy of the action and by the violence of the attacks of the characters upon each other. It is a powerful instance of theatre's demand on its audience to go where the dramatist takes them and to suffer in the process. Pinter provides little relief from the horror, except moments of grim comedy and the disturbing pleasures of identification with perverse states of mind. But there is also the completeness of the dramatic whole, as the family comes full circle, and the brilliance of the language.

All of the dramatists we have discussed in this book have in our view brought audiences face to face with critical issues both in the individual and in the larger social experiences of their audiences. Pinter, acutely sensitive to the cruelties and disorientations of mind that are one aspect of contemporary times, is no exception to this. His plays have thus created a space for reflection on states of acute crisis, and for the deeper understanding of ourselves and others that can follow from this.

This, we think, is not only Pinter's achievement, but a quality his work shares with all of the great plays that we have been exploring in this book.

REFERENCES

Alford, C. F. (1993). *The Psychoanalytic Theory of Greek Tragedy*. New Haven, CT: Yale University Press.

Aristotle (1951). *Poetics*. In: *Aristotle's Theory of Poetry and Fine Art*, trans. and notes by S. H. Butcher, Introduction by J. Gassner. New York: Dover Books.

Alvarez, A. (1968). *Beyond All This Fiddle: Essays, 1955–1967*. London: Allen Lane.

Alvarez, A. (1973). *Beckett*. London: Fontana.

Anderson, P. (1992). *A Zone of Engagement*. London: Verso.

Barber, C. L. (1959). *Shakespeare's Festive Comedy*. Princeton, NJ: Princeton University Press.

Beckett, S. (1986). *The Complete Dramatic Works*. London: Faber.

Beckson, K. (Ed.) (1970). *Oscar Wilde: The Critical Heritage*. London: Routledge.

Bell, D. (1961). The racket-ridden longshoremen. In: *The End of Ideology: On the Exhaustion of Political Ideas in the Fifties*. New York: Collier.

Bertaux, D., & Thompson, P. (1997). *Pathways to Social Class: A Qualitative Approach to Social Mobility*. Cambridge: Cambridge University Press.

Berger, P., & Kellner, H. (1964). Marriage and the construction of reality. *Diogenes* (Summer 1964).

Bick, E. (1968). The experience of the skin in early object-relations. *International Journal of Psycho-Analysis, 49*: 484–486. Republished in E. Bick & M. Harris Williams, *Collected Papers of Martha Harris and Esther Bick*. Perthshire: Clunie Press, 1987.

Bigsby, C. W. E. (1992). *Modern American Drama 1945–1990*. Cambridge: Cambridge University Press.

Bigsby, C. W. E. (Ed.) (1994). *The Cambridge Companion to Arthur Miller*. Cambridge: Cambridge University Press.

Billington, M. (1996). *The Life and Work of Harold Pinter*. London: Faber and Faber.

Bion, W. R. (1959). Attacks on linking. *International Journal of Psycho-Analysis, 30*: 308–315. Reprinted in *Second Thoughts*. London: Heinemann, 1967.

Bion, W. R. (1961). *Experiences in Groups*. London: Tavistock Publications.

Bion, W. R. (1962a). *Learning from Experience*. London: Heinemann.

Bion, W. R. (1962b). A theory of thinking. *International Journal of Psycho-Analysis, 43*: 306–310. Reprinted in *Second Thoughts*. London: Heinemann, 1967.

Bion, W. R. (1967). On arrogance. In: *Second Thoughts*. London: Heinemann.

Bion, W. R. (1970). *Attention and Interpretation*. London: Tavistock Publications.

Bloom, H. (1999). *Shakespeare: The Invention of the Human*. London: Fourth Estate.

Bourdieu, P. (1993). *The Field of Cultural Production*. Cambridge: Polity Press.

Bowlby, J. (1981). Psychoanalysis as a natural science. *International Review of Psycho-Analysis, 8* (3): 243–256.

Britton, R. (1998). *Belief and Imagination: Explorations in Psychoanalysis*. London: Routledge/Institute of Psychoanalysis.

Brooks, H. F. (Ed.) (1979). *Arden Shakespeare*. London: Methuen. Reprinted London: Routledge, 1988.

Brooks, P. (1984). *Reading for the Plot: Design and Intention in Narrative*. Cambridge, MA: Harvard University Press.

Cohen, T. (1999). *Philosophical Thoughts on Joking Matters*. Chicago, IL: Chicago University Press.

Copley, B. (1993). *The World of Adolescence: Literature, Society and Psychoanalytic Psychotherapy*. London: Free Association Books.

Cronin, A. (1996). *Samuel Beckett: The Last Modernist*. London: Harper Collins.

Dennett, D. (1995). *Darwin's Dangerous Idea: Evolution and the Meanings of Life*. Harmondsworth: Penguin.

Dodds, E. R. (1951). *The Greeks and the Irrational*. Berkeley, CA: University of California Press.

Douglas, M. (1970). *Natural Symbols*. London: Barrie and Rockcliff/Cresset Press.

Douglas, M. (1982). *In the Active Voice*. London: Routledge and Kegan Paul.

Douglas, M. (1992). *Risk and Blame: Essays in Cultural Theory*. London: Routledge.

Durkheim, E. (1915). *The Elementary Forms of the Religious Life*. London: Allen and Unwin.

Easterling, P. E. (Ed.) (1997). *The Cambridge Companion to Greek Tragedy*. Cambridge: Cambridge University Press.

Ellmann, R. (Ed.) (1969). *Oscar Wilde: A Collection of Critical Essays*. Englewood Cliffs, NJ: Prentice-Hall.

Ellmann, R. (Ed.). (1970). *The Artist as Critic: Critical Writings of Oscar Wilde*. London: W. H. Allen.

Ellmann, R. (1987). *Oscar Wilde*. Harmondsworth: Penguin.

Empson, W. (1986). *Essays on Shakespeare*. Cambridge: Cambridge University Press.

Esslin, M. (1968). *The Theatre of the Absurd* (rev. ed.). Harmondsworth: Penguin.

Esslin, M. (2000). *Pinter the Playwright*. London: Methuen.

Figes, O. (1996). *A People's Tragedy: The Russian Revolution 1891–1924*. London: Jonathan Cape.

Finley, M. I. (1954). *The World of Odysseus*. Harmondsworth: Penguin.

Finley, M. I. (1983). *Politics in the Ancient World*. Cambridge: Cambridge University Press.

Fisher, J. (1999). *The Uninvited Guest: Emerging from Narcissism towards Marriage*. London: Karnac.

Fonagy, P. (2001). *Attachment Theory and Psychoanalysis*. New York: Other Press.

Freud, S. (1900a). *The Interpretation of Dreams. Standard Edition*, Vol. 4–5. London: Hogarth Press.

Freud, S. (1905c). *Jokes and Their Relation to the Unconscious. Standard Edition, Vol. 8*. London: Hogarth Press.

Freud, S. (1905d). *Three Essays on the Theory of Sexuality. Standard Edition, Vol. 7*. London: Hogarth Press.

Freud, S. (1909c). Family romances. *Standard Edition, Vol. 9*. London: Hogarth Press.

Freud, S. (1909b). Analysis of a phobia in a five-year-old boy (Little Hans). *Standard Edition, Vol. 10*. London: Hogarth Press.

Freud, S. (1916d). Some character types met with in psychoanalytic work: (II) Those wrecked by success. *Standard Edition, Vol. 14*. London: Hogarth Press.

Freud, S. (1927c). *The Future of an Illusion. Standard Edition, Vol. 21*. London: Hogarth Press.

Freud, S. (1930a). *Civilization and its Discontents. Standard Edition, Vol. 21*. London: Hogarth Press.

Freud, S. (1939a [1937–39]). *Moses and Monotheism. Standard Edition, Vol. 22*. London: Hogarth Press.

Ganz, A. (Ed.) (1972). *Pinter: A Collection of Critical Essays*. Englewood Cliffs, NJ: Prentice-Hall.

Giddens, A. (1981). *A Contemporary Critique of Historical Materialism*. London: Macmillan.

Gide, A. (1901). *In Memoriam*. Reprinted in R. Ellmann (Ed.), *Oscar Wilde: A Collection of Critical Essays* (pp. 25–34). Englewood Cliffs, NJ: Prentice-Hall, 1969.

Gilman, R. (1987). *The Making of Modern Drama*. New York: Da Capo.

Gilman, R. (1995). *Chekhov's Plays: An Opening into Eternity*. London: Yale University Press.

Girard, R. (1991). *A Theatre of Envy: William Shakespeare*. Oxford: Oxford University Press.

Goldhill, S. (1986). *Reading Greek Tragedy*. Cambridge: Cambridge University Press.

Gottlieb, V., & Allain, P. (Eds.) (2000). *The Cambridge Companion to Chekhov*. Cambridge: Cambridge University Press.

Gordon, L. (Ed.) (1990). *Harold Pinter: A Casebook*. London: Garland.

Graver, L. (1989). *Waiting for Godot*. Cambridge University Press.

Hall, S. (1965). "Home, Sweet Home." *Encore*, 56 (July–August).

Harris Williams, M., & Waddell, M. (1991). *The Chamber of Maiden Thought: Literary Origins of the Psychoanalytic Model of the Mind*. London: Routledge.

Hirschman, A. O. (1981). *Essays in Trespassing*. Cambridge: Cambridge University Press.

Honan, P. (1998). *Shakespeare: A Life*. Oxford: Oxford University Press.

Hrdy, S. B. (1999). *Mother Nature*. London: Chatto and Windus.

Jaques, E. (1965). Death and the mid-life crisis. *International Journal of Psycho-Analysis, 46*: 502–514.

Jones, E. (1949). *Hamlet and Oedipus*. New York: Norton.

Jones, S. (1999). *Almost Like a Whale: The Origin of Species Updated*. London: Doubleday.

Kermode, F. (2000). *Shakespeare's Language*. Harmondsworth: Penguin.

Kitto, H. D. (1961). *Greek Tragedy*. London: Routledge.

Klein, M. (1930). The importance of symbol formation in the development of the ego. In: *The Writings of Melanie Klein, Vol. 1: Love Guilt and Reparation and Other Works 1921–1945*. London: Hogarth Press, 1975.

Klein, M. (1935). A contribution to the psychogenesis of manic-depressive states. In: *The Writings of Melanie Klein. Vol. 1: Love Guilt and Reparation and Other Works 1921–1945*. London: Hogarth Press, 1975.

Klein, M. (1963). Some reflections on the Oresteia. In: *The Writings of Melanie Klein, Vol. 3: Envy and Gratitude and Other Works*. London: Hogarth Press.

Klein, M. (1975). Envy and gratitude. In: *The Writings of Melanie Klein. Vol. 3: Envy and Gratitude and Other Works*. London: Hogarth Press.

Knowlson, J. (1996). *Damned to Fame: The Life of Samuel Beckett*. London: Bloomsbury.

Kott, J. (1964). *Shakespeare, Our Contemporary*. London: Methuen.

Lan, D. (1994). *Euripides: "Ion"—A New Version, with Introduction*. London: Methuen.

Mann, M. (1986). *The Sources of Social Power. Vol. 1: A History of Power from the Beginning to A.D. 1760*. Cambridge : Cambridge University Press.

Matthews, S. (2001). Change and theory in Raymond Williams's *Structure of Feeling. Pretexts: Literary and Cultural Studies, 10* (2).

Mayer, A. (1982). *The Persistence of the Old Regime: Europe to the Great War*. New York: Pantheon.

McCarthy, M. (1963). The unimportance of being Oscar. In: R. Ellmann (Ed.), *Oscar Wilde: A Collection of Critical Essays*. Englewood Cliffs, NJ: Prentice-Hall, 1969.

McDougall, J. (1986). *Theatre of the Mind*. London: Free Association Books.

McFarlane, J. (Ed.) (1994). *The Cambridge Companion to Ibsen*. Cambridge: Cambridge University Press.

Meltzer, D. (1992). *The Claustrum: An Investigation of Claustrophobic Phenomena*. Perthshire: Clunie Press.

Meltzer, D. (1994). *Sincerity and Other Works: Collected Papers of Donald Meltzer*, ed. A. Hahn. London: Karnac.

Meyer, M. (1967). *Ibsen*. London: Rupert Hart-Davis.

Miller, A. (1978). *The Theatre Essays of Arthur Miller*, edited and Introduced by R. A. Martin. Harmondsworth: Penguin.

Miller, A. (1987). *Timebends—A Life*. London: Methuen.

Milner, M. (1987). *The Suppressed Madness of Sane Men*. London: Routledge.

Money-Kyrle, R. (1968). Cognitive development. *International Journal of Psycho-Analysis, 49*. Also in: D. Meltzer and E. O'Shaughnessy (Eds.), *Collected Papers*. Perthshire: Clunie Press.

Money-Kyrle, R. (1978). *Collected Papers*, edited by D. Meltzer & E. O'Shaughnessy. Perthshire: Clunie Press.

O'Shaughnessy, E. (1993). Enclaves and excursions. *International Journal of Psycho-Analysis, 73*: 603–611.

Parker, R. (1995). *"Torn in Two": The Experience of Maternal Ambivalence*. London: Virago Press.

Parsons, T. (1937). *The Structure of Social Action*. New York: McGraw-Hill.

Pilling, J. (Ed.) (1993). *The Cambridge Companion to Beckett*. Cambridge: Cambridge University Press.

Pinker, S. (1997). *How the Mind Works*. Harmondsworth: Penguin.

Pinter, H. (1991). Introduction. Writing for myself. In: *Harold Pinter: Plays 2*. London: Faber and Faber.

Pinter, H. (1998). *Various Voices. Poetry, Prose, Politics 1948–1998*. London: Faber and Faber.

Raby, P. (Ed.) (1997). *The Cambridge Companion to Oscar Wilde*. Cambridge: Cambridge University Press.

Raby, P. (Ed.) (2001). *The Cambridge Companion to Harold Pinter*. Cambridge: Cambridge University Press.

Rayfield, D. (1997). *Anton Chekhov: A Life*. London: HarperCollins.

Ridley, M. (1994). *The Red Queen: Sex and the Evolution of Human Nature*. Harmondsworth: Penguin.

Ridley, M. (1997). *The Origins of Virtue*. Harmondsworth: Penguin.

Rustin, M. E., & Rustin, M. J. (1994). Coups d'états and catastrophic change: Shakespeare's *Julius Caesar*. *British Journal of Psychotherapy*, 11 (2).

Rustin, M. E., & Rustin, M. J. (1987). *Narratives of Love and Loss*.

Rustin, M. J. (1991a). *The Good Society and the Inner World*. London: Verso.

Rustin, M. J. (1991b). Thinking in *Romeo and Juliet*. In: *The Good Society and the Inner World*. London: Verso.

Rustin, M. J. (2001). *Reason and Unreason: Psychoanalysis, Science and Politics*. London: Continuum.

Scott, M. (1986). *Harold Pinter: The Birthday Party; The Caretaker; The Homecoming: A Casebook*. Basingstoke: Macmillan.

Segal, H. (1952). A psycho-analytical approach to aesthetics. *International Journal of Psycho-Analysis, 33*. Reprinted in: *The Work of Hanna Segal*. London: Free Association Books, 1986.

Segal, H. (1986). *The Work of Hanna Segal*. London: Free Association Books.

Segal, H. (1997). *Psychoanalysis, Literature and War: Papers 1972–1995*. London: Routledge.

Shapin, S. (1996). *The Scientific Revolution*. Chicago, IL: Chicago University Press.

Sharpe, Ella Freeman (1950). *Collected Papers on Psychoanalysis*. London: Hogarth Press.

Simon, B. (1988). *Tragic Drama and the Family: Psychoanalytic Studies from Aeschylus to Beckett*. New Haven, CT: Yale.

Snell, B. (1953). *The Discovery of the Mind: The Greek Origin of European Thought*. Oxford: Oxford University Press.

Spinoza, B. (1963). *Ethics*, trans. A. Boyle. London: Everyman.

Steiner, G. (1967). *Language and Silence: Essays, 1958–1966*. London: Faber and Faber.

Steiner, J. (1985). Turning a blind eye: the cover-up for Oedipus. *International Journal of Psycho-Analysis, 12*: 161–172.

Steiner, J. (1990). The retreat from truth to omnipotence in *Oedipus at Colonus*. *International Review of Psycho-Analysis, 17*: 227–237.

Steiner, J. (1993). *Psychic Retreats: Pathological Organisations Psychotic, Neurotic and Borderline Patients*. London: Routledge and the Institute of Psycho-Analysis.

Stokes, A. (1965). *The Invitation in Art*. London: Tavistock.

Stokes, A. (1978). *The Critical Writings of Adrian Stokes, Vols. 1–3.* London: Thames and Hudson.

Stone, L. (1977). *The Family, Sex and Marriage in England 1500-1800.* London: Weidenfeld and Nicolson.

Styan, J. L. (1981). *Modern Drama in Theory and Practice, Vol. 1: Realism and Naturalism; Vol. 2: Symbolism, Surrealism, and the Absurd; Vol. 3 Expressionism and Epic Theatre.* Cambridge: Cambridge University Press.

Thompson, M., Ellis, R., & Wildavsky, A. (1990). *Cultural Theory.* Oxford: Westview Press.

Turner, V. W. (1969). *The Ritual Process.* Harmondsworth: Penguin.

Turner, V. W. (1974). *Dramas, Fields and Metaphors: Symbolic Action in Human Society.* Ithaca, NY: Cornell University Press.

Tydeman, W. (1982). *Wilde Comedies: A Casebook.* Basingstoke: Macmillan.

Vellacott, P. (1954). *Euripides: The Bacchae and Other Plays (Ion, Helena, the Bacchae), with Introduction.* Harmondsworth: Penguin.

Vellacott, P. (1963). *Euripides: Medea and Other Plays (Medea, Hecabe, Electra, Heracles).* Harmondsworth: Penguin.

Vernant, J.-P., & Vidal-Naquet, P. (1990). *Myth and Tragedy in Ancient Greece:* New York: Zone Books.

Weber, M. (1930). *The Protestant Ethic and the Spirit of Capitalism.* London: Allen & Unwin.

Weber, M. (1965). *The Sociology of Religion.* London: Methuen.

Wilde, O. (1891). *Intentions.* Reprinted in R. Ellmann (Ed.), *The Artist as Critic: The Critical Writings of Oscar Wilde.* London: W. H. Allen, 1970.

Williams, R. (1961). *The Long Revolution.* London: Chatto and Windus.

Williams, R. (1966). *Modern Tragedy.* London: Chatto and Windus.

Williams, R. (1968). *Drama from Ibsen to Brecht.* London: Chatto and Windus.

Winnicott, D. W. (1971). *Playing and Reality.* London: Tavistock Publications.

Wright, N. (1988). *Mrs Klein.* London: Nick Hern.

Young, M., & Willmott, P. (1957). *Family and Kinship in East London.* London: Routledge & Kegan Paul.

INDEX